A Dying Art II

By
Jack Allen Powell

Best Wishes !!
Thanks !! *Jack*

Airleaf
Publishing
airleaf.com

ISBN: 1-59453-346-6

Contents

Dedication

This humble book is dedicated to my "Angel" wife who stayed and stood behind me. When times were mean, lean and just plain rough, Mary Annette Wright Powell was there. Thank you Mary!!!

Thanks to daughters, Trenda, husband, Doctor John McGavock Jacocks, Colonel, United States Army (Special Forces). Andra, husband Martin Hayes McKown, Captain, United States Navy Reserves and United States Naval Aviator, and six grandchildren, Brittany Virginia Jacocks, Mary Carter Jacocks and Martin Hayes McKown III, Connor Braxton, Carson Lee and Bailey Wright McKown.

It is further dedicated to all LAW ENFORCEMENT OFFICERS that I have had the privilege to work with, be it Local, State and Federal.

A Dying Art II: Part I

Chapter One

A Branch Of The Past

Maybe it is a paradox of epitome to say that moonshining is a dying art in the United States especially in the thirteen southern states. Dying Art or not, the world's largest multi-blackpot illegal stills were captured in Virginia in 1993 at Cool Springs, Virginia, in Pittislyvania County, one mile from the Franklin county line. The huge distillery consisted of 36-800 gallon, black-pot, wood and galvanized stills and 28,800 gallons of live fermenting mash. The stills were capable of turning out 2,800 gallons of "moonshine whisky" a day.

Before prohibition, moonshining was just a practiced art in these Blue Ridge Mountains and the foot hills of the southeastern states especially along the Appalachian Mountains that stretch North Carolina to Georgia and from Arkansas to Alabama and from Virginia to Florida.

We harken back to the eighteenth century, leaving the south, going back to England and Scotland where excise tax laws caused man to make moonshine illegally.

Judge Blackstone abruptly put it this way. "From the beginning of its original time to the present, the very name of excise tax has been hateful to the people of England, Scotland, and Ireland."

From that day to this, two hundred and fifty years have passed and the "Dying Art" still goes on.

Revenue Gaugers made it miserable for those mountain people with those little "pot-teen stills." Moonshine proper was confined to the poorer class of people, especially in

Ireland where they lived in the wild and sparsely settled regions, which were governed by a clan feeling stronger than their loyalty to the central government. These poor people could not and would not share their profits with the government gaugers.

In the rich and popular districts around London, Edinburgh and Dublin, the common practice was to bribe government officials.

As time passed, these poor mountain moonshiners with arms in hand, they defied gaugers or excise officers. They were later to be called "revenues" and in America they would be called "Revenueers" and many other names.

These makers of fine Irish whiskey fell out with the British government and migrated to America settling for the most part in western Pennsylvania.

Between the Scotsman, native Irish, and the Pennsylvania Dutch, they drove out the Indians, formed our rough rear guard to the American Revolution and won that tough mountain region for civilization, then left it when the game got too scarce and their neighbor's houses got too close. These mountaineers followed the mountains southward, settling in West Virginia, North Carolina, and then forged a vanguard westward into Kentucky, Tennessee, Missouri, and still onward until there was no more West to conquer. Some remained behind in the wilderness of the Alleghenies, the Blue Ridge and the Unakas. Their descendants are still here.

The first generation of these Dutch-Scots-Irish frontiersmen knew no laws but their own. England didn't care as they faced a revolution. These backwoods men were loyal to the new American government, as was one man, George Washington.

They fought off the Indians from the rear, then sent their best riflemen to fight at the front. These first English speaking poor people were the first to use the weapon of percussion, the rifle, introduced by the Pennsylvania Dutch in 1700. They were the first to employ open-order formation in modern warfare.

These whisky makers were the first outside colonists to help their New England brethren at the seize of Boston. They were the first to serve under a federal banner as the first "regiment" of the Continental Army; and they were the first troops enrolled by our new Congress.

They made General George Washington's day at Saratoga, Cowpens and Kings Mountain, but this would change drastically. These whisky makers were the first rebels against the authority of the United States government, "George" himself. commander-In-Chief who had the ungrateful job of bringing them to order by a showing of Federal bayonets against their chest.

After Tom Tinker showed himself and Washington squelched the "Whisky Rebellion", Alexander Hamilton suggested an excise tax in 1791.

It was opposed by many noble men including the "Red Headed," squeaky voiced Thomas Jefferson. He never offered a tax on his own still at beautiful Monticello, Charlottesville, Virginia. The tax he opposed, passed anyway.

Mr. Hamilton had to pay for the revolutionary war. It is no doubt in many minds that is what started the trouble in the mountains of Southern Appalachia.

All frontier communities had a scarcity of money. All trade was by barter. Any cash received was saved for sugar and gunpowder and was brought across the mountains by "pack trains". (Mules & Horses) consequently, a "moonshine still" had to be set up on every farm.

A strong horse could carry twenty gallons of liquor on its back across the rugged mountains, equaling nine bushels of grain. That doubled the value of this new "Mountain Dew," which outsold the cheap New England rum.

Our new government continued to interfere with the poor mountaineer's enterprises by sticking its nose into private business. Our new Congress placed another heavy tax on the hard working mountain folk while letting the wealthy Eastern farmers pass without, "nary a cent of charge."

Again in 1791 Washington was informed that the nation was ready to revolt. To tax stills seemed a blow at the only thing which was "hard of heart" nature, and had given these mountaineers, a lot harder in comparison to the wealthy people of the Atlantic seaboard.

Who made up the Western mountains of the Eastern South? Mainly those of Pennsylvania, Maryland, North and South Carolina, Georgia, and Virginia, but not the rest of the Southern highlands, they came later, much later.

The irony of this story is, not any of the "moonshiners" of today know or care why history reveals the saga of them never paying taxes on their illicit manufactured moonshine. They will have learned after two hundred and three years President Washington was as cracked as their grain. Those heavy taxes on a gallon of whisky in 1793 placed eleven cents more on a gallon to distillers and nearly caused a civil war.

Then came the savior. The "Federal Amnesty Act." It was the governments way of freeing those who violated the liquor laws or better freeing those who violated tax laws. Even then there were some who did not participate.

Stubborn malcontents of these mountains moved farther South. No serious attempt was made to collect any taxes at this time and the mountaineers practiced their own "Dying Art."

Chapter Two

Extravagant Taxes

America now has a new president who was redheaded and had a squeaky voice. He probably wouldn't be elected today on his own charisma. He attempted to make good his earlier opposition on taxes after being elected in 1801.

President Thomas Jefferson repealed the taxes in 1804, but that didn't last too long either. The War of 1812 came along and caused extravagant taxes. In 1817 he repealed the taxes again and everyone was happy, especially those who were working by the "light of the moon."

For the next thirty-five years, no specific tax on liquor occurred. The marketplace of whisky remained fourteen to twenty-four cents a gallon.

Spirits got so cheap, the people were mixing turpentine with moonshine and using it for lamp fuel. Moonshining almost went out of business! They did find out though, that the two of them were good for something other than lamp fuel, "snakebite." Just don't drink the two of them together, and light a match, oooooh doggie!

What next? A rumbling in the North, meant that Civil War was eminent. In 1862 another heavy liquor tax burdened the public and ladened the Southern moonshiner with more grief. Taxes went from twenty-four cents a gallon to sixty cents a gallon.

Late in 1865, whisky went from a dollar fifty a gallon and then to a prohibitive figure of two dollars a gallon. Stills are a "boiling and troubles are a brewing."

Shortly after the Civil War, the moonshining got so bad that by late 1865, President US Grant, sent his less favorite General to the Southland to eradicate illicit liquor manufacturing.

General Armstrong Custer commanding several battalions of worn out, but "crack" soldiers attempted to flush out these mountaineers and destroy the only "art" they knew. To the contrary, General Custer met the same fate that he was to meet at the "Little Bighorn" by the Sioux. He was sent with his tail wagging back to Washington and then West to meet the Sioux.

In 1867, the government thought the moonshiner would throw in their buckets and go to raising cotton and tobacco, but they thought wrong. In 1869, the newer administration removed most of its old Revenue officials.

In 1872, taxes were reduced to seventy-five cents a gallon, on one hundred proof whisky, however, in 1875 it went up to ninety cents a gallon for one hundred proof. In the mountains of the Southern states illegal distillers were building and storing more "white lightning."

For some reason or another the government paid little or no attention to those tobacco spitting country boys, who bathed once a week in the creek, while slopping mash all the way to the still to the tune of one hundred and ten proof.

Uncle Sam worried about those good old boys who were making whisky so strong that it would take the enamel off your teeth.

The tax jumped again to two dollars a gallon, while corn brought twenty-five cents and at its best fifty cents a bushel. A bushel of apples or peaches cost no more than ten cents a bushel.

These were the only crops that could be grown on ridges and rocky valleys. Transportation was very difficult, markets remote, and so what was left they added to their corn, apples, peaches, and what not, putting them together in a jar, equaling one hundred proof.

The new Internal Revenue Commissioner started surveying information on illegal whisky and its manufacture in the mountains of the Southeastern regions and urged vigorous measures to suppress it.

He said, "the extent of these frauds, would startle any belief. In the past year more than 3000 illicit stills have been in operation in designated districts of the South. They are producing ten to fifty gallons of moonshine a day and something must be done about it."

These moonshiners are located at in-accessible points in the mountains away from the main line of travel. This is pretty much the same today, but; the moonshiner is running out of real estate to put their stills on. This is due to the development of rural areas by giant mountain and lake building entrepreneurs such as those along Smith Mountain Lake in Franklin County, Virginia.

Stills are hidden underground, or in "prefabed" buildings, in these counties as the one previously mentioned. The largest was found about one mile from the Franklin county line in Pittslyvania County, Virginia, in a huge 'prefabed" building especially built to hold those 36-800 gallon blackpots.

The stills of yesteryear were owned by unlettered men of desperate character as opposed to today's tax dodging characters who may be a pillar of the community. Those of bygone days were armed and dangerous and ready to resist the law.

In 1879, the hierarchy of the Revenue Department was made up of some duke's mixture of government officials. They were the tax collectors. U.S. Marshal's of the United

States, and District Attorneys, and United States Commissioners were paid a fee by the commissions on collections. Then there were the subordinate agents whose income depended upon the number of illegal stills they cutup and the number of arrests they made.

Some of the officials were brutal and desperate characters who were also armed and dangerous before they were deputized. They were ready to seek out the moonshiner. The government collectors could authorize up to ten additional deputies, while the most experienced Revenue Agents of great perseverance and courage were assigned to duty.

United States Marshal's made a name for themselves hunting moonshiners and desperate characters. They were frequently called upon to accompany tax collectors along with the Revenue Agents. Their sole duty was to seize and arrest all persons known to violate the liquor laws. You can forget about the Sheriff's in those days because the "stillers or shiners" were most time kin folk.

In certain parts of the country many people didn't make or sell corn liquor, but sympathized with those who did. There are all sorts of stories about Revenue Agents. One such mountain man was asked about the Revenue Agents that came through. "Low down scoundrels, every one of 'em, plum ornery, lock stock, barrel and gun stick. They will suck up yore 'squeezings', lie to you, cut up yore still, break up your stash, and have been known to run off with your daughter and even take your wife if they could!"

Most mountaineers say the revenue men were runners themselves before they "ginned" the service. In late 1879 and early 1890, it was getting incredible at the amount of moonshine whisky that was being made and distributed in this country.

The Internal Revenue service reported at one time, "It is with great difficulty to enforce the liquor laws and the mountain regions of West Virginia, Kentucky, Virginia, Tennessee, North and South Carolina's, Georgia, Alabama, Arkansas, Mississippi, Florida and Texas. We are satisfied that the annual loss to the government from this source has been nearly if not equal to the annual appropriation for the collection of the tax throughout the whole country."

You can imagine what the moonshiner had to say about that. Very few could write the government in those days, and wouldn't if they could. They would say this, I am certain," Stick it in your ear, Uncle Sam."

Maybe so, however, the bearded old man was going to get tough with these people. There were known to exist over five thousand illegal stills strewn out through the "hollows" and hills of the South. Moonshining was getting bigger and bigger and more profitable as larger stills were being built and operated as opposed to those small "pot-teens."

Revenue agents seeking out the moonshiner and their illegal stills got in so many gun battles with those desperate characters that they finally armed us with Breech Loaded Carbines. It finally got so bad that "posses" had to be organized, numbering from five to sixty to affect arrest and warrant seizures.

It wasn't a one-sided affair, with some one hundred and twenty agents being killed, seventy-five wounded, and some were never able to ride a horse or walk again. One hundred and nineteen were wounded due to liquor related incidents and accidents, not to mention drinking accidents. Four hundred Moonshiners or illegal distributors were killed or wounded, from West Virginia to Georgia, and Arkansas to Mississippi.

Revenuer's finally reached the conclusion that the "fraud of illicit distilling was an evil of the devil, to be ferreted out and that it must be endured and we are sure it has been."

It had been concluded in those days that it was an economic thing and not a tax thing.

State officers including Judges on the same bench have sided with illegal distillers (1880) and even in 1989, they said they "weren't criminals" however.

In January of 1994, a judge in Pittislyvania county, Virginia, gave the maximum sentence under the new sentencing guidelines. If you have been convicted of illegal distilling, you can get the maximum sentence of five years, and he handed out the first in the history of illegal distilling. The judge reprimanded the "criminal" by saying, "Maybe this will deter moon-shining in Pittislyvania County, Virginia. Remember this also, it was just across the line from the moonshine capital of the nation, in Franklin County, Virginia.

The law enforcement was in shambles in the bygone days. State officer's wouldn't investigate cases where US officers were in ambush and killed and where conflicts were common, especially where the revenue officers killed violators.

They were arrested and prosecuted by state authorities. State and local officers never received any medals for the way they treated U.S. Government and U.S. Officials, either.

To show the increased magnitude, eight thousand unlicensed distilleries were destroyed between 1877 and 1880.

In January 1880, a combined movement of armed bodies of the Internal Revenue department and its officers were to suppress untaxed liquor and unlicensed stills from West Virginia, southward through the mountains and foothills infested with "moonshiners" and bootleggers.

The effect of this movement was to convince violators of the law that if was the determination of the government to put an end to illegal liquor making and it's resistance of government authority.

One hundred years later, January 1980, in Henry County, and Franklin County, Virginia, a combined movement of armed bodies, "mustered."

They were made up of United States Revenue Agents, Alcoholic Beverage Control Agents, Sheriff's deputies of both counties, and the city police of Martinsville, Virginia. Both the US Marshals and the police from North Carolina and other small surrounding towns made a wide sweep westward into the both counties to bring bootleggers, drug dealers, and illegal distillers to justice.

Our task force "80" and task force "90" used the same philosophy that we used one hundred years ago, concerning liquor enforcement in the Southeastern United States. We apparently didn't learn a thing!

Illegal distilleries declined in 1882-85. Revenue agents and the moonshiner's casualties became far and between, however, just for a little while, as the government couldn't keep its nose out of private enterprises. In 1894, they increased the taxes on spirits from the old ninety cents a gallon to one dollar a gallon. Once again, seizures tripled and blood shed increased.

The turn of the century was around the corner and because of powerful anti-saloon leagues and the women's temperance movements, the nation was pulling away from the Civil War philosophy that there would be no need for prohibition.

According to these leagues stating prohibition in some areas of the nation looked like they were heading for complete dryness.

A turn of events changed the entire domestic scene when seventy-nine years ago to the date of January 1917, Germany announced that its submarines would sink any vessel bound into or out of any allied port. America wasn't going to stand for that, and we didn't. It declared war on Germany on April 6, 1917.

World War I is here and so is prohibition. President Woodrow Wilson has both an international and national mess on his hands. All able-bodied men went to the military, shipyards, and munitions plants.

Churches gained political power and utilized it. The eighteenth amendment was passed and the Volstead Act came in. Prohibition put a premium on illegal whisky making. The profit of moonshine jumped from seventy-five cents a gallon to three dollars a gallon.

In 2004, tax on a gallon of legal whisky both federal and state taxes, totaled twenty-four dollars and fifty cents. Sale of untaxed whisky and brandy runs from twenty dollars a gallon to forty dollars a gallon, while brandy is anywhere between ninety and a hundred twenty-five dollars a gallon.

Chapter Three

The Great Experiment

Moonshiners of the thirteen southern states of this new union put up a tremendous fight against the United States government. That is why southern doughboys of World War I and II, Korean, Viet Nam, and Desert Storm and Mid East Wars made the best guerilla fighters.

Now, guerilla warfare erupts again in the Southern Appalachian. This time, moonshining wasn't just for those old country boys chewing black maria and pitching horse shoes while the mash ferments in those wooden boxes and barrels.

The Great Experiment had begun. Wartime prohibition had begun in 1917. Congress passed the Lever Food and Fuel Act, prohibiting the manufacture of distilled spirits for beverage purposes, especially from grains, cereals, fruits, and all food products. To top this off, the government decreed all existing stocks of beverage alcohol taxing it at three dollars and fifty cents a gallon. Remember those good old boys were paying a dollar ten cents a gallon? Their uncles and grand-dads are making enormous profits on a gallon at half the price of the tax alone.

Bootleggers were smiling all across the Southern Moonshine Belt (supposed to be the Bible Belt), not to mention racketeering because grinning to the North of us, was the mafia.

The Volstead Act gave President Wilson's government ample enforcement powers and the National Prohibition Act became law on October 28, 1919. Strange as it may seem,

Sigmunds Freud and Statesman William C. Bullits booked a Psychological study of President Woodrow Wilson, and not a word was mentioned about the National Prohibition Act.

A thirsty public, the advent of bathing suits, fast cars, and trucks was the important issues of this era. World War 1 had ended and our doughboys, at least the ones who made it, came home less sober than they left. Cognac and those French women taught them some tricks.

President Wilson and his cabinet were preoccupied with the League of Nations and International Politics, not even giving the Volstead Act a "hiccup." That waiting period before prohibition went into effect on January 20, 1920, which further complicated matters.

Existing liquor stocks had risen to be taxed at six dollars and forty cents a gallon. Virginia moonshiners saw the handwriting on their "buckets" and worked day and night "running the mash."

Northern bootleggers were working frantically to "screw" the government out of taxes by finding a new way to distill whisky coming up with the "column still." These "column stills" speeded up the distilling process. This was to out smart those old cockfighting-overall wearing, dumb southern country boys in the delivery of corn whisky to those city slickers. The battle was on.

At the beginning of prohibition, illegal stills seized in Virginia jumped from a few hundred to several thousand. The enigma goes on and on. By 1924-25, Virginia was the third ranking moonshine state in the nation and Franklin County, Virginia was proclaimed and publicized the "Moonshine Capital of the World," and remains the "Moonshine Capital of the Nation."

In 1925-26 seizure of illicit stills reached an all time high in the nation and new moonshiners had surrendered with more than four thousand six hundred stills to the "Revenueers" and Law Enforcement Officers, along with eleven million dollars worth of equipment, vehicles, wagons, horses, mules and oxen.

During this era, whisky makers received a yield of one hundred and ten proofs, especially on the second run, or commonly known as the "second twist." This was done without the use of sugar, however.

They gradually caught on, that if you put sugar in the mash, it would boost the amount of alcohol and proof-age. Through the extensive use of sugar and a thing called a "doubler" and "Thumper Keg," they would have to run the whisky through only once.

Then came the bigger stills and the copper pots were put on the back burner.

Later came the Multi-Blackpot or submarine type stills. These Multi-Blackpot stills can produce more illegal whisky faster than the old steam outfits, and are easier to construct and a lot cheaper.

These Multi-Blackpots of "submarines" came into being in the late forties and early fifties. This last frontier of moon-shining was still flourishing in the sixties and in the eighty's and even today, and will continue most likely until the end of time.

In the "Free State of Franklin County, Virginia," this idea seems to remain right up on top and at specific dates in time. They offered ample proof-age which they took the appellation seriously and to be quite frank about it they do it today, sixty-three years after prohibition.

Thomas Jefferson once said, "The best governed were the least governed," and also advocated and hoped the United States would be a nation of small farmers, for in his opinion, only this could insure independence and liberty.

President Jefferson found reason to modify his attitude but the average farmer of the south stuck to the original text for years because comparatively speaking, most residents of the south operated small farms.

Mr. Jefferson wasn't aware that the red clay of Franklin County and the South made it difficult to raise a crop, or to harvest tobacco and cotton which was then a cash crop, Marijuana is the cash crop of the nation now requiring strained labor and long hours in the fields.

Further, the Free State of Franklin County, Virginia, as well as many other Southern Counties found that their soil formation did not lend itself readily to the construction of good roads thus later on causing some of the population to put their rows of "corn in fruit jars."

The North was "dry." It was noted that only qualified voters participated in the election, so by far, the great majority had no say one way or the other. Assertively, the "wets" sought illegal sources and for the many good folks it seemed like the Millennium had come.

With illegal distilleries and in spite of an increase in Federal and State Law Enforcement Officers, a steady stream of whisky poured into the cities of the Eastern Seaboard and elsewhere and with this illegality came corruption.

Roanoke, Virginia became one city with headquarters of the gaunt Norfolk and Western Railroad (Norfolk-Southern) and tattled many a story that crews on the Roanoke-Winston-Salem NC, divisions, made unscheduled stops at lonely crossings, faking inspections of the train and engine. There, liquor was loaded and sent on to Winston-Salem. Some drops were made at the "Franklin Road Crossing" and along the "pumpkin line."

None were wiser and dozens of five gallon "tins" of moonshine was dumped for pickup and distribution. Fleets of whisky running cars, private carriers and even horses drawn milk wagons were delivering something a little "stronger" than sweet milk.

At the Franklin Road Crossing, in South Roanoke, fleet type vehicles brought thousands of what was termed good whisky to the North and East. Thousands of gallons are leaving Franklin county every month in 1996. Just recently, a noted moonshiner was stopped for speeding through radar in Dinwiddle County, Virginia. The trooper using his police sense of smell, detected the odor of untaxed whisky, emitting from the rear of the "camper pickup." Investigation revealed four hundred and fifty gallons of illegal whisky.

Another noted violator from Franklin County, was stopped for running through radar in Rockingham County, Virginia. Again another sharp smelling Trooper smelled the odor of untaxed whisky and this "transporter" had deodorizers hanging in the "camper pickup." An investigation revealed three hundred and fifty gallons of "white lightning" which was supposed to be heading North.

In 1996 between February and March three heads of "White Lightin" were seized in Northern Virginia total of thirteen hundred gallons, all coming from "the hand between the lakes and home of sixty thousand springs" Franklin, County Virginia going north to the thirsty public seventy-one years after prohibition.

While many types of vehicles were confiscated and thousands of dollars imposed in fines, the traffic increased. Remember we said, "Hard surface, secondary roads were coming?" There were few, hard and long coming.

Revenue Agents tried getting off trains far below where they suspected leads of whisky were to be stashed. Some tried racing their chase cars to cut off the trains and intersect the crossings. These methods just set the "grapevine" in motion and county telephone began to "crackup."

Law Enforcement Officers crossing the county might come upon a still running, "hot as a fox, trying to out run the hounds," but could not find operators of the still anywhere.

Government Raiders were becoming exasperated until the old man with the white whiskers quietly built up the winning hand starting around 1929-30. Investigations of invoices, shipments of certain commodities continued until February-March of 1935. A little known law was passed in 1929-30, called the JONES LAW. It was empowered to provide fines up to ten thousand dollars for offenses against the Prohibition Laws. It also provided for imprisonment from one to five years or both fine and penal time. Prohibition ended December 6, 1933. Was this the end of "The Dying Art?"

Many in this nation thought that the moonshiner would throw his stills and barrels onto the "scrap-heap." Southern moonshiners had just begun to "soak" the public.

Chapter Four

End of the Fee System

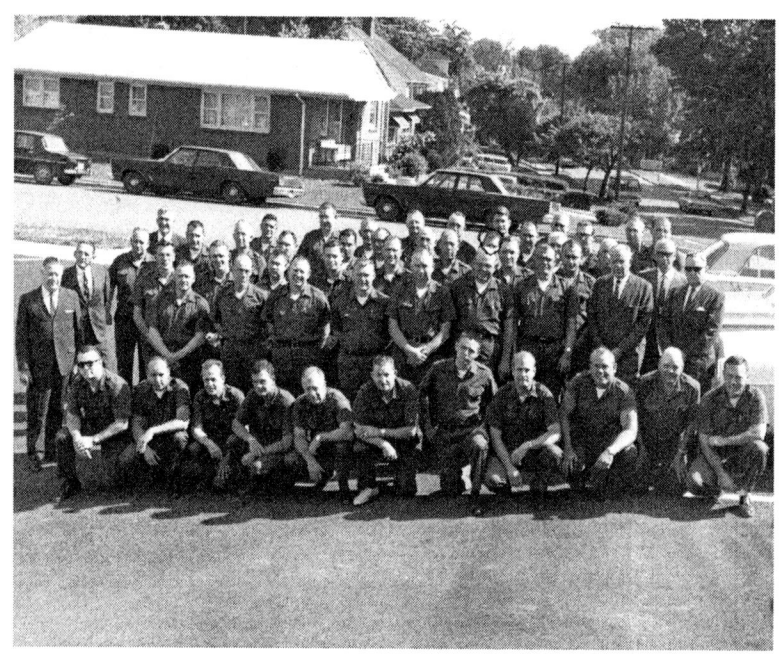

1967, Enforcement Division, annual meeting, Lynchburg, VA

The ending of the old prohibition system caused Monopoly State systems concerning the sale of Alcoholic beverages. Virginia was one of the many that ask for the vote of confidence and in March 1934 Virginia became a Monopoly State and opened its first State operated liquor store in Richmond, Virginia, on Broad Street.

There were that vast number of people who thought that the moonshiner would break up all their bottles and succumb

22

to the government's wishes. Instead the "bootlegger," found out they could fill up their bottles with something else, which is government bonded liquor already charred and ready for resale. Government Agents now had a three fold problem, not just in Virginia, but also in twenty some other states.

Virginia's growing untaxed whisky trade was getting out of hand again and Virginia had to create its own law enforcement agency and I might add second to none until November 21, 1994.

We pioneered undercover work in the thirties, teaching federal agents how to comb the woods for stills and survive in the rugged mountains of the Appalachian, Blue Ridge, Unakas, and the Great Smokey Mountains.

When I said, "We pioneered undercover work I meant we brought to the "bootlegger" the quiet, smooth talking "Fish-Man."

He drove a '37 model truck loaded with assorted Mackerel, Cod and "Salt" fish for sale, that is if "you" had something for sale. He would even trade or barter for untaxed or now taxed liquor.

The other pioneer type of undercover agent that was introduced into the undercover world was "The Watermelon Man" who had a huge '38 Ford Truck loaded with watermelons and chickens and he did business with anyone who had corn in a jug or one hundred proof bonded government whisky. He received plenty of business, catching hundreds in his net.

What brought all this about was that the Governor appointed a three-man ABC board and the Board appointed a Director and fifteen men wee selected to make up the Enforcement Division.

Later they merged their inspection and the enforcement to make up the Enforcement Division because there was only a handful of licensed establishments to monitor. In the hot summer of July 1937 they now had twenty-five men to enforce and to concentrate on the rising untaxed liquor business with the legal whisky bootleggers. The newly appointed director was Mr. C.W. Saunders of Richmond, Virginia and a graduated class of the Virginia Military Institute. He served in the United States Navy as a gallant pilot.

As the years went by, the Enforcement Division grew to fifty-two men, which consisted of a director, an assistant director, four supervisors, (for the four geographical territories, Tidewater, Northern, Central & Western Districts).

Later in 1982 the ABC board again merged forces creating the Regulatory Division and after fifty-seven years not only is monitoring nearly twenty thousand licensees and continuing to battle the "moonshine enigma" with only one hundred and thirty seven Special Agents. That is the total of all the agents doing a magnificent job without any additional help.

In fifty-seven years we have had only three directors. Mr. C.W. Saunders, Mr. Stanley E. Gaulding, and Mr. John M. Wright. Mr. Gaulding was a graduate of hard knocks. Mr. Saunders saw merit in a hard working Mr. Gaulding and promoted him to Assistant Director-Director.

As I said, Mr. Saunders was a graduate of Virginia Military Academy and the third director is a graduate of VPI and SU, Blacksburg, Virginia. He is also a graduate of the Federal Bureau of Investigation (112 Session) Academy, in Quantico, Virginia. The current Director is Mr. Chris Curtis, Director of Bureau of Law Enforcement (ABC), FBI Academy, Session 180. The liquor enforcement priorities were three fold in those days.

1. Suppression whisky (manufacture transportation, and illegal sale).
2. Illegal sale of government bonded whisky (ABC liquor)
3. Illegal importation of Bonded Whisky in bonded warehouses.

This threefold purpose still exists today with certain other priorities concerning the use and possession of alcoholic beverages by persons under twenty-one years of age. Robberies and burglaries of the new self service of ABC stores.

Now we have "total agents" in Virginia. Moonshiners of Virginia and of the South who boasted once of the best makers of white lightning in the nation, and many who made millions of gallons of corn squeezing's in a few short years, bragged about how they never got caught.

There were different types of stills being invented all the time in the dear old South. Virginia went from the Copper Kettle to the copper Pot, then on to Steam Stills, to the Multi-Blackpots which are popular today. Tennessee was the first to employ the famous "Silver cloud." It's a funny looking thing. It looks like a rocket!

Alabama stuck with the "crude" steam still.

There were all sorts of stills being utilized through the South. Again the whisky business was growing at such alarming proportions that the Federal Government revamped its old prohibition program and called in some of its "legal whisky" store keeper gaugers. These guys knew the process of fermentation and nomenclature of distilling. They armed and ordered these new agents on the scene to combat the new techniques and more sophisticated equipment at the disposal of the moonshiner.

More and more states were organizing their own enforcement agencies eliminating the "Old Fee System." Horses were replaced by slower cars and now slower cars are replaced by the faster cars and trucks to provide new links to the thirsty public.

The New National Liquor Industry had now as yet become organized enough to exert any pressure on the now running rampant moonshiner, especially any legislation to effect the liquor issue.

Illegal liquor operations continued to flourish and state and federal agents teamed together to continue to battle the makers of the untaxed mountain beverage.

The real battle was being fought to keep us out of the next war. World War II was on top of us. The illegal whisky mobsters were getting worried. What about sugar? The "life blood" of the moonshiner. Would sugar be rationed? Yes!

World War II erupted December 7, 1941. Most of the our "boys" had to answer the beckoned call to save their country. If you were ever convicted of moonshining, which is a felony, you were not eligible for the service, however, many went and died for their country.

The Law verses the Lawless. Mountaineers went right on making whisky using molasses and Karo syrup. Thousands of rusty gallons of Karo and molasses buckets are lying in the woods today. They are a reminder that there was a way that sugar when rationed or-not, was used for making liquor.

The war ended and the boys came home to a real celebration. Ticker tapes and all. There were many unemployed men looking for work and they found it. Yeah!, with Daddy, Uncles, and Grandpa's in the hills and hollows of this great Southeastern United States.

Their philosophy was simple, and I quote from them, "If I am good enough to fight for my country, then I am good enough to get into the liquor trade." There is nothing wrong with it, except when there is a little tax dodging and if they can cheat the government in any way they can, then they will do it.

From 1920 to 1996, the moonshiner continues to fortify themselves in Franklin and Pittislyvania Counties and it is the "only" county in the nation where four law enforcement agents, are stationed to enforce the liquor laws.

Of course, there are other counties in the South that produce vast amounts of untaxed whisky.

Chapter Five

Statistical Still Data

The moonshiner was getting more sophisticated with the faster cars and better communications in the 1950's. There would never have been NASCAR, if it had not been for some moonshine-race drivers such as Turner, Johnson, Flocks, and many other good drivers.

Some of their wildest and bravest deeds were on the back roads of Virginia, North, and South Carolina, Georgia, Mississippi, and the boonies, "running wide open" most of the time with their lights off and the liquor law hot on their tall, long before the Premier Southern Racing Circuit or northern racing circuit was established.

Some of the very first racers were the liquor runners, who never got their debut on the "dirt tracks" or the "asphalt turns," because they spent most of their time in jail.

There's a nice story that the old timers say is true about "Lakewood," which is the old dirt track in Atlanta. They banned everyone from that area who had been arrested for "transporting moonshine."

They wouldn't let one of the Flock brothers race at "Lockwood" so he waited until the race started and they were running very fast. He then came out onto the track from the back of the straightaway. When the cops found out he was in the race, they started chasing him. Those race cars came sliding around that old dirt track, pushing, bumping, some crashing, as dirt and dust flew with the cops in the middle of all the action. After several laps, Mr. Flock gave the high sign and came down through the pits and out the back gate, right down through Main Street in Atlanta, cops and all.

The distribution of illegal whisky was flourishing to the degree in the early fifties and sixties that we all thought the whisky was coming from Franklin County, Virginia, but little did we know that Virginia was not the first in the production of mountain spirits.

Fulton County, Georgia was first, and next in line was Haleyville, Alabama, following after that was Wilkes County, North Carolina, and in the following processions came Harlan County, Kentucky; and Franklin County, Virginia.

Virginia was sixth or seventh at times but has rose to the number one spot again with the help of neighboring Pittisyvania County, along with Johnston County, North Carolina, to the tune of 1500 gallons a week going to Washington D.C., New York City, and New York State, etc.

The worlds largest illegal multi-blackpot stills were captured at Cool Springs, Pittislyvania county, Virginia about one mile from the Franklin County line. The stills were in a new prefabricated building with an elaborate pumping and cooling system. They consisted of 36-800 gallon, wood and galvanized submarine type stills that were holding 28,600 gallons of fermenting mash. One person has been arrested and convicted of illegal distilling along with several major drug violations.

In the twenty-first century, moonshine, cocaine, and other drugs seemed to go together. Law breakers support the determination and defiance of the moonshine drug dealers but few enforcement assignments are comparable with the job of running down and eradicating the illegal distiller, and dealers permanently.

Statistic data, in Virginia, reveals that in 1993-96 there were a number of illegal distilleries seized and destroyed, but of the sixteen distillery sites there were great numbers of individual blackpots destroyed also, however, it has not reached any comparison to what was seized and destroyed during the thirties right on through the nineties.

In 1937-38, one thousand seven-hundred stills of various sites were seized and destroyed along with twenty-five million gallons of untaxed whisky, and ten million dollars worth of equipment and motor vehicles, along with twelve million pounds of assorted brands of sugar.

In 1956-57, Virginia enforcement agents seized and destroyed nine hundred and fifty-eight stills, three hundred and fifty-one vehicles, seventy-seven thousand, three hundred and ninety pounds of sugar, one hundred and eight thousand, three hundred and twelve point three gallons of untaxed whisky and live fermenting mash that was condensed to whisky at a ratio of ten to one which amounted to thirty thousand, seven hundred and ninety-nine gallons of corn liquor, along with twenty million, two hundred and fifty-nine thousand, six hundred, point three dollars worth of miscellaneous equipment.

In 1967-68, four hundred stills, one hundred and thirteen vehicles, twenty-two thousand, and two hundred and ninety-five, point five gallons of illegal "hooch," seized and destroyed.

Fifteen thousand one hundred and eighty pounds of sugar, one jeep, one tractor trailer, one horse, one wagon, one goat, one saddle, and one hundred and ten thousand gallons of fermenting mash ready for distillation.

On March 17, 1968, near beautiful Concord, North Carolina, something suspicious was going on underneath a huge barn in the community of Midland, in Cabarrus County.

After a long surveillance by State and Federal Revenue Agents, and the Sheriff's department they raided the massive underground distillery, arresting two and one escaped.

This unique operation is believed to be the world's largest illegal steam type distillery. It was housed under a huge barn in a room three hundred and twelve feet long and three hundred and eighteen feet wide. According to Bob Martin, ATU agent, it was the most elaborate set up he had ever seen in his career as a government agent.

The still had a total mash capacity of thirty-three thousand gallons of mash. It could produce three thousand gallons of whisky at a ratio of ten to one. (Ten gallons of mash to one gallon of whisky or one gallon of whisky for every ten pounds of sugar used.)

The mammoth conglomerate actually consisted of thirty-three individual stills, each having a capacity of approximately one thousand, one hundred gallons of mash. The giant distillery had been in operation for several years. The illegal factory was located on Sossomans Road, on the Elfiard farm and was taken care of by a man named Gregory of Wilkes County, North Carolina. Efiard and Gregory were taken into custody and charged with the possession of an unregistered distillery, possession of illegal distillery equipment, along with the illegal manufacture of untaxed whisky.

The distillery was completely underground and could only be entered from a concealed hatch in the old barn and through a compartment at Mr. Efiard's home. It was hidden well, because a search of the premises years before failed to turn up any clues of such an operation.

It was a "blue print job" probably designed by an engineer and was constructed from prearranged plans. A trap door leading into the huge underground chamber was hidden under a large stack of hay, the underground room extended from the rear of the barn to the front of it, and thirty-three vats lined the right side of the room with hundreds of cases of fruit jars along with two thousand seven hundred and twenty-three gallons of white lightning, surrounded by a twenty-seven thousand gallon of fermenting mash. Viewing the still from above ground was virtually impossible to detect "any" signs of such goings on in a grown up pasture with cattle grazing on it.

The still contained a special filtering system to prevent odor escaping from it to the outside. Underground pipes extended nearly a quarter of a mile to a creek. At the creek, moonshiners placed a large water pump and buried it far beneath the ground level, with heavy insulation to keep it muffled. The pump could be switched on at the still providing cold water to cool the condensers.

The huge vats were made of steel, the piping was galvanized, the condensers were made of old truck radiators. They even stole the electricity from the power company, Duke Power company. They connected the wires from the house, and tapped them to the back of the power meter, leading the cables to the underground still. It would cost approximately one hundred thousand dollars to construct a still of this kind. The dismantling of this monster drew thousands of curiosity seekers when Kiser Salvage Company, demolished it. Efiard and Gregory both said, "We don't know what was going on under there."

The Cabarrus Company, still seemed to overshadow every still in the nation, however, ten years after that notorious capture was the largest box-type, coke fired, super-preheated seizure, just up the road from North Carolina in Floyd County on the Paynes Creek Church Road about one mile off the beautiful Blue Ridge Parkway.

It was the day after Memorial Day, June 1, 1957, a day I will never forget because it was my first still raid as a State Agent. It was a quiet area, off the Blue Ridge along the Little River. The biggest things sitting near the Parkway was a quaint little white church with a small yard and gravel parking lot.

We crossed an old steel bridge that dated back to 1898, and as rusty as hell. Running parallel with the river was an old road, and at the entrance of this road we noticed many pine laps laying across the road covering up any travel leading to an old weather beaten house that seemed abandoned. Beyond the house was a family cemetery. Mr. George Martin, group leader for ABC enforcement, dropped ATU Agent, Walter W. Elmore and I off near the bridge and cautiously we made our way down the river bottom and up to the old house. The travel on the road was well worn by the vehicles.

We went around to the back of the old house and over to the family cemetery. At first we thought the road going to the cemetery was busy because of the Memorial Day holiday, as there were wreaths and flowers placed on the graves of loved ones.

As Walter and I approached the old house we could see clothes hanging on the make shift line on the porch. The rusty gate had been oiled and there were chickens running on the porch as well as little pigs under the house.

We were out in the open and if anyone had been anywhere around, we would have been "caught" but no one came to the half-fallen front door. We went directly behind the house and into the woods, when we weren't there but a few minutes and I stumbled over a huge black plastic pipe buried under the leaves and ground. At that time, I knew nothing about stills. I had been a Roanoke City policeman for a year, working liquor and vice with Sergeant Jack Heath. Mr. Elmore had been a government agent for twenty years then and knew every aspect of illegal distilling. He was the first state police motorcycle rider that ever chased "moonshiners" down US Rt. 220 in the thirties, before he became a federal agent. Walter whispered to me, "Jack, I think this is a big one."

We followed the black hose further into the woods and onto an area that became a "bluff." Down the bluff came the river and buried in the bank of the river were two large Briggs and Stratton engines, attached to the large Demming pumps. The pumps were muffled in the river by two large "crocks."

We went back up the bluff and through the woods until we heard voices. Walter said in a whisper, "Jack, you go back up to the main road and get Mr. Martin and wait on Mr. Prillaman, then return here "pronto.""

I made it back to the main road and hid under the old steel bridge. We didn't have any walkie-talkie's with us because the only one we had was in the hands of Agent Harless Taylor and Jim Bowman, and they were in Franklin county. It was an old "link set" with an antenna twenty-five feet long.

We used the old "boot leggers method." Wait sufficient time, then start looking for us. We put a stick out on the main road so if our people came along they would see that we signaled them. Agent Wayne Prillaman was in court on this day, but he didn't want to miss this part of the action.

While I was waiting for Mr. Prillaman and Mr. Martin, a 1946 Chevrolet sedan pulled up to the bridge near an old mail box someone had placed there. A few minutes later a 1950 ford pickup pulled behind him. Being new, I didn't recognize either of the people in the vehicles and I had to stay low under the bridge.

Apparently, they heard something and drove off quickly. It was Wayne in our 1957 Thunderbird Interceptor and I came out and jumped into the car and we took it down the old River Road and hid it in the bushes. We called Mr. Martin on the State Police radio who was in the car to get out of the area. He was affirmative and we ran up the hill into the woods and joined Mr. Elmore.

We could hear someone working not too far from us. The giant black hose led to that direction and we were attempting to get into raid position. We got closer and we could see it was a very large illegal distillery. We could see a huge smoke stack in the air and something large mounted on a platform. Mr. Martin had brought his black Interceptor down the road and had joined us. He placed me in the woods about one hundred yards from the still.

It was in the Spring of the year and the algae on the leaves and trunk of the trees were eating me up. I wanted to sneeze but knew better, and a good thing too, because I had glanced up in front of me, and there stood a man in bibbed overalls and he was unhooking the galluses. I guess nature had caught up with him. I muffled a cough and he stood up and looked all around, quickly he buckled his overalls and just stood there, looking all around. I was hiding beneath a big log and I didn't move a muscle. He then went back to the still and back to work. Now, I had the stuff running down my leg, I was so excited. I didn't want to "screw" up my first big raid.

After they settled down, we raided the still and I had the pleasure of running down the guy that came out in the woods where I was hiding. I asked him if he heard me, and he said, "I am hard of hearing and I didn't hear a thing."

Mr. M. Shively, was a nice man who had been caught seven times. Mr. J. Sigmon was the total opposite of Mr. Shively, and he had been caught fifteen times and it wouldn't be his last before court.

When we reached the still, it was staggering to the mind. It was very huge, and it was no doubt it was the largest in the Southwestern part of Virginia ever, and now we think it was the largest Box-type-Coke fired-Super-Preheated, concept in the world. An illegal still of course! There were fifty four four by four wooden pine box fermenters containing approximately twenty-five thousand gallons of live mash. It would produce one thousand five-hundred gallon's a day-pre-heater concept.

There were seven hundred gallons of white lightning to be taken out. This huge still gained the attention of a popular Magazine, "Male Point Of View" and the "Jack Parr" show on NBC.

Those participating in the raid were Mr. A.L. Fulcher, Wytheville, Virginia, Supervisor, ABC, Western District, (now deceased), State Troopers Walter Moore and Tom Gibbs, (former ATU) (both deceased.) both defendants are deceased, (Sigmon and Shively) ATU Elmore and ABC Prillamen (deceased). Only survivors of the raid are Mr. G.A. Martin (deceased) and myself.

Both defendants at the time of the raid were told to come to the United States Commissioners hearing on a certain date on their own recognization. They were as good as their word and reported that morning at 9 a.m. Most old timers were highly reliable and honest. They usually worked for someone else who was beating the government out of taxes.

Then came Federal Court time with The Honorable Judge John Paul presiding. It is to date the largest federal court term in the history of Western Virginia, with one hundred and forty-seven defendants standing in the hallway of the second floor of the old United States Post Office Building. One of the chief prosecutors was Mr. H. Clyde Pearson now The Honorable H. Clyde Pearson the Federal Bankruptcy Judge (retired). The only other large trial of notoriety was the "Franklin County Conspiracy" in 1934.

Those defendants standing around in the hallway of the court house were thirsty because they brought with them their own whisky to drink, keeping it in their "bibs" and in the men's toilet and hallways.

It kept us, the US Marshal Chief Deputy Boyer and his lone Deputy Marshal, George Rasnick busy taking bottles of corn liquor away from the defendants as well as keeping them sober enough to be tried plus maintaining order.

Mr. B.A. Davis was the senior defending lawyer, along with his young son B.A. Davis Jr. There was a host of other good lawyers but Mr. Davis probably stands out among most of the others because of his love for Franklin County and its citizens.

The case that brought the most attention in this court were the Shively & Simon cases. They had no lawyer and said they didn't need one.

As the court clerk, Mr. Gentry looked on, the government witness testified about Shively & Sigmon working in the still and running from it during the raid. They testified to the enormous capacity of the illegal distillery and that the defendants stated that the still was huge and bigger than any one they had worked at before.

After the State and Government agents had testified to the surmounting facts, defendant Shively wanted to testify. Mr. Shively took the witness stand wearing a brand new white shirt neatly ironed and a new pair of bibbed overalls. He had a new handkerchief in the upper bibbed pocket. He was astute. Sitting on the front row was his entire family which consisted of his wife, children, mother, daddy, neighbors, and friends.

Mr. Shively proceeded to testify, looking Judge Paul directly in the eye and expressing himself dramatically. Remember Judge John Paul twenty-two years ago was the presiding federal Judge that heard all the conspiracy testimony in 1935. You would think he was getting callas to personal stories, however, as tears flooded Mr. Shively's eyes, he told the honorable Judge Paul that he had several small children. "Your honor," he said clearing his throat and wiping the tears from his eyes with his new handkerchief, "There they sit, you can see them, I don't have any education or skills. I don't know anything but to make liquor, and I am forty two years old and I hope you will sentence me to a long prison sentence to Mill Point West Virginia where I can learn a trade, maybe I will be worth something then, (tears streamed down his face) and taking his new handkerchief he wiped the tears away. U.S. Attorney, Mr. Strickler was speechless.

"I want to be worth something to my wife and family. I have been caught seven times in still houses and I need to learn something besides "stillin." Mr. Shively wrung out the tears in his new handkerchief. Judge Paul listened intently. You could have heard a pin fall in that courtroom.

Everyone was crying, the lawyers, the spectators, law officers, and the court staff. "I know I am going to do wrong," Judge Paul said.

He was rubbing his bald head, and said, "Mr. Shively I'm going to give you another chance. Don't let me down."

Mr. Shively was given three years probation and never made liquor again, to my knowledge. Mr. Shively although a mountain moonshiner was truly a gentleman.

After 35 years of being a "revenuer" I have thought of what he said that day, many times, and when I grabbed him by the gallis of his overalls running from that huge still, he turned to me and said, "Please don't beat me like the other revenuer have when they caught me at the "still house."

Mr. Shively's co-defendant wasn't as lucky as he. Mr. Sigmon had been caught fifteen times and was on the bond waiting trial for having been caught at a big still in Appomattox County, VA, thirty days after being caught at the world's largest super-pre-heat still. The one in Appatomox County was a pretty big one too.

Judge Paul wasn't as understanding as he was with Mr. Shively. Mr. Sigmon was currently under three bonds for making whisky. He was told by Judge Paul. "I hope you have your tooth brush because I am sentencing you to eighteen months in the Federal Pen at Mill Point, West Virginia. (Most all liquor convicts were sent to Mill Point, in those days. It no longer exists.) That was Mr. Strickler recommendation, he was the U.S. Attorney for Western Virginia.

Judge Paul ordered the Chief Deputy Marshal, Mr. Boyer, to take charge of Mr. Sigmon and put him in lockup for transportation to Mill Point.

That was the two larger box-illegal distilleries we ever captured, however, they by far weren't the largest newer type of illegal distilleries captured in Virginia and classified as not only the World's Largest Black Pot still concept, but they were "born" in Virginia in the fifties.

The World's Largest blackpot type of illegal distilleries was captured in the nations finest county, population forty thousand. It was found on a land between two fishing lakes. Smith Mountain Lake and Phillpott Lake home of the best sun cured tobacco in the world, and naturally the best "corn

In A Jar" that one could see coming out of a rusty truck radiator and if you poured it down a drain, it would take the hide off any rat down there. Oh yes! There had been some good apple and peach brandy and lots of good corn sprouted whisky made by some old timers who took pride in making good whisky and not this new breed of distiller and bootleggers who wanted to make it for quantity and not for quality.

It seems from the looks of this conglomeration of black-pot stills that someone was manufacturing for quantity rather than good old quality.

The "Still House" was located off Rt. 778, four point five miles of Ferrum, Virginia, in Franklin county, at the Republican church area. The huge still shed housed twenty four eight hundred gallon blackpots with nineteen thousand two hundred gallons of mash. There were two hundred gallons of un-taxed whisky sitting in front of the operation ready to be taken out.

Government and State Revenue agents watched the big still or series of stills. Then they got "hot". Something went wrong during the fermenting process or someone saw government investigators in the area. They didn't come back so we put the world's largest blackpot stills high in the air. It is the largest assembly of stills ever raided in Franklin County since I have been here in all my twenty-one years said, Kenny Stoneman, law enforcement Supervisor and Chief of Enforcement for Southwest Virginia that encompasses approximately twenty counties.

Just across the county from Ferrum and Henry ATU and ABC agents destroyed 18,800 gallon stills under a fake cemetery. We arrested one at the time attempting to escape from the distillery with 443 gallons of untaxed whisky. The still contained 11,200 gallons of ready mash." The stills were concealed under carefully constructed underground structures which were covered over by a "fake cemetery" with fake tombstones and planted with fake flowers and grass.

It wasn't the world's largest stills as we have portrayed, but it was unique and shows the ingenuity of those old mountain boys. Then there was a 20 pot still captured about the same time with 14,363 gallons of live mash and 300 gallons of liquor was seized. This "outfit" was located 6.5 miles west of US Rt.220 near Phillpott Lake, just the opposite of Smith Mountain Lake, in February 1972.

It goes to show you that the distillers continue to make untaxed whisky in the 1970's because sugar prices dropped a little, making illegal whisky more profitable.

As we move up the mountain into "Floyd County" where there has never been a railroad or track laid. The water runs down into Franklin County and no where else. Floyd County has lent its good name to whisky making and always prided itself of having the best distillers. At one time they were the best until the advent of the Blackpot Still.

Floyd County was the leading county in the nation for having more mineral mines than any other county in the country. They eventually closed all of them, which consisted of copper, nickel, gold, arsenic, lead, silver and zinc. However, they didn't close all of their stills because on April 6, 1973 the world's largest Blackpot operation was raided in Floyd County.

The huge whisky manufacturing plant was in a large black patch, just 2 miles east of the town of Floyd. The ironic thing about this was that the town drunk went around preaching there was a still within site of the court house.

Apparently, no one believed him. He was forever bumming money from everyone including the Sheriff and myself. We didn't take him seriously about anything, but an informer who had been reliable in the past gave us information that a noted convicted bootlegger had several cases of corn whisky hidden in a "trap" in a closet. (False bottom of a closet). We got a search warrant for his house and executed it.

This wasn't just any ordinary bootlegger. He was confined to a bed and a wheelchair, as he was a paraplegic who had lost his legs. He had been in the whisky business for over 40 years. He's deceased.

We caught him at least twice a year so he paid a fine instead of a license. He was a rather good guy but he kept a pearl handled pistol under his pillow and he had mirrors set up so he could see who was coming down the driveway. He didn't like what he saw that day when we presented him with the warrant to search for the "trap."

It wasn't in the closet, however he did have 28 gallons of assorted whisky behind the sofa. We didn't bother that and he was highly perturbed and wanted to know if we looked over the hill from him. I said, "Over the hill? Where?" He never answered me, but we had looked over the hill repeatedly and would come out eventually on his property. We had looked between his property and a black man's just a few days before this and found nothing, and the 82 year old black man saw us come out on the road, but I think he couldn't see too well so he didn't know who we were.

After the search of the house and premises we left and the Deputy that was with us said, "Take me back to the Sheriff's office, I need to be working on those burglaries." Troopers Tom Higgins and Roger Abshire and I were in the patrol car. I said, "Let's go back on the Pike and drive up to Sam's new house."

We drove onto this new road he had bulldozed out which we went through from a hardtop road to another and he maintained it until the state took it over.

We entered from the Franklin Pike side and drove up to a metal building he had placed on the side of his new road about 200 yards from his new home. We could hear a tractor running. I told them to let me out down here near a cattle shute and for them to go directly to the house and if he asked any questions, tell him they were looking for a stolen car.

There was an electric line running off a pole near the silver building, and that didn't look right because the electric line went directly into the ground. I went to the left and hugged a dirt bank down the hill to the left. When I get to the bottom of the hill, there was a black pickup truck parked near a creek. There was a large roll of three inch black plastic hose on the back of the truck. There were no tags or stickers on the truck, as I examined it. Carefully, I went around to the front of the truck from the left and I could hear a faint sound coming from a large mound of dirt heaped nearly as high as the front of the truck.

Troopers Higgins and Abshire went straight to where the tractor was grading. There was snow still on the ground and the ice was thawing as Mr. Sam's worked frantically from where I could see. It was warm that day because I was in civilian clothes and not in my customary field greens.

It was Spring of the year and the birds were chirping along with those water-pumps laboring and the putt, putt, putting in the underground. I heard something "clink" and through some thick alder bushes I could see someone working. He was covering up a trench that was holding a large black hose. He had his back to me at first and then he turned around. We saw each other simultaneously. I didn't know him and I felt he didn't know me. He had on heavy clothes and galoshes.

He also had a large shovel in his hand, and said, "What are you doing here?"

I told him, "I am here to survey some timber." I then continued to ask him, "What are you doing?"

"Building a watering trough at the top of the hill and I'm burying the hose."

Good story I thought as I started to walk a little bit closer to where I had first spotted him. As I got closer, I reached in my pocket for my credentials. I had my stub-nose .38 to the small of my back so he couldn't see it.

He was backing up and I was coming forward, and now by that time I had identified myself. He took off, lickety-split, up the hill trying to kick off those heavy galoshes. I finally got one hand on him and with the other I fired up in the air. Troopers Higgins and Abshire came a running. They jumped across the cattle shut and up near the house where Mr. Sam's was working. Troopers Higgins and Abshire and I finally wrestled him to the ground and placed the "cuffs" on him.

He couldn't tell us his name. I went directly toward where the hose was being buried and when I got there I could hear "blowers" going and when I got near the still site, I was awed by what I saw.

Mr. Sam's left the tractor and when Tom and Roger got over to the still they couldn't believe their eyes. There was so many 800-Gallon blackpots situated throughout the grove of black pines and there was also 1300 gallons of untaxed liquor to be taken out, along with jugs, jars, tubs and strainers.

Large canvas' covered up some of the stills and it was camouflaged from the air. It had three truck radiators as condensers and they buried it with about one thousand feet of hose, when they completed it.

There was some good news for the distillers, because when I fired my pistol not knowing where the still was at that time, the hired help fled, leaving five overall jackets behind hanging on those pine trees.

There was approximately 17,600 gallons of fermenting mash ready for distillation. That is why Mr. Sam's was working so hard, to get a path for the liquor to be taken out and the other mash was ready. It had been bad weather and they had gotten behind. Most of the time they placed two sets of chains on a four wheel drive vehicle and go with it anyway.

Both distillers were tried and received suspended sentences and four year's probation. They made thousands of gallons of untaxed whisky which was converted into thousands of dollars and only received four year's probation.

"The Evil Is Still With Us." This should be the title of a Moonshine Racketeering movie but not as much as it would have been two decades ago. Figures on seizures have shown a decline of 40 to 60% in the last 30 years, of course, reflecting good liquor law enforcement.

If a man moonshine's today, it's by choice and not by necessity. It was a matter of economic significance to many years ago, however, in this day and age, if times get hard enough, some of these banjo picking, guitar strumming country boys might turn to something besides singing to the moon.

It was almost a forgone conclusion, that if Pop and Grand-paw moonshined, his sons followed in their footsteps. A person is not forced into the business today. It is a lucrative and attractive business, but the dues you pay, are ones that may land you and your family into the clinger. The liquor business is buoyant to the economy.

Some twenty-six years ago, in 1970, there were 613 stills seized and destroyed in Virginia, as contrasted with seizures in Alabama, which were 3,847. Georgia had 3,169, while North Carolina had 1,850, leaving Mississippi with 776 and South Carolina a little under that with 691 stills.

Total seizures over a period of 28 years, from a high of 25,608 in 1956 were astronomical. Seizures were down in 1960, and I believe that was because of the Viet NAM War. In 1965 it rose to 19,958 that was down 13,065 in 1968. It went lower and lower and by the year of 1970 to 1980 there was only a slight upswing.

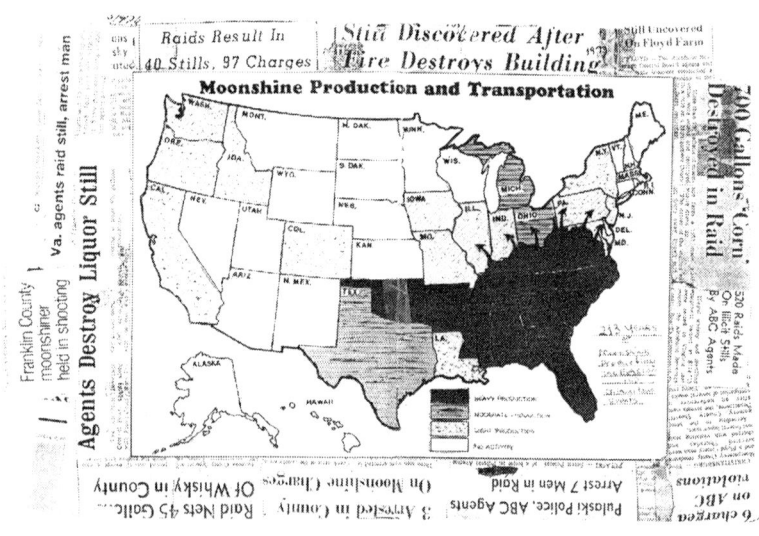

These swings brings to mind as to what class of people "moonshiners" are. We have categorized the poor old moonshiner in every conceivable way, but the "moonshiners"

of today's generation are not your regular "Git the shotgun Maw, there is a revenuer coming over the hill" hillbilly, hobbling down a rickety porch to defend his still. No, he's not that type of "tobacco-chewing" good old boy in a spitting contest to see who can hit the potbelly stove down at the local general store.

Moonshiners are organized specialists in untaxed liquor production, the clandestine transportation of spirits and finances conceived by shrewd minds to evade the nations taxes through criminal activity.

They now have taken some of the illegal liquor money and invested it in a half gallon of marijuana seeds that can be transported in someone's coat lining, planted where there is some sun and water and harvest it whenever you want to, before the frost naturally.

We had two additionally big distillers who are brothers that wanted to get rich quicker by diversion of "likker" money to a suitcase of "coke" and we obliged them by waiting on them to return from Florida with their converted merchandise. They received 25 years just for being greedy.

Years ago a study revealed that 10% of all liquor consumed in the United States from illegal distillers diverted 600 million from public taxes. The estimated loss to Federal, State and Local treasurers since 1965 is approximately 50 billion dollars.

With a reduction of 40 to 60% in the manufacture of illegal spirits, the legal whisky moved forward by virtue of mixed beverages in states that didn't allow them and self service liquor stores in monopoly states and more licenses with both beer and wine, especially in the 1970's and 1980's. These elicit entrepreneurs still beat the taxpayer out of 30 billion dollars over a time.

How did government agents "gauge" the way of illegal distillers that defrauded the taxpayer? Back in the good old days, distillers used wood and coke for fuel, so we would measure the amount of ashes and through a formula calculated figure we accessed the illegal distillers with the appropriate tax.

The smart old country boys then hauled away the ashes and in these modern days with the use of oil and propane fuels it presented another problem until 1987. One of our agents by the name of Barney Arthur got the idea to measure the "mash trails." So, he and tax collectors and a Chemist and photographers went to work. We had located this huge illegal distillery in Botetrout County being operated by some "good old boys" from Franklin County. It was in a large barn, filled with 12-800 gallon blackpots fully "mashed in."

We apprehended the "Crow Brothers" who later plead guilty and received punishment for violating an unpopular law.

However, behind the barn was a trail of mash, one eighth of a mile long, and forty feet wide. That told Special Agent Arthur and the tax collectors something. They measured the length times the width of the "mash trail" and then the depth, and did that from the barn doors throughout the length of the "mash trail."

They also took samples of the mash and had it analyzed at the consolidated laboratory in Richmond, along with the new spent mash that had an alcoholic content which meets the statutory provisions for the definition of distilled spirits or alcohol. These same illegal distillers were assessed a specific amount of taxes and they have paid it or will pay it, or they will lose some of their possessions, such as their cars, trucks, and other non-liquid assets.

Most people would think that these moonshiners would have given up by now, but this was not the case. They starting placing their stills in places where they could easily dispose of the mash, such as diluting it, and letting the mash flow over the bluff into a creek. They hauled it off in trucks, but you had better believe they weren't going to get caught with their pants down.

In the 1980's, the classic American confrontation between the revenuer and the moonshiner was thought to be buckling under the pressure of inflation and the poor economy.

Many families suffered from the rising costs of inflation, and so did the illegal distiller, because sugar, which is the life blood of the moonshiner, kept going up in price. President Carter once said that "Inflation is eating us up," and President Reagan said, "We are putting a lid on inflation." However, the moonshiners in the south said, "Stop this inflation so we can put our profits back in the jar."

The federal government decided to help inflation hoping the two of them along with the state and local law enforcement officers would succeed in taking over a small southern county, which is known as the "Land Between the Lakes."

General Armstrong Custer didn't come back, however, there came a battalion of reporters and government agents from the Bureau of Alcohol and Tobacco, Firearms, and the Virginia ABC Investigators and some lawmen from all over the state and the nation were down here to put the final "Stamp Out" on moonshining in Virginia. If we had been successful, it could have settled the matter in the entire South.

It was classified as a "**Media Bust**" rather than a moonshine bust. An editorial in the Franklin County News, in January of 1980, characterized the issue as "**Still**

Waiting," "**Fly By Night**" and "**Stumble**," through Franklin county to make a big show. The government drew sharp criticism of the way it handled publicity prior to the start of that operation. The procedure for the way the government had national news media on hand to cover the events was very immature.

Word was that the stills were seized several days before the action began and guarded by government and state agents until the Washington Post and other high-powered news media arrived. The rumor was that moonshine in one gallon plastic jugs were seized from other locations and held and brought to the location of the stills where the new media were to set a new record. There were reports that several stills had been blown to bits before the "**Blitz.**"

The stills were credited as being part of the effort to eradicate the terrible demon of the "Moonshine Capital of the Nation."

The "**Blitz**" what did it actually cost in the end? It was estimated to be about one million, five hundred thousand but no one will really know. Many national newspapers from all over the country reported the seizures as sixty stills seized and blown to bits, while forty were arrested in the roundup called, "**Operation Dry Up.**"

George Teston who was second in command of the BATF in Virginia said, "They estimated the stills destroyed in the investigation have bilked the public out of about eight million dollars. That estimate is based on federal alcohol taxes of $10.60 per gallon and Virginia alcohol taxes of $3.50 a gallon. Mr. Teston continued to say, "It's not just a matter of tax money but a health problem. Moonshine is potentially deadly. Ninety percent of the moonshine that the federal authorities tested contains lead salts. They produce physical and mental disabilities and sometimes even death.

He continued to comments that, "Agents have busted three major moonshine production and distribution operations that were distributing to the southern states. Some people said only the surface was scratched, however, only a third of the active stills were destroyed in the six county area of the raid which encompasses Franklin, Floyd, Pittsylvania, Halifax, Henry and Patrick counties, and perhaps maybe even Carroll county.

This was the last of the biggies for a long time to come and was until 1990 when we had the mini-blitz finding a mini-amount of the stills and arrest warrants. Again, many saw the 80-Blitz as a publicity stunt. It was ill-conceived and poorly executed, which dovetailed straight to the news media for the US-BATF, VA-ABC, and the NC Liquor Enforcement Agents. Many people said that the agents muddled the water, and minnows got caught while the big fish got away. The number of stills seized were minuscule compared to the volume of moonshine produced in Franklin County.

An editorial in the Franklin County Times indicated that in 1980, "**Operation Dry Up**," of the Media Blitz was just a show put on by desk jockeys in Washington who apparently was set up by a story in this particular newspaper depicting the fact that Franklin County leads the nation in the production of illegal whisky. And the enigma goes on, while being graphically illustrated by a former moonshiner. His statements were uncanny in the sense that he commented, "A moonshiner is like a groundhog, you find his hole, and cover it up, and he will dig out another."

G.R. Dickerson of the federal enforcement (BATF) agency also replied, "We are going to keep our eye on Franklin County and if this "**Blitz**" doesn't have an impact, we will return." Twelve years of statistical media copy and eye after eye impacted on the county, resulting in a thousand of the gallons of illicit liquor a month, leaving Franklin County, (which is the land between the lakes) and the home of sixty thousand springs, with a population of 40,000 happy citizens. After sixty-three years of prohibition, where do you think that wonderful poison is going?

Chapter Six

Wonderful Poison

Much has been written about why individuals have made illegal liquor, and who are continuing to make both legal and illegal distilled spirits. Has anyone ever stopped to think where it came from? Who created it? God, of course. Who invented it? Not the Wright brothers nor the Smith brothers and certainly not the Japanese.

The intrigue and intoxication of the human race have been around for the past ten thousand years. Was it discovered by accident? The mixing of grain, honey, fruits, which are left standing in a puddle or a container comes by way of diffusion through yeast organisms causing the process of fermentation. After fermentation, the liquid product contains ethyl alcohol that affects human beings and their behavior.

Alcohol has been known to people of all walks of life, from the cave men to the twentieth century. From north, south, east and west of this wonderful world of ours. From present to past, such as the Spanish conquerors looking for gold and the new land, fermenting corn by smashing whole corn and placing it in containers made of clay, calling it "Indian Beer." Later it was proclaimed to be the first alcoholic beverage. Captain James Cook, a noted English navigator drank a product made from fermented peppers in the south Pacific in 1778, while Africans were found in the 1800's drinking wine made of palm leaves.

While I was in the Navy, stationed in the West Indies in the 1950's, we sailors would bury coconuts in the sand and wait for them to ferment, so we could drink the fermented coconut milk. Oh, what a headache, along with a terrific buzz.

Probably the Greek word, "Mead" fermented from honey is the oldest word associated with getting drunk. It was a special kind of beer and was recorded as being the oldest alcoholic beverage, which was noted on clay tabloids uncovered from Babylon some five thousand years ago. By the way, those master brewers were women priests. These breweries go back to the Tomb from Babylon, in 3000 BC, where workers and peasants were only allocated three jugs a day by the Egyptian Pharaohs. They were the master brewers and made the best and purest beer.

It seems that eventually everyone caught on because the northern European tribes also brewed beer, then came the Allemanies, which are a German tribe, who also brewed beer, under the supervision of a priest, who blessed it before it was gulped down.

The Vikings inhaled ale on every occasion feast, or no feast.

When man began farming he learned by on-the-job-training, about how to make beer and when the grapes were plentiful enough, to produce wine.

Way back in King James era, they hid the grapes in a root cellar and told everyone they were poison because they turned a liquid purple. One of the women in the town decided to commit suicide one day, and went down in the root cellar and drank the purple juice that had rotted and fermented. She started to feel fairly good, and after thinking about it for a while, decided that if drinking this stuff made her feel better, she didn't want to kill herself. She eventually passed out from drinking so much, and the next day she told the King about it. The King began to drink it and then he named it "A wonderful Poison." He decreed it and henceforth it became wine. That was 7000 years before Christ. While we are on the biblical aspect, Noah had planted the first vineyard when he left his ark, first by sending his doves to see if the water had subdued, after the great flood.

A Benedictine Monk, between 1665-1670 is credited with the discovery of that wonderful bubbly stuff, not pink, but just plain Champagne.

Spaniards made corks from the cork oak tree and the Romans corked their brew with them. For over ten thousand years all denominations have been drinking mead, beer, and wine, and feeling good while doing it. Medicine doctors of these tribes, and ancient doctors of long ago, used to use this alcohol, or wine for medicinal purposes to heal their patients, or to make them just feel good. Later on down the road, and Arabian, by the name of Jabin Hayyah or later on you may know him as Mr. Geber (Jeeber) devised a process that paved the way to stronger beverages in the eighth century. He was an alchemist, or in other words a scientist who discovered nitric acid and other compounds that would cure all diseases and prolong life indefinitely. He was experimenting one cold wintry night with metals and later developed a medicine that he accidentally caused to the world, as the "Art of Distillation." It was this process in which a substance is thoroughly cooked until all the impurities are separated and the essential substance remains.

Mr. Geber burned away all the impurities that formed wine during its natural fermentation process and isolated the essential liquid. What a whale of a discovery!

When the plough-boys of the Appalachia mountains learned this from the same methods the farmers used way back then, they went into business for themselves, as you have already read.

Dr. Francis Sylvus, Ph.D. of the Medical University of Leyden, Holland, burned the liquid alcohol in an attempt to "doctor it" he discovered that by adding "Juniper" berries to it, and rapidly boiling the concoction, you would get Gin. That idea spread to England and Russia. The "Huskies" took the Juniper berries out of the liquid and Wala! Vodka. However, the Germans and the Scandinavians fermented potatoes. And the Scots and Irish made "usquebaugh" later naming it "Whisky."

The Whisky process began with barley, malt, and water, then it germinated and heated, to dry it out. If you add the yeast to make it ferment, you will have a much stronger beer. By distilling this mash you create raw whisky. If you place it in wooden barrels and age it you have seasoned whisky, with a mellow taste.

In 1832, an Irishman by the name of Coffey made a new type of still that produced Scotch Whisky quickly and inexpensively. Both rye and bourbon were found in the 18th century, after an Edinburgh distiller blended gin and whisky, which resulted in the arrival of blended whiskeys. There have been some fancy drinks from this process. So, where did the old moonshine come in? Well, they brought that stuff with them and their stills, and stored it on the Mayflower that brought people from England to the good old United States of America.

All that cold spring and mountain water vaporized to plain whisky has never caused anyone to catch fire, as many were lead to believe during the temperance days. Such as in 1890 there was a play entitled, "Ten Nights In A Tavern". In the play one of the characters said, "I'm not going to get close to the bar owner because of "Spontaneous Combustion" may occur."

There were stories about moonshine that has caused cancer, tuberculosis and heart trouble. Whenever typhoid or cholera occurred those who worked for the dry causes would assure the public that those who drank, would be the first to become ill and die.

However, whisky had the reputation as a remedy for coughs and colds, and many say it still does to this day.

What does alcohol really do to the human body? Does it stimulate you? Does it cause depression? Where does it go when you drink it?

Ethyl Alcohol is classified as a drug, a depressant, which anesthetizes the central nervous system.

I received this information from my son-in-law who is a doctor with the United States Army, he relayed this information to me.

Dr. John McGavock Jacocks, MD, of Wytheville, Virginia and the United States Army says that alcohol is not like a food because these different fruits, vegetables and meats that contain many calories, will make energy. This energy contains vitamins and proteins that provide the body with much needed nourishment.

Alcohol contains none of those great things, it takes away what those fruits and vegetables give us to make our body run the way it is supposed to. Actually the chemical process is called Oxidation, and when that occurs with the food, the alcohol burns off the original chemicals and ingredients, which reduces it to carbon dioxide and plain water. Oxidation destroys about 95-99 percent of alcohol in the human body as it passes through. The other 1-5 percent is eliminated through the natural discharges, the lungs by exhaling, kidneys by urine depletion, body fluids such as stomach juices, bile, sweat, and even a tear or two.

Food digests slowly, while alcohol oxidates at one hour per ounce, and it oxidates it in the liver. Alcohol is absorbed unchanged in the stomach and intestines, while the blood is actually the main vehicle that carries it to the liver.

Now depending on the size of your liver, the average liver can oxidize two drops of alcohol a minute. That is about one half an ounce per minute or a tad more. If alcohol oxidation takes place a second after it reaches the liver, some of the unoxidated alcohol will then reach into the blood stream.

Law officers that work undercover are given implicit instructions not to consume but one ounce of alcoholic beverages, for an hour, before they take another drink. It burns off an ounce an hour. It keeps the blood alcohol level low. If a person has many drinks, it will take eight to 10 hours to burn off. In the blood stream it will dilute the vessels in the lining of the mouth, then to the stomach. Once the alcohol is in the blood stream, and minutes after the first drink, it is pumped up to the brain where it not only stimulates the brain, but also depresses it.

When it becomes a depressant, it depresses the cerebral cortex. this part of the brain has control of the judgment and social functions, restraining that segment, that is. You become more lively and talk more freely. Does it stimulate you? Yes, at this point, but only to this point. If one continues to drink more and faster than the body can burn off the alcohol will then depress the brain's cerebellum which controls the balance, vision, speech, and coordination. The cerebellum is located behind the major part of your brain.

When all parts of the brain are affected, even the heart, and respiratory system, it also either slows down the organs it dominates, or makes them beat faster. By depressing the

Medulla Oblongata results in sleep, loss of consciousness and near death. Thanks, Dr. Jacocks, now we are "Plum Drunk."

In the fifteenth century, the lawmakers passed laws to protect drinkers from themselves. In England they devised party drinking to protect others or somehow to control their drinking altogether. In 1490 judges in England regulated beer and ale houses, and in 1550 another law was passed that ale and beer houses must obtain a license. The licensing fee was designed to cut down on the number of "alcohol houses" and enable the government to withhold licenses from the beer and ale sellers who may get drunk, and breach the peace more than any of their patrons.

Even with all these new laws, excessive drinking continued, which became a nuisance, and will continue to affect us more so in the next century than it has in the past. With the English Parliament making new laws on the selling of beer and ale, more drunkenness continued, it was a catch twenty-two situation. They were damned if they did, and damned if they didn't oppose the drinking laws. From 1605-1630, dozens of laws were passed against drunkards. If a person was caught drinking a little excessively, you were fined money, which was given to the poor. If you couldn't pay your fine you were placed in jail.

And, anyone drinking on Sundays, were definitely put in jail. The specifically had Church Wardens who patrolled the local pubs to see if they could find any serious drinkers. They had made a "Drunkards Coat" out of a barrel with a hole in the top and on the sides. The drunkards were required to wear it in public, which made them feel so ashamed of themselves and embarrassed, they never drank again.

However, that never really stopped a drunkard. When you are drunk, you really don't give a damn, who sees you in an ugly costume. In fact you play along with the idea, as if it were a joke. In England, the "Gin Act" was enacted into the lawmaking system, and then the gin houses had to be licensed as well. The tax was so high that the lawmakers forbade the sale of gin in containers less than one gallon. This was to deter the poor man because he couldn't afford it.

The great 17th century philosopher, Thomas Hobbes boasted, that he had been a drunk more than a hundred times in his life, and he was a mildly temperate man. One witty person in England had said it for everyone, "People are drinking to everyone's health to impair their own."

England was a nation of drunks for two centuries, and we all know that the beer and ale didn't always stay in England. It found its way to the thirteen colonies and excessive drinking became a way of life in America.

George Washington issued two cups of rum to his troops every day, while he was enforcing the tax laws. Thomas Jefferson brought Bohemian brewers to Virginia to help train Americans in the art of making good beer. He encouraged people to drink beer instead of whiskey. Americans turned to a variety of mixed drinks, such as wine coolers, beer with a whiskey chaser, Sherry and Bordeaux, and I'm sure you could think of many others.

By 1930, scientific studies of alcoholism had begun physically and otherwise. Alcoholism is compulsive, and estimated 75 million Americans are afflicted with it. Five out of six alcoholic men between the ages of 22 and 55 years of age are included in the age group. It is one of the most prevalent diseases in the United States and is a leading cause of death and major health problems today.

Chapter Seven

Strange Phenomenon

High in the Blue-Ridge Mountains of Virginia, moonshining takes a different sighting. On or about November 1, 1975, we had located an illegal still which consisted of 6-800 gallon blackpots of fermenting mash. In blackpot distilling, one puts the "**daisy mettlings**" in the huge pot and saves the flowery sack for making a new dress. When adding yeast, water and loads of sugar, (1-pound for every 10 gallons of water) and some malt, letting it sit for a spell, you get the "**daisy mettlings**" (**mash ready for distillation**).

The assemblies of stills were sitting in the middle of the road, which had been rendered un-passable by the highway department back in 1955. We could barely run a liquor car down the road in 1956, and as the years went on it grew up and the people from that area moved out except those "hippies" who came later with their communes and marijuana growths. In the 1960's they found a haven in the heaven of Floyd County and Franklin County. It was a mile or so of extreme remoteness, and deep in the hollows the "ginseng" is free if you know what to look for and where to dig. Runnet Bag Creek, where the assembly of stills where located starts as a trickle of water in Floyd County and cascades its way down the rough mountainside that people in the 18th century tried to grind out a living in the mountain terrain.

The stills were being fired by propane and the water gravity fed into from a mountain ledge of water pouring into the Runnet Bag Creek. The long black plastic hose was taken high into the rocks so as to get a good fall onto the water and it was gushing out at the stills cooling box that housed two rusty truck radiators. We checked the stills several days and decided to move into the area because the mash was getting ready for distillation. We dropped off on the Blue Ridge Parkway and went afoot down County Line Road and down to where Runnet Bag Creek started. From the parkway to the stills site, is about three miles straight down the mountain laurels until you get on the old road bed. We left two men in a government car at an overlook on the Parkway, namely "Smartview". The distance between the car and the stills is approximately four miles. We had taken turns about staying in the car so that everyone won't be completely worn out, however, Investigator J. B and Investigator R.D. and I had been on the ground for several nights and we welcomed the car duty.

Investigator J.B. had since retired and is now deceased. R.D. is working somewhere in Franklin County. I saw him not too long ago in the department store and we talked briefly about the strange object. On November 9. 1975 it was our turn in the car. J.B., R.D. and I.R.D. was in the back seat and Bowman was driving, and I was in the front passenger seat.

We were driving Federal Agent Don Hall's government green Chevrolet. We had eight good hours of sleep and we were perfectly sober and rather in a good mood. The other agents had already been dropped by another car and radioed that they were in place, which was approximately 200 yards to the left of the still site and were settling in for the night. We were hoping that they would come on and run the "outfit." We had an idea who it belonged to but we weren't sure.

The night wore on and R.D. and J.B. went to sleep and I took the radio watch. At about 3:30am, I observed a brilliant light descending just above the Blue ridge. At first I thought it was a satellite or a meteorite, or perhaps a passenger plane with its landing lights on, however, it became brighter and brighter, then moved from side to side, and than back upwards. I tried to get a definition of the object through a pair of 50 power Navy binoculars but I could not bring its contour to be anything definite because of its motion and mostly because of the brightness it produced.

I woke up R.D. and J.B. and called to their attention to the strange object. I tried to radio the crew on the ground to see if they saw the same thing. They apparently were asleep in their bags, and they never responded to any of the radio calls. Then J.B. called our attention to the object. At this time the brilliant light or object seemed to have been dancing. R.D. then looked at the object through the Navy binoculars and we all three of us awed at the bright light moving the strange object. It looked like it was about two or 3 miles out in the night sky about a 60-degree angle. Then R.D. spoke up and said, "Federal Agent Hall has a view finder or Infra-Red "Scoope" with tripods. The instrument is very sophisticated in magnification," and will be very useful to us."

I studied the object through the high power magnifying glass, as it rested on the trunk of the car, which was stabilized by a tripod.

At the top of the bright ball I saw what was a set of rockets or brown cylindrical type piping. Below the area of the ball was another set of piping and the bright dancing effect of the ball was enhanced by the movement of the contour of the ball clockwise at a terrific rate of speed. Then it appeared that the rockets were reverse and went in a counter-clock wise position. It would then change to a vertical position with rapid movement both clockwise and counter clockwise. I further studied the bright ball of its rotary motion of brightness, and at the top of the ball there seemed to be a tubular type structure running up several feet, having a telescopic effect. Above this was the ship's structure, shaped like a rocket ship or balloon type ship. Gray in color and pointed on the ends about 30 to 40 degree angles. Above the center of the ship was what looked like a cabin or cockpit of some sort.

There was visible light through the Visa-Vant, although I could not see it visible with the Navy binoculars and certainly not by the naked eye, not even the tubular device could be seen without the use of the Infra-Red glass.

I watched this object rise and move to the right and left, but now it was not descending, it was ascending, and moving slowly and upward and by 6:30am, it had just started to turn daylight. After awhile it went up and out of sight.

I told my story to many, including noted news commentator clay Peters of WSLS TV, who w anted me to go on television and tell my version on the six o'clock news. I couldn't do that because I had serious court cases coming up and I didn't want to jeopardize my court cases. People took a dim view on UFO spotters in the 60's and 70's.

To further complicate truthful matters, Clay Peters placed me in touch with a world renown UFO Investigator and the technical director of a famous movie about UFO's. The UFO scientist was located at the Ferrun Junior College for a lecture of no other than UFO's. That was several weeks after my encounter of the "Foo Fighter". "Foo Fighter" got its name from the Air Force pilots, who could not recognize unidentified flying objects. The first unidentified flying objects were reported by American pilots in 1946. Since then there have been thousands of reported flying saucers and recently strange field mowing designs depicting some foreign phenomenon.

The noted doctor and astrologist called me from Woodrum Airport and we talked about the object over a cup of coffee. He asked me to send him a schematic of the so called "Rocketship." I did just that and he never got back to me, but I will tell you what he later told Commentator Peters. He said, "Mr. Powell must have gotten into some of his moonshine or he had stayed too long at the still they were watching."

J.B. and R.D. came by my house several weeks after the strange phenomenon incident and I pleaded with them to publicly confirm our sighting, since they saw the same thing I did.

Jim and Ron readily admitted that they saw the brilliant object dancing in the sky, the rocket type ship and the tubular device, and even the faint light coming from what appeared to be a cabin as well. The ship didn't light on the parkway or parachute any green little men nor was there any forceful magnetic absorbing gulp. I saw what I saw and I haven't seen it since nor anything like it.

On November 21, 1975, just twelve days after my sighting, the Federal Aviation Administration investigated a report by two pilots that they saw missiles near their passenger jet as it flew south of Richmond, Virginia.

Raymond G. Belanger, then chief of FAA's Air Traffic Service said that an Eastern Airlines pilot reported seeing what appeared to be missiles a couple of thousand feet above his DC9 plane. The co-pilot also saw the object. Angelo Vlsilli, then Chief of the Washington Air Traffic Control Center in Leesburg, Virginia, said that computer and sound tapes of air traffic activity were being examined, and if it was a missile, it shouldn't be there, and then he said, "We can't handle rockets."

The Eastern pilot at the time was identified as Captain C.S. Wilson, of Hollywood, Florida, and the flight was Eastern 852, from West Palm Beach, Florida to Washington DC.

The plane was descending from an altitude of 15,000 feet as part of its approach to National Airport. The sighting occurred about 60 miles south of Richmond, Virginia over Emporia, Virginia. The officials said military missile firing is restricted to areas over the ocean and is definitely prohibited in regular commercial air corridors.

A complete check with military officials and all commands in and around the area failed to suggest where a missile could have come from. Mr. Belanger, said the air traffic controller at Leesburg, Virginia reported only one military plane in the vicinity at the time of the incident and that it did not have missile firing capabilities. It's never been determined what they saw except that it looked like a rocket of some sort.

In 1985, nearly ten years later in another part of the world, and amazed crew and passengers say they saw a huge star like UFO beam a "dancing-dazzling" beam or ray on the aircraft they were traveling in. the co-pilot of the Aeroflot flight radioed air controller in Minsk about the sighting and was told at first there was nothing on the radar screen. In other words, they must be saying that they weren't normal, the co-pilot was quoted as saying.

The Soviet ground control said the Aeroflot flight was not crazy that there were splashes of an unidentified object on the radar screen in the same part of air space. The "Newspaper Trud" interviewed the crew and passengers, and also the Russian controllers, too.

It drew the attention of the Soviet Academy of Sciences and its Deputy Chairman of State Commission on unexplained phenomenons. He told "Trud" it was indeed an interest, although the commission already knows of similar cases.

He was further impressed with the fact that this object could reverse its course instantaneously and reach the ground with a brilliant ball of light of unusual intensity from such a high altitude. This is undoubtedly abnormal he related to the news-people. He then continued to tell everyone concerned that the Soviet plane was flying from the Georgian Capitol of Tblisi to Tallinn in Estonia and was approaching Minsk when what appeared to be a large object suddenly shed a dazzling-dancing brilliance or light from an altitude of 25-30 miles toward the ground. That is undoubtedly as abnormal as what I proclaimed to have seen without the corroboration from my fellow investigators in 1975, some 20 years ago. It is undoubtedly strange as the Eastern pilots saw from flight 852 in 1975, remind you just several days after my sighting despite the circumstances.

The commercial Russian pilots saw a "dancing-dazzling" light surrounded by concentric colored rings. The UFO then came toward the airliner at tremendous speed and brilliant light or flashing light. It left a green cloud in its wake and instantaneously hovered over the plane and next to it, at an altitude of 33,000 feet for the rest of the flight.

Nervous passengers asked the attendants what was happening and the Captain reportedly told them that it was a reflection of the Northern and Polar lights.

From 24,000 feet to 15,000 feet what did Captain Holland and his co-pilot see? What did the Russian commercial Areoflot pilot-co-pilot and passengers see? What did Jack Powell, J. B and R.D. see high over the Blue Ridge Mountains of Virginia? They all saw something!

> *Deep in the Blue Ridge, I saw a brilliant light*
> *It wasn't fire at a still sight...*
> *Maybe the moonshiner cast the sight...*
> *To make the revenuer's not too bright*

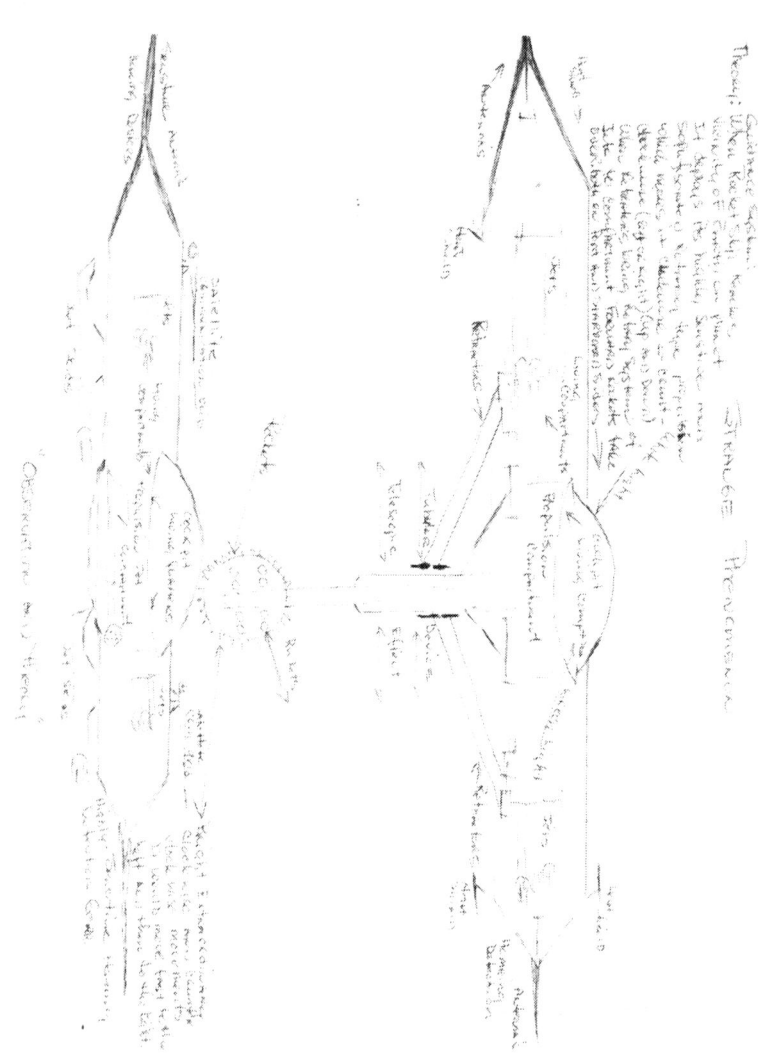

This page represents what we saw as the strange phenomenon, the so-called U.F.O. Story.

Chapter Eight

The Enigma Goes On

Enigma - a puzzling problem, that's what the Webster Dictionary defines. Why didn't the whiskey tax dodging business in England, Ireland and the Normadic countries just stay where they belonged?

Why didn't General Washington and others teach the real "Tom Tinkers" a lesson? Why didn't General Armstrong Custer teach those "Clodbusters" of the South and those mash swilling mountaineers something? Why didn't prohibition cure the liquor riddle? Why haven't Government agents marching four abreast across the Southland stop the illicit liquor trade, along with the drug traffic that has interwoven the clandestine dual money making problem?

So goes the problem, so goes the stories, that have been American folklore, or legends, so say the practice of the Art of Moonshining and the distribution of it. It's Enigma has been the controversy of the Federal and State governments for 216 years, and who is to say that is not just American folklore but a criminal violation to avoid government taxes on whisky and the use and distribution of it, breeding other crimes as well.

These stories reflect a revenuer's view of that enigma. The plight of the moonshiner-bootlegger and the Revenuer's fight has lasted forever and is an everlasting puzzle. We have just about swept the liquor thing under the rug so we can let the drug thing run overtop of us.

Moonshining and bootlegging hasn't been confined to the rural areas and the substitute use of the over-worked soil of the mountains has found its way in the urban area, following its destructive path to schools, colleges and universities.

I had a very fine old doctor friend who treated me for a skin problem. He always told me it was due to too much yeast in my blood. I told him he had yeast on his mind and he told me a story. He said, "My daddy was an engineer on the railroad in Florida during prohibition and he had a friend who was a revenue officer. The revenuer would leave ten gallons of whisky between boxcars and my daddy would bring it home and hide it. Then I would pint up several pints of it in my doctor's bag and take it to Atlanta where I was a medical student."

He said all of this while in his office, which was a small room, not too much larger than an eight by ten room. He dragged on his cigarette, puffed out a few rings, and flopped his feet up on his desk, "Yep, I can remember it all now," he continued to say, "I worked my way through medical school, supplementing the cost by selling liquor to my friends. I really didn't mean to violate any laws, I just needed a little more help than my daddy could provide from his small railroad job. After graduating and going into practice, I have not sold any liquor, or drank any of it. It will kill you if your not careful." Then he smiled at me, and I replied, "In more ways than one."

The illicit sale of alcoholic beverages and other supplementary commodities have long been the savior of the financial aspects of thousands of students in the 1960's and 1970's. Undercover agents didn't limit themselves to the bootleggers and moonshiners of Blackburg, Virginia and Montgomery County. Those agents in 1964 targeted thirty "Frat Houses" selling whisky, wine and beer illegally and without a license too. About twenty-five Tech students were charged with various liquor law violations and most of them pied guilty to the illegal sales, possession, and other infractions of the law.

It was an unfortunate price to pay for such an unpopular law, however, the ABC laws in Virginia are very implicit and the complaints were that we were looking the other way because it was VPI and students as opposed to the noted bootleggers who thrive off beating the government out of taxes.

One "Hokie" employed the services of a well known attorney from Pearisburg, Virginia to defend him in a twenty-five cent sale of beer to an ABC man. The defendant stated that he received the money for the beer as a contribution to the Alumni.

The noted and highly respected attorney pleaded the case before a seven person jury, wearing a white Gardenia in his lapel while his explicit silver hair shone like a white dime on fire, and was falling down, like a sunset in his face. He had a white handkerchief in his hand that had an odor of onions, which when he wiped his face with it, it would make him cry. His summation was this, "My client took a measly twenty-five cent contribution and told the investigator to throw the money into a cigar box and he then "drew" a large draft. My client never looked to see where money was going.

The attorney also stated that if his client was convicted it would ruin him for life. Maybe not for life, but I know of a person who was a defendant in these cases, and then went on to become a Navy pilot and Captain, and recently in 1991 sought highly sensitive clearance in the Navy and was subject to a complex background investigation by the Department of Defense and they ran "every liquor case down" that concerned him. They did this because it was a long time ago that these things took place in his life. And the Navy authorities wanted to make sure this fella's background was impeccable. If we had not kept records on him, then there wouldn't have been any for them to check into. And guess what? The clerks office couldn't find his records, they were missing, vanished into thin air.

The University President at the time said, "the institute is deeply concerned over the matter and each person is independently liable for their actions." He also went on to say that, "Virginia Tech standard procedure is to withhold disciplinary action until the outcome of any legal action occurs for such parties."

He didn't speculate on the degree of disciplinary actions until after court was over.

The jury found the Virginia Beach student not guilty and there was plenty of action in the hallway when we came out of court. The boy's mother lamblasted us and then spit at us for our tactics of catching people who broke the law. It didn't stop the Frat Houses. in 1974 ten years later, they did the same thing. The Frat Houses sold liquor again and the students at the Tech also sold the beverages and twenty-three people were charged in that raid. It may have gotten better because some of the houses have been able to get banquet and special event licenses to sell the alcoholic beverages. Other events have taken place to alleviate Frat House problems, I think!!

Making liquor isn't just for those old poor mountain folks nor we can't blame it all on those Frat Houses and students who occupy them either.

About a mile down the road from Virginia Tech, a unique illegal distillery was seized from a motel room being used by some Tech students. It was a Coco Cola pressure fountain container to concoct the mash. They used a second container to condense the beverage, inserting a coil into the container, and then they used a third container for a cooker, a copper tube to the "L" fittings, which then they ran the tube to the condenser. The formula is: Place H20 in the condenser, cook the mash on the stove, bottle it in the room then find a party to crash.

Investigation revealed two former Tech students had occupied the room at the motel. They were tracked to Northern Virginia but were not arrested because possession or ownership couldn't be proven. Of course, they never came back for their report card either.

Small mountain stills usually are hidden in the mountain near the operators home, using the cold mountain springs to ferment the cracked corn, or corn sprouted mash in a couple of Oak wooden barrels. Most of the mild, mellowed whiskey is consumed in the community. Oh, they might let a couple of gallons go for a good price. Speaking of price, on November 24, 1970, the Prices Fork Community, in Montgomery County found and seized a complete copper still and the apparatus at the home of a man we never suspected of being in the stilling business, however an informant told us otherwise. We arrested a nice old gentleman and charged him with possession of distilling equipment.

He went to court and he testified to the Honorable Kenneth DeVore, who was General District Judge then and is the Circuit Court Judge now, that he was using the still to cook pumpkins in. They were for Thanksgiving. The expression of the judge's face was a questionable one, and he didn't dispute the old man's tale but did give him a minimum fine for possession of distilling equipment without a permit.

A few farms down the road in the Prices Fork Community, there was another gentleman who was nicknamed the "Preacher." He was a big man, no doubt of Irish decent, because he didn't take to "a-liken" to the "giverment" intrusion.

We went there with a search warrant based on reliable informant's information, who very seldom, might I add, failed to relate faulty ideas to us.

Preacher wasn't at home because he held down a good job at Virginia Tech and would be home shortly after we got there. In his ice box he had moonshine and RC-Cola already mixed. To the rear of the house he had a chicken house with two locks on it and tar paper covering all the cracks from the inside. A strong odor of fermenting mash was permeating from under the door and covered the rear window area.

The Preacher finally arrived home and right away the offensive started into a raising Hell of fury. He had in his hand a set of keys to his pick-up truck. He was asked about the keys to the two pad locks on the chicken house. The Preacher never answered and clenched his fist tightly. I attempted to get the keys from him but he gave them a heave into some honeysuckles and briars. Consequently, the locks had to be removed by the "Devil". (Our trusty axe). My partner chopped the locks, and hinges, and everything came off, even splinters from the wooden door.

And what to my wondering eyes did appear? A pure copper still and several barrels of fermenting mash, all housed in the tar-paper building. This small community could turn out at least six gallons of whiskey a day. It just seemed that everyone in the community had their own little "pot-teem" just like they did in their native land.

Preacher was tried in Montgomery County and he told the Honorable Judge DeVore that he found the still and took it home, and he was going to cut it up himself but his axe wasn't sharp enough. But, as we went back to his farm to see if there was anything else we missed, we couldn't help but notice the several hundred gallons of live mash found some three hundred yards from the shed covered up with the same type of tar paper we found on his chicken-coop. Well, the Preacher was read his rights, but he declined he wasn't going to jail and put up a terrific fight for a man in his sixties. It took four officers to subdue him, without hurting him, of course. He then quoted the Bible all the way to jail.

Judge DeVore did take into consideration that he had a good job at Tech and was a hard worker, and was supplementing his income while practicing the "Art", but not as a preacher of course.

*   *   *

It's brandy time, constantly in the mountains. The Sheriff of Floyd County had given us some information on a still three miles north of the town of Floyd. We had searched out an area behind Hatcher's Restaurant, just off Rt. 221.

We were returning to be picked up when we heard fire trucks running up and down the road with their sirens blaring, their red lights flashing, and people screaming. We thought it was a brush fire, although we made comments about the smoke. Eventually we got picked up and returned to Roanoke, then about a half hour after we returned to Roanoke we received a call from Trooper Higgins to come back because we had missed something. "What in the dang Hell did we miss?" I thought to myself.

The Floyd County Fire department is a loyal bunch of guys, they never told us a thing, and that's quite understandable. Their job is to put out fires, not start them. We could see the smoke from where we were looking for the still on the other side of the road. We joked about it saying, "I guess we were looking at the still burn in the grove of pines, a half mile away."

We returned to the scene of the crime and found that a huge barn had blown up, and appearing from the evidence it was hanging in the surrounding trees, along with the melted tin on the ground. There were barrel emplacements (12) and smoke and debris strung out in the trees, for a moment you could have sworn it was Spanish Moss. Pieces of tin roofing, copper tubing, fragments of an oil heating device all were dangling in the air. When the wind blew, it sounded like a wind chime. The only thing salvageable was a lone apple grinding mill and a quart of Brandy with a note on it saying, "This is for you, Jack." The quart of Brandy was sitting next to the apple mill.

Below, the ruins of the barn down through the pines was a house. An electric line went down through the pines and just this side of the barbed-wire fence the wire hung. It had been connected to a box attached to the house. We couldn't prove it, but we found out who was renting the place and we went out to a quarry where this huge bearded mountain man worked. God, he was bigger than Smokey the Bear.

He was the quarry blasting man. When we found him he was up on top of the quarry looking down into the rock and gravel pit. We interviewed him but he didn't know anything about the suspected barn-still explosion. We got a little too close to him, physically, and he told us to move back, and he didn't have anything else to say. I didn't want to tangle with him, cause he was meaner than a grizzly bear and just about as big as one.

The owner of the property said he didn't know his renter, but he didn't think he was involved in the illegal distilling business.

Consequently, we couldn't arrest anyone due to the lack of evidence, including the fingerprinting of the quart of brandy and some other items. We couldn't make a case, but someone was smart enough to make a poem out of the ordeal. The thanks goes to Mrs. Roger Abshire, a Trooper's wife.

Dew Its Ruins

Down the road I hear tell
there was a still on a hill
where they ran off a gallon or two.

To someone's dismay, fire took it away
now, no more mountain dew.
The fireman wouldn't talk
no one would squawk
on the makers of mountain dew.

They call it old mountain dew,
and many refuse it, they do.
So, if you know of a still,
you really shouldn't tell,
on the makers of the mountain dew

Over the years law enforcement officers encountered many unusual circumstances. However, it is not kosher when State and Federal Agents are watching the same violator at the same time, and they don't know it. If they are trying to catch the main transporter and distributor, so are we.

On this one particular evening, the perpetrator backed his black pick-up to the distributor shed and unloaded his whisky. Then a little while later another black pick-up came into view, which made us a little confused as to which one our man was, because it had gotten dark. The first one stayed awhile and departed and then the second one stayed a little longer and left.

The whisky had been loaded and both agencies didn't react to the delivery. The next night we surveiled the building and determined that the shed was full of cases of liquor. We obtained a search warrant and at approximately one in the early morning hours we attempted to execute same. Melvin Whiteside and I were the first to knock on the door, and identified ourselves. We could hear water running in the house, however, no lights were on, and no response to our inquiry. We advised them unless someone answered our knocking, we would attempt to kick the door down. We finally kicked a hole in a 3/4 inch plywood door and reached for the doorknob and forced our way in. He finally answered our beckoned call with a .12 gauge shotgun. There, in the dark with just a flashlight beam, stood a huge black guy with a shotgun pointed in our direction, and he had his fingers on the trigger, but nothing happened. We wrestled him to the floor and took the shotgun away from him. He was strong and drunk and good thing because he couldn't get his safety off the gun. One hundred and thirteen gallons of untaxed whisky was seized that night.

Back in the land between the lakes and the home of sixty thousand springs and captioned on the "tee" shirts and ball caps is the moonshine capital of the nation. This publicity is not the life blood of the moonshiner, as sugar is to a sweet tooth, but it is a free enterprise in Franklin County, Virginia.

On March 15, 1971, shortly and swiftly after court opened, Franklin County Circuit Court Judge, Honorable Langhorn Jones leveled criticism at the publicity the county had been receiving on illegal moonshining stills, and those stills destroyed in the county were warned that he meant business in stopping what the moonshiners lividly expressed as a way to make a living.

The remarks were made during the trial of illegal whisky and most of the remarks were directed to the ABC Agent V.K. Stoneman, who was Supervisor in charge of western Virginia's Enforcement Division. Mr. Stoneman was the Chief prosecuting witness in the case and did an admirably good job. Due to the publicity, the Judge claimed that when people heard the community Ferrum mentioned, they didn't think of it as an outstanding college community, but rather as a moonshine producing community.

Judge Jones made note that Georgia was now the leading moonshine producing state and Mississippi was second with Virginia following right behind, and the Carolina's fourth and firth. He went on to say that he wasn't proud of the fact that more stills were destroyed in Franklin County than any other county in Virginia. He was avid in his speech when he said he was going to make an effort to see that publicity on the stills would be halted and he added that he had already spoke to the State Alcohol agents stationed in Franklin County about the matter.

In the distilling case Judge Jones handed the defendant a three year suspended sentence for illegal manufacture of untaxed whisky.

Franklin News Post editor, then, Kermit W. "Red" Salyer had something to print about publicity and illegal bootlegging, moonshining and so stated in an editor's note: "Despite the Judge's claim, the annual report issued by the Licenses Beverage Industries Inc., of New York, shows that Virginia ranked seventh in 1970, among thirteen southern moonshining states. This report also showed three hundred and twenty-four stills were destroyed in Virginia as compared to the two thousand, nine hundred and thirty-two in the state of Georgia. Franklin County however, was still the leading moonshining producing county in Virginia in 1969.

Franklin County Rights and State Circuit Court Rights vs. First Amendment Rights is what is at issue now, however, for the judge's information the publicity on the seized stills and the bootlegging activity is not going to stop, no matter what he says."

Editor Salyer went on to note: "We consider the destroying of illegal distillery a legitimate news and we shall continue to give publicity to such. We don't blame Judge Jones for being ashamed of the bootlegging activity in Franklin County, for it is within the power of Judge Jones to stop it if he would hand out a few still sentences, and then perhaps the bootlegging would decline."

The present case is an example: After criticizing the publicity and giving Franklin County an un-reputable name, the judge hands out a suspended sentence. Mr. Salyer, then asked Judge Jones if this made any sense. "This bootlegging has got to stop" instead of "this publicity has got to stop."

The situation with Judge Jones, the editor, and the publisher, reached the high courtroom, and only upon Mr. Salyer's persistence did he emerge a victor as he continued reporting the news as it happened. He also attacked the procedure in which we use to destroy illegal stills. At one time we "Blew" stills for years, and when the United States government got touchy with explosives, we started axing them again, like we did at the turn of the century. The Revenuers developed a special cut with their "devils" called a **"Keyhole Kut."** they would know if a Revenue officer had been there or someone else and it was supposed to have made the still inoperable.

Mr. Salyer, thought "Keyholing" wasn't enough to destroy them and reported that the unlicensed distillers were patching the stills up and running them again. We again started to blow them to smithereens.

The moonshiner went right on manufacturing illegal whisky and tax dodging the government to the tune of several hundred millions of dollars since that noted skirmish between the Judge and editor in 1970. Thousands of bundles of newspapers have been sold and recycled through "**Johnny Houses**" one way or another since then and that literary enigma went on and is still going and going, right on up to the new year of 1996, and this is what we call "A Dying Art."

Ten years later the turn of events of making whisky got so sophisticated that in 1980 the distiller went to "**Triple Piggy Back-Doubling.**" One such still operation was located in the Hardy section of Franklin County, Virginia. There were three still operations going on in one location cutting down their "Running" (distilling) time.

The stills were staggered "**Catty-Cornered**" in a heavy pine grove with large vines hanging down around them, making it thicker than the hair on a dogs back. Maybe that was their escape plan and it almost worked. They had dammed up water for about twenty-five feet and approximately twenty feet wide. The water looked milky and the quality of whisky they were making looked even worse. It must have been real bad because they came one day to heat up the mash so that it would ferment in the cold November weather and brought a fifth of Canadian Mist with them and drank it. They left the bottle with a "**Swig**" in it sitting up in one of those blackpots, and they didn't even have a chaser to go along with it. It is pretty bad when you can't drink your own liquor.

There is bad liquor, and there are bad men who drink the liquor, and the man I'm telling you about was a pretty bad man, moonshiner, informer and assassin. He was the most violent and dangerous man I've ever had any law enforcement dealings with. He killed his first wife and poisoned the second one, beat the Hell out of the one he was living with, he shot his brother in the throat (smack in the Adam's apple). He served time and he hadn't been out too long, (we dreaded his return to the mountain).

He returned to his mountain home and went back to bootlegging in full gear. He went to Floyd County one day and picked up a load of whisky. Trooper Tom Gibbs got behind him and noticed that his blue 1950 Ford was sagging mighty low in the rear. He decided to stop him on Route 8, north of Floyd, Virginia, near the Montgomery county line.

Trooper Gibbs had been ground hog hunting and still had his rifle in his police car when he spotted the suspect's car. He followed the old blue Ford a little ways, and then attempted to pull him over but the suspect kept going and went out into a field of corn, with the trooper following him. As Officer Gibbs approached the car the suspect crouched down by the driver's side of his car. He had in his hand a butcher knife and lunged at Gibbs. Trooper Gibbs for some reason or another had his hand on his ground hog rifle. When the suspect jumped forward, Trooper Gibbs, cracked the suspect across the head, which bent the barrel of the trooper's gun, as told to me by the suspect himself. It bent his head alright, and that is where I interviewed him at the Montgomery County Hospital.

We seized his car and charged him with transporting one hundred and twenty-five gallons of untaxed liquor, based on Trooper Gibbs sharp observation and alert response to a dangerous situation.

Let's call the suspect, "**Mr. H.**," who we now had charged with a liquor violation and naturally him being the informant he was and the kind of person he was, made us a deal, and what a deal he made!

He said he could order a load of "**white**" from some of his buddies in Ferrum, Virginia, and he did just that. He had set the game plan to go down in his large garage on Catawba Mountain. He then ordered thirty cases of "**corn**" and his buddies couldn't wait to deliver it. Mr. "H.", told us they were coming and they would be driving a 1956 Oldsmobile which had a Cadillac motor, four carburetors, progressively linked, so we had better had a powerful vehicle as well in order to catch them should they decide to take off and leave us in the dust.

At approximately 6pm, on August 12, 1958, the transporters arrived. They were brothers, one was the wheelman and the other the whisky man. They backed their Olds-Cad back into the garage and the driver never got out of the shaky, "lopping" Olds, as he gripped the steering wheel tightly, and accelerated the gas so that if he had to take off in a hurry, he would fly out of there, so to speak. The car shook so badly that it shook the walnuts off a tree nearby.

We had the garage surrounded on foot and a chase car up the old Catawba Road, waiting, just in case. The whisky man had unloaded about seven cases when Mr. H. screamed, "It's the God-damned law! Run fer it!"

Needless to say, the driver floored it and the tires started smoking and crying, while splinters flew high in the air, as the garage door parted and fell on top of the top of the Oldsmobile they were driving. Well, we started yelling to each other that they were getting away, and called to Car 233 that they were coming their way. The whisky man fell back in the back seat, and was squashed like a sandwich between the liquor.

The liquor car was in a cloud of smoke and headed up Catawba Road at an unidentifiable speed with our chase car a considerable distance behind. The chase car obtained speeds on that curvy road of about ninety miles an hour. He was sliding around a curve when he saw the Olds hit a huge Oak tree. (Which is no longer there, I wonder why?)

The Olds catapulted after hitting that huge tree and all of the liquor, some twenty cases came forward and cut the driver's head off. Miraculously, we got them to the hospital and the doctor sewed his head back on. It was only held on by the jugular vein in the back of his neck.

They both lived, and were eventually convicted and apparently have lived a long life, despite the dangerous lives they were living.

Mr. "**H**", attempted to shoot me on that raid, along with Investigator Wayne Prillaman. Later, I found out in the course of time, he killed someone else and went to the penitentiary, and as I am told, he died there. May God rest his soul.

An alert Special agent of ours, Warner Osborne, noticed an advertisement in the Roanoke Times, and the World News that a man in Giles County, Ripplemead, Virginia, had a still for sale and gave the phone number. (Isn't that one for Ripley's Believe It or Not, it's like advertising your criminal behavior, then asking the law to come get you). Anyway, the next day my partner and I arrived in Giles County and we contacted the man about the still he had for sale at his residency. We were told to meet him at his home, and when we got there he greeted us at his door. My partner asked him if he was the one who had the still for sale, and he replied, "I certainly do and it hasn't been used very much either. You will really like it."

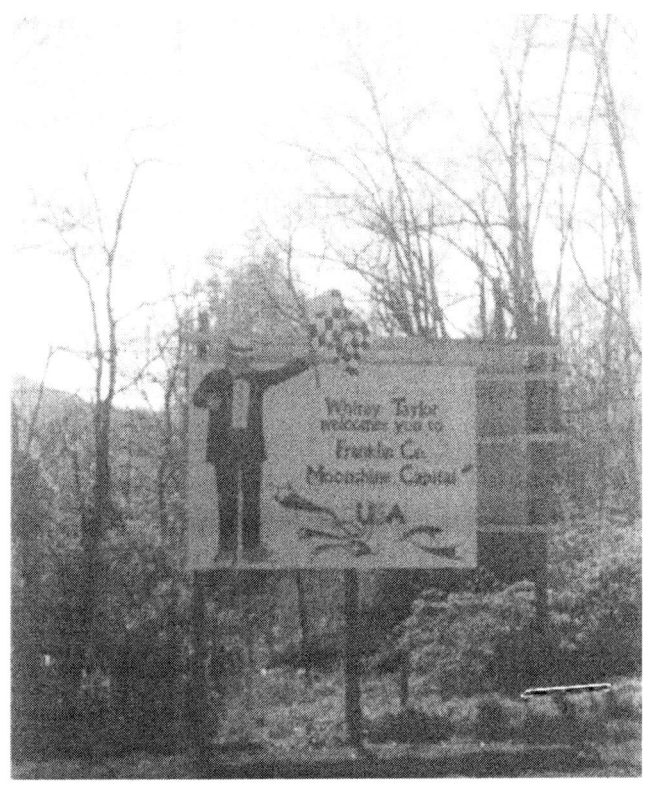

Mr. Whitey Taylor (Franklin County Speedway owner) put up this
sign of invitation to all, to come to Franklin County. Sign was
erected just at the Roanoke County line over in Franklin Co.

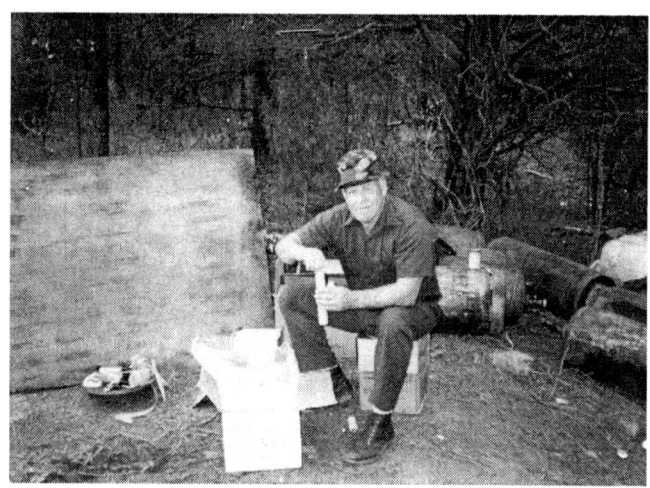

Smith Mountain Lake, Franklin County.
Assistant Special Agent in Charge Jack Allen Powell preparing explosive to "put this baby high in the sky"—a large illegal distillery!

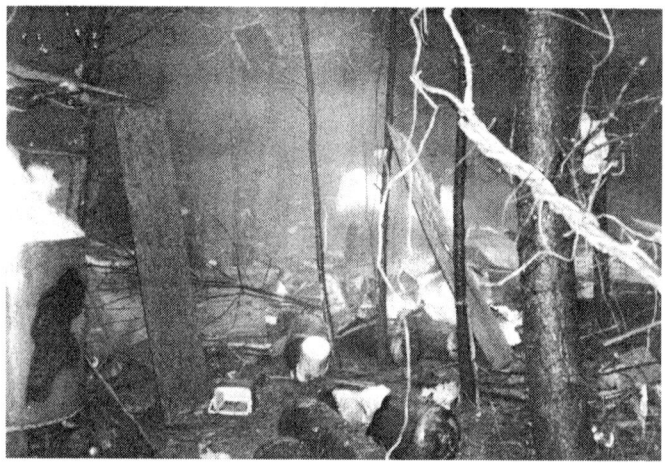

Smith Mountain Lake, Franklin County.
The aftermath—demolition after the explosion and fire. There are only pieces left up in the trees!

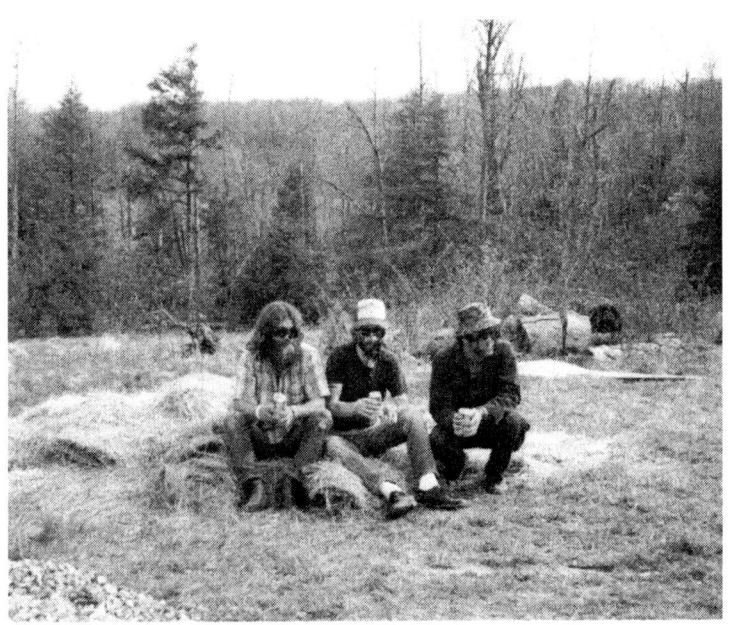

Still hands captured May 1993 in Floyd Co., VA. Just off the Blue Ridge Parkway were 12,800 gallon black pot illegal stills.

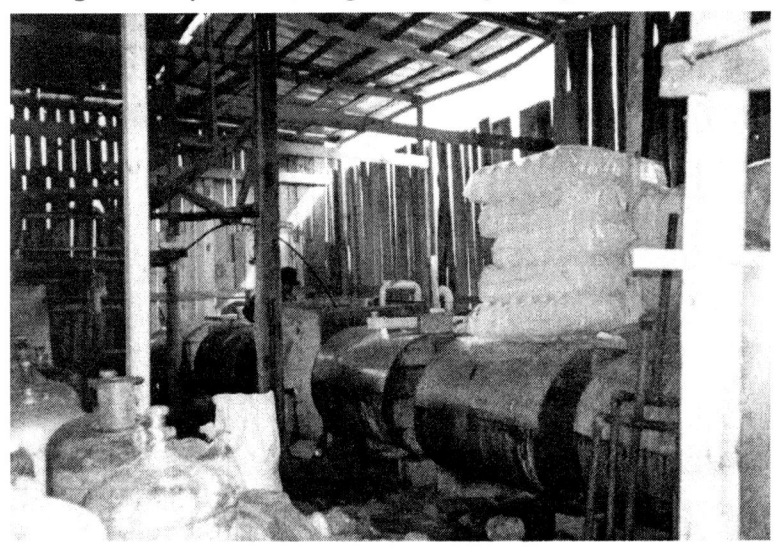

May 1993 in Floyd County, VA.

87

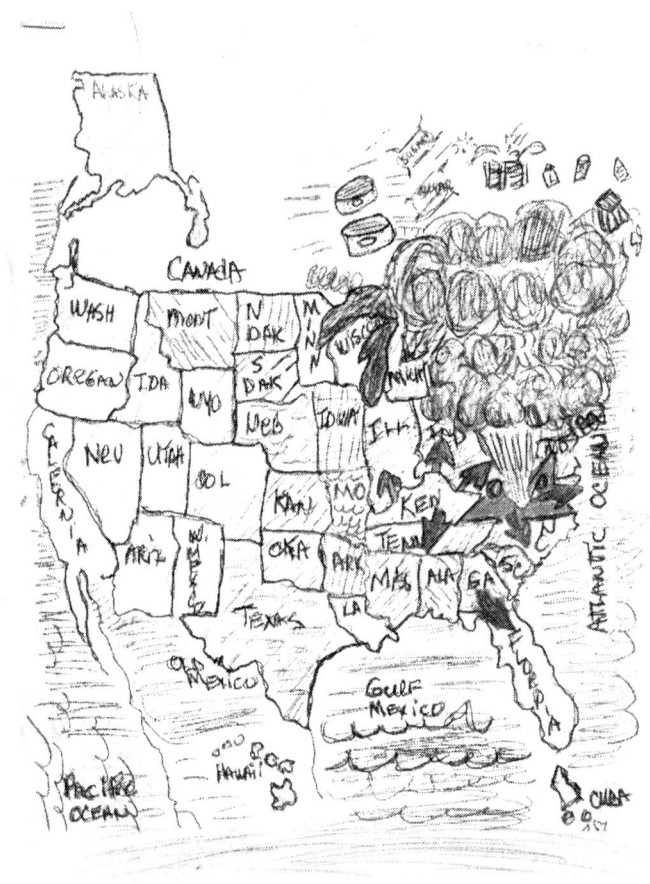

Moonshining production and transportation in the southeastern United States as indicated by the arrows. Activity "still" prevalent in the following Southern states: Virginia, North Carolina, South Carolina, Georgia, Tennessee, Alabama and Mississippi.

I answered him, "Well, I do want a good one, but how old is it, may I ask?"

He had to think on that one for a bit, then replied, "This damn thing hasn't been used since 1937 young fella! I also would like to add, that I used to make a little "**likker**" for my boarders back in the old days."

I glanced at my partner and we shook our heads.

"How old are you?" I asked of him.

"I'm only 92 years old."

I whispered to my partner that I think we might have stepped into a world of pooh-pooh.

He led us down the basement and showed us a pure copper still about a ten gallon cylinder type, with the cap apparatus in perfect shape. We then flashed our badges and credentials and told him who we were. He replied, "Well, I'll be damn!"

We told him we had to take his pretty little still, and he told us to go ahead, but to put it to good use. We never arrested the old gentleman, and later we discussed the matter with Commonwealth Attorney Robert Powell, and later the still was put to good use. It was used as an antique decoration for plants.

Chapter Nine

The Molasses Saga

I crawled on my belly listening for moonshiners. Buckets rattled. I could hear voices murmuring.

I knew the anonymous tip was good. The information was someone was making liquor behind some thick alder bushes off the Blue Ridge Parkway. I whispered into my walkie-talkie, alerting nearby Federal agents that I was ready to flush this moonshiners in their direction.

I gave out a blood curdling scream and a wild whoop. I charged through the thicket and saw an elderly couple, who probably thought they were being invaded by a band of wild Indians. She had on a bonnet and he had on coverall, stirring a large pot. I hear a horse wheezing, very common in use of manufacturing illegal whisky years ago.

What I saw, and to my dismay, that these two elderly people were making molasses. I ran right by them and when I passed them the lady said, "Paw, I think this guy is crazy, in those green clothes."

When I reached the Federal Agents, I excitedly told them, "Oh, God, it's an old woman and man making molasses. We have raided a molasses outfit."

This was a story told by David Poole about me. He is a Reporter for the Roanoke Times Paper, stationed in Richmond, Virginia.

*   *   *

High in the mountains of Giles County, north of Gold Bond, more than fun was brewing up in big Stoney Creek. After an hour's climb to Mrs. Reed's general store we located a small distillery and four barrels of fermenting mash, They had set the still up at the top of a small ravine and there they had driven a pipe back into the ground gravity feeding the cold water to the still site for the cooler barrel.

The not so antique but unique thirty gallon still made of a carbide can with a small copper cap had been jugging the liquor up in those slim brown pharmocolial jugs. They were just sitting around the still, It was a week-end and a night time operation from the looks of the flash light batteries and lanterns hanging on the trees.

Mash at Big Stoney Creek in barrels took a week to ferment and they usually set it to run on Saturday and Sunday night. We checked it one week toward the end and the mash had fallen three rings and the mash crust had almost cleared off.

The mash was ready and so were we. We were hidden in the heavy laurels and brush surrounding the still that overlooked the Jefferson National Forest and the Big Stoney Creek. This was in the afternoon and dark fell, we could hear people talking in low tones. We let them settle down and then we crawled toward the sounds and could see a flicker of light. We sprung from the darkness and could see that they were eating dinner and during the excitement one of the distillers started to choke on something. He was coughing pretty bad and I was hitting him on the back and finally he coughed up a big country ham biscuit.

When I grabbed him he swallowed the whole thing, and it wasn't funny either, but after we got ourselves organized from the raid we all had a good laugh about the incident. We told the judge about it and he gave the two distillers probation. The judge thought that the still was the most rickety operation that he had ever heard of. We eventually cut the still with their own mattock, The judge wondered if they were making some kind of medicine due to the bottles. "No your Honor, just rot gut!" one of them casually replied.

From the beautiful rugged mountains of Giles County to the coal regions of the great southwest in the late 1950's when times were sort of hard and they had their share of bootleggers, along with some trading their homebrew, (wine and liquor) for food commodities they had. If a man had plenty of money and a guide, it went far. I had a fellow who showed me around Lebanon, Cleveland, Honaker, Wise, Pound, Applachia, Norton, Big Stone, and just about everywhere in that country. Especially where bootleg liquor and country music was. That is why country music is popular, because they were humming more than one tune! Back in those days the popular sounds were vibrating the jukeboxes into a nervous prostration. There were so many bootleggers in the regions that they had to wear badges to keep from selling each to each other.

One such place was a little community of Ramsey. There lived a woman and a man named Flannels or something like that. My guide told me they sold good bootleg liquor. We went to their little white house in the center of their quiet community. Mrs. "F" came to the door and I asked her if she had any good whisky. She replied "No, but I have some good raisin homebrew."

I told her I wanted a gallon. She then poured it from a large brown crock, and said it was fifty cents a fifth. (There's five fifths in a gallon) so I paid her $2.50 with a five dollar bill. Then she gave me my change. We went our way and later returned to find Mr. "F" at home, while the Mrs. went on an errand.

I never saw her again until we went there to arrest her and her husband. I had been told she actually sold the liquor to raise money for some kind of medical treatment she needed. I accompanied the deputy Sheriff to Mr. and Mrs. "F's" home, and when we got there she was sweeping off her porch which was considerably higher than the ground. I told her who we were and that we had a warrant for her and her husband. She kept on sweeping with that old timely "sage-broom", and she never looked up as I went up the steps to take her into custody. Just about the time I got to the top step, that broom of hers went into a rotary-halo motion and she whipped the daylights out of me before I knew what was happening. The Deputy was bewildered, as we finally subdued her and after that I never saw her again. I think she eventually died because she couldn't get the medical treatment she needed, but couldn't afford.

I need to tell you the entire story or it wouldn't make sense and it didn't make sense to my wife regardless, however, two of our investigators working undercover with two female informants bought a lot of whisky, stills and some drugs. Through their escapades they inadvertly burned one of the ladies underclothes and may have scorched her a little on the thighs.

Our investigators returned to their respective bases to find out that the two bleached blondes had reported their activities into the allegations. The two waitresses were going to file criminal assault charges against our men but struck a deal with the authorities.

The deal was for the supervisor to arrange for two different investigators to work with the ladies. My partner and I arrived on a Friday afternoon and contacted the women informants at the Norton Cafe. In those days you had to know a little bit about Norton, Virginia to appreciate the atmosphere and environment, with all those hundreds of "coke ovens" going and the mist that lay overhead, it almost looked like the smog in California.

When we were introduced to one of the blondes, they asked me if I was the same one that interviewed them before. The other guy and I did resemble somewhat because we both had crew cuts and were twenty-five years old. She must have been in good shape when her clothes were burned off of her not to know the difference between the other guy and me.

After awhile, all four of us loaded up into a 1957 Chevy and headed out of Norton. We had gone just a little ways when they told us to stop at the funeral home and pick up a wreath of flowers.

Their cousins told them that their uncle had died and we needed to take that wreath to the old home place up Guess River. They also proceeded to tell us that we could buy plenty of liquor and an old copper still from their kinfolk. One of the girls said, "Uncle Ned won't need the still any longer, not where he is, unless his kitchen is too hot," she giggled about the whole matter like it was a big joke.

After we had drank a fifth and a half of the Vodka, the road in which we were traveling got a little bit smaller in size as we made our way in the ruts to Uncle Ned's community of kinfolk.

The road finally started to spread out a little further where it was passible for a few cars, and then we came upon a house and just stared at the side of the coal stripped mountain next to it. The people in that area were as drunk as a skunk, falling off Uncle Ned's porch. There were some sitting on the rickety steps holding a gallon syrup jug of corn liquor. I thought we were at Snuffy Smith's place.

The car radiator was getting hot and spewing hot muddy water from under the hood, which attracted the attention of the women's cousins who then jumped off the porch and steps with the gallon of whisky they were holding. They gave us a swig and it tasted pretty good.

I asked him how much did he want for the rest of it and he said it was only his drinking whisky, but after the funeral he would definitely get us some.

It was a small family cemetery, behind the house. We fell up the hill to the burial dropping flowers from the beautiful wreath. We actually fell on the ground, got up, walked a distance, and fell again, dropping flowers, and by the time we got to the burial, there were no more flowers on the wreath, so we sat on the ground and finished what was left of the Vodka, and then poured the rest on Uncle Ned's flowers.

The women told us to take off our wedding bands because their kin wouldn't take kindly to married folk being with them. So, I placed my ring down in my watch pocket and forgot about it being there.

We finally went to the burial, bringing plenty of liquor with us, and Uncle Ned's old copper still was producing at least five barrels of that good old corn whisky, but we didn't have any additional space for the barrels, so we left them down at the house. We then returned the women back to the Norton Cafe, they went to the upstairs apartment, and finally we went home, half stewed in a bag, so to speak. Anyway, remember I told you I forgot my wedding band in my watch pocket? When I walked in my door my wife, Mary asked me, "Where in the hell is your wedding ring?"

Sheepishly, I explained to her it is in my watch pocket my little pumpkin pie, and I had to take it off at the funeral.

Mary replied, "If you don't find that damn ring in a hurry and place it on your finger where I put it, you will be going to another funeral. Yours!"

It has never been off my finger since.

Chapter Ten

Lu-Lu's

I had worked with some lu-lu's at times, but one informant I worked with one particular time, took the cake. He had worked for government agents before and had nearly been killed by bootleggers for turning them up, but he was at it again.

He started working with me, and at one point in time when we were watching one of the bootleggers, he said, "I'll catch my kin folk at their own game, you watch and see if I don't." So we headed for Dickerson County in the heart of liquor and coal making country.

"I can't buy coal, but I sure can buy liquor, drugs, and some stills," the informant said.

This guy had just gotten out of the state pen and was real thirsty. He said he could catch the die-hards if given but the chance to do so. It was a Sunday morning. The birds were chirping, and the morning sunrise had just drifted over the mountain, as we traveled up the creek towards this guys uncle's house which was near the West Virginia line. He said his cousins and uncle would have a big poker game going on every Sunday morning and as he said that, his 1967 Chevy puttered up that mountain where everyone was supposed to be at. We then stopped about seventy-five feet from where the game was going on.

Both of us being half-drunk, staggered into that card game like we just got off one of those crazy amusement rides, and started playing right along next to them.

Jack Allen Powell

Although I was wearing bib-overalls and a doodlebug hat, I seemed to fit right in with those hillbillies. I was a complete stranger to these hicks, however, they watched me very closely. Just in case, I happened to have a .25 automatic in my back pocket wrapped up in a handkerchief just in case one of those hicks got ornery.

There were about ten people around the circular table, my informer sat on a log to my left and there was an old man sitting on my right. The informant, blatted out that we had two barrels of mash but no still, and he wanted to know where we could get one.

The old man on my right replied in a southern drawl, "I have one, a one hundred gallon rig. I gave a pocket watch, a shotgun, and a coon's dick for it, and I will take one hundred and twenty dollars cash fer it right now."

To my surprise, my informant pulled out several one hundred dollar bills. (And he told me he didn't have any money). Well, that old man's eyes twinkled and he jumped from that log and said with excitement, "I'll take it!"

Then, a bearded man from across the circle who had been watching me like a hawk said, "I don't like your looks, mister."

He didn't say anything else, just stared at me with his beady eyes, and slowly pulled out from behind his back a long barrel gun, shot and the projectile cut off a small limb over top of my head. I was sweating bullets, while my heart beat like a fast clock.

My heart nearly stopped and a lump came rising up in my throat, and I almost pissed in my pants. I numbly thought about that .25 caliber automatic, but I quickly forgot that thought because I certainly did not have any chance in Hell. He would have put a hole in me big enough to drive a steer through.

After awhile, things settled down and the informant told the old man he would be back in a little while. He wanted us to go up into the house and load the damn thing into the car, as he had it out back in the ground cellar with his canned goods and potatoes.

I told him the law was running the roads and we would be back by dark as soon as the traffic quieted down.

"You had better hurry, or it won't be here when you git back," he replied. "I'm taking it to West Virginia to my grandson's."

It was a "**shinny**" rectangular pure copper still with the cap and coil. It was a piece of this **Dying Art** as a **still artist** would describe. We left and they followed us a little ways, just to make sure we weren't up to anything. We looked for trouble and could have easily found it, but we stopped the car, raised the hood and acted like the car broke down. I conveniently stopped the car near an old phone booth that no doubt was dated back to the early 1920's and a little old general store that had an antique coke cooler and some Redman tobacco hanging on the wall behind it, along with some little traveling packs of aspirin.

I had such a hangover and needed some tomato juice or something to get rid of this buzz. I did get the juice and aspirin, then I called Mr. Caney Farmer who was the agent in charge, who was the supervisor in charge of the whole district, and I asked him if he wanted me to pay the one hundred and twenty dollars for this still, and if the **Feds** would reimburse us. He proceeded to tell me to stay put and he would call Jim Hunt, the supervisor in charge of the ATU and now retired.

What a mess, for just a few dollars, but the state didn't necessarily reimburse us for still buys unless the circumstances were unusual, and unless the people we arrested were on the spot in most of the cases. I thought this was an unusual case.

Mr. Hunt said he would have to call Washington or Philadelphia to confirm buying a still to reimburse us. Well, I'm going to confirm something right now that I didn't know existed then. The Federal Government informed us by phone (via Mr. Farmer) that it wasn't against the federal law to possess a still or equipment, per say. I would have liked to fell over, as I know there is and always has been a law on possession of illegal distillery or apparatus. That is the state law. I was quite perturbed by then and I told Mr. Farmer to get the Deputy Sheriff, and some state troopers to go to this old man's house before he took the still to his grandson's which is over near the Virginia state line. We left the area and never went back and later I found out from Mr. Farmer that he finally did get a Deputy Sheriff who knew the moonshiner, and the Deputy and the state trooper went to the house supposedly with a search warrant, but it turned out that the sly Deputy actually had a piece of toilet paper inside his jacket and showed it to the old moonshiner, and the old man led him around to the cellar where he showed the still to me, but it wasn't there. Apparently, the old man couldn't read and since the Deputy knew him fairly well, he believed the deputy about the search warrant.

The moonshiner told the officers that the still and equipment had been taken to West Virginia, but his trusty friend of the law knew the farm well and asked him what he had in the chicken house. "Oh, nothing but chickens," the old moonshiner replied.

"Then, you won't mind if I go have a look-see," replied the Deputy.

"It's full of lice and rats, are you sure you want to go in there?" The old man asked him, trying to disillusion him from going in there.

"Look, old man, you go climb up the loft and throw the still down, I know it's in there," replied the deputy.

He reluctantly did, and they hauled his still and him away with it.

You may wonder why I told you about this incident, a little still, not worth anything, especially one hundred and twenty dollars if that at all, and the government wouldn't pay for it. All and all the old man lost his still, pocket watch, shotgun, and his coon's dick, and yes, he got fined a whopping sum of ten dollars and that's what we call **Mountaineer Justice** in the southwestern region of Virginia.

*　　　　　*　　　　　*

My partner, who was a former Marine and I had just met. I had been assigned to duty in Rockingham County, which is the turkey capital of the world. His nickname is Bulldog, a short handsome fellow who always wore a huge western hat, which always hung over his brow and then you couldn't tell who he was. He also had a terrible temper and a mean left hook, so I was very careful of what I said to him.

At that time, I lived in Harrisonburg, Virginia and we worked in the counties of Rockingham, Paige, Highland, and Augusta. We worked the towns of Stanley, Shenandoah, and Monterey.

One day we got some information on what was considered to be a large still, up "**Cubbage Holier.**" This Cubbage Holler was located in the vicinity of Stanley. Well, we had been walking for sometime now looking for this large still, and it was one of those dog days of July.

You either sweat your ass off in the summer months in this region of Virginia, or you freeze it off in the winter. We were drenched with sweat as we made our way through some thick woods and down to a flat where a cold spring ran through a cluster of laurels. There, hid by a **lawyer green** was a beautiful copper-turnip type still sitting on a metal furnace, along with two butane gas bottles, lying directly in line with the still. We decided right then and there to stay a while because there were also two barrels of fermenting mash covered and it was just about ready for distillation.

We got ourselves a drink of that mountain water which ran into a barrel that had the copper coil inserted down into it. The coil was there to cool the hot vapor via the cold mountain water which turned that vapor back into a fiery liquid, which helped win the West and caused tax dodgers to try and get richer whether in small stills or in large steam outfits.

We concealed ourselves in some of the honeysuckles and bramble briars and prepared to stay until someone came to operate this small mountain community still. We waited and waited. Finally, after many hours and impatience, we hear some cussing and someone coming. Their buckets were rattling and Bulldog punched me in the arm and pointed in the direction of the two men making their way down the sparse mountainside that was covered with blackberries and rattlesnakes.

These men would pick a few berries and then ease on down the mountain towards us, looking not at the berry vines but all around. They were getting closer and closer to us. We held our breath and didn't move a muscle as they passed nearby and made their way cautiously toward the illegal distillery. They took their work seriously, as so did we.

Once they got to their still, one of the berry pickers picked up a **gunny sack** and his friend said, "Let's go. I got an inkling that something just ain't right."

When he said that we rushed out of the bushes and arrested both of these gentlemen for the manufacture of illicit whisky. They made no statements, and the identification they had on them was quite clear of who they really were. These men could make bond at the Rockingham County Court House, because they were well established businessmen of the community, who would have guessed they were doing this kind of work? These men weren't caught red handed stirring the mash or pouring the liquor, they were caught red handed with a sack in their hands which contained a butane bottle. They could have easily said they were camping and stole the gas bottle. We didn't catch them in the **Art** that they were schooled in, which was producing this white lightning.

We knew we had some heavy duty investigating to do to make a bona-fide liquor case on these two professional bootleggers who had a long record of making **hooch** by the light of the moon that shadowed through the cracks of old turkey houses.

Through our investigation, we had nothing but circumstantial evidence, however, we had put together a good case as we placed both men in the still on two different dates and their purchases of sugar, malt, two packs of bologna, and a propane gas bottle, lead them through a grand jury and before a circuit judge.

The ironic aspect of this case will forever go down in the minds of Rockingham County citizens. The day we tried Mr. Goode and Mr. Short, they waived a jury trial and was casually standing beside two other men similar to themselves, except their counter parts had stolen turkeys from a turkey farmer in Harrisonburg.

Did you know that both turkey stealing and illegal distilling are felonies and carry long term prison terms? If someone steals a turkey in the turkey capital of the world, it is the worst thing you could "possibly" do in this part of the country, and turkey thieves get prison sentences and are specifically told not to come back into the county when they finish serving their prison term.

The two culprits of illegal distilling wound up in front of the judge and was asked what kind of whisky they made.

"Oh, we make "goooo...d" whisky" one of them said in a long southern drawl.

"Well, you take your "goooooo...d" whisky out of these parts, especially in the turkey capital, and never set foot here again. I don't want to see either of you come in front of me again. Do you hear?" reprimanded the judge.

They heard, and were fined a large sum of money, and I believe they did probation, and never laid foot back in turkey country.

*   *   *

These small community stills are quite a contrast from the large illegal distilleries to the south of the growing northern sprawl that was developing, and also where those "poteen" type stills now sits, are huge shopping malls, patio houses, town houses, new highways, byways, and a heck of a lot of change.

The turkey business is not the same and the huge dairy, chicken and turkey farms are in the days gone by era, making root for the fast food chains and real estate developments that are vastly gulping up the beautiful environment and mountain scenery, smothering the cold springs that was once a haven for the moonshiners artistic ability.

However, complex as it may seem, those moonshiners were making liquor and hauling it out in antique Chevy's and 1950 Ford pick-up trucks, to a thirsty any, motels and hotels which were only in cities and towns. consumer, not too far from Hopkins Gap, a few miles out of Harrisonburg.

One particular gentleman, with an age of ninety-one had never been arrested for a still he had set up in Hopkins Gap on a two-way creek or branch. He had an immaculate copper still and cap and coil tied together on a nice metal furnace with a spout running white liquor into a funnel over charcoal. The funnel was sitting in a glass-fountain syrup jug.

He was caught red-handed, but under extraordinary circumstances. I know he is still up there somewhere, to this very day, and will probably own up to the still when he sees a picture of it.

Bulldog dropped me off on the hard top road not too far from this noted distiller's house. He could walk to the area or drive, I preferred for him to drop me off. I walked a dirt road that lead toward the mountain, and there was a field parallel to the dirt road, and then it went into the woods and stopped. I had to find the water so I could track where the still might be located. I finally came to a small branch and creek intersection. I got down and started to crawl up the creek parallel to the branch. When what to my wondering eyes did appear, but a barbed wire fence at the intersection of the creek, and the branch where it meandered into the creek. This was their security. A triangular affair, where small bull pines and the barbed wire directed itself towards a field. Apparently, one strand or two had deliberately been lowered for the rascal's escape in case they sighted the Revenuers.

I continued to crawl up the creek and I could smell smoke, mash cooking, and whisky. As I crawled closer, I could see a man's lower half of his body, and part of his upper half. He had on overalls, and a jacket. I could see clear gallon jugs and a spout coming out of a cooling barrel, and over that a funnel that was filled with charcoal. The funnel was sticking down in the neck of the jug. The small copper still was sitting on a metal furnace, supported by metal legs, complete with copper cap attached. There was a small tempered fire under the still.

I crawled under the lower strand of the barbed wire, as the branch changed directions on certain angels. I thought to myself I had it made, and it would just be a matter of time before we grabbed this lone distiller who kept his trade a secret from the world. "God, I would love to bash his quaint mountain still to pieces, and I can hardly wait to do it" my thoughts ran excitedly through my mind.

I am lying on my belly, like a pancake to a grill, in the middle of the cold branch and there staring me in the face was two marbled eyed baby beagle hounds. Their innocent faces and speckled bodies seemed like little babies needing a bottle. I whispered to them, "Hi, little puppies," but their response might just as well been a roaring lion's.

The yelping was music to the distiller's ears. He never panicked, at all. He just stepped over slowly and as nonchalantly as could be, over those two strands of barbed wire and went running through those little bull pines, and right on into the open field.

"Damn!" I said out loud.

I had my trusty six shooter, which is a Colt revolver in my hand and I was holding it in the air and fired it. The distiller's hat came off his head and he turned up a little yelp, like one of those beagles, and fell over a brush pile going over a small ravine. He screamed, "Oh! God! You could have shot me in the back!"

"Oh! My gosh! How could that have happened?" I asked him, laughing all the while.

I pulled him out of the brush pile and examined his clothes and body and found no bullet holes at all. There was a break in his skin, on his heel. Something had penetrated his high top shoes and he continued to accuse me of shooting him.

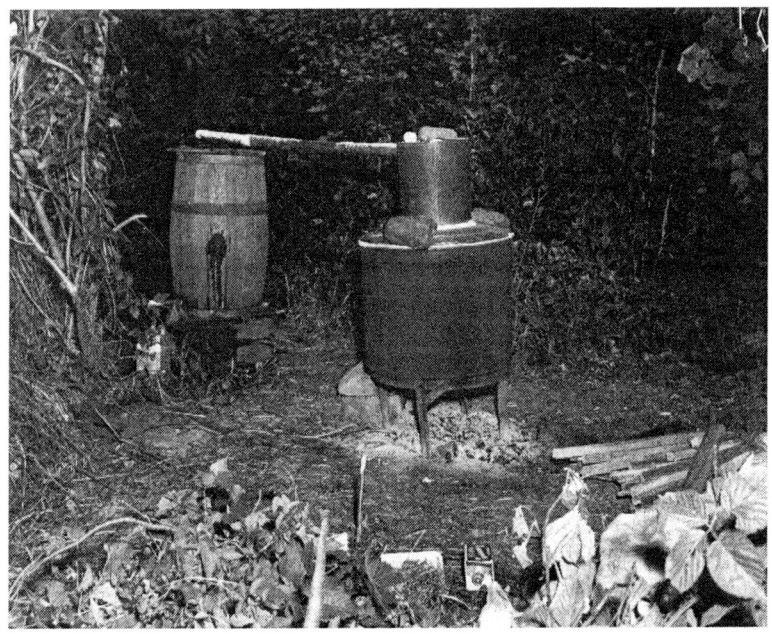

Morris ran from the still and across a field and turned up a little ravine, falling over the brush pile. Though a shot was fired into the air, Morris claims he was shot in the foot.

The sad part of this whole story was that I never had seen the man and I certainly didn't know him. Only the lower part of the body was the only part that I saw at the illegal distillery and I even lost site of him momentarily so I couldn't positively identify him. Imagine trying to identify someone from the waist down? So, I couldn't charge him with making whisky illegally, and he had been shot. We made a pretty good case against the old geezer but the Commonwealth won't prosecute the case, because I couldn't positively identify him. He said he didn't know who was making the whisky, and he got scared while walking in the field nearby, when he heard a shot, he then ran up the holier and across the ravine. Next time I identify a suspect, I'll make sure to look above the belt and not below it.

Chapter Eleven

Moonshine Short Shorts

On December 22, 1954 just six miles north of Floyd, Virginia, Liquor Enforcement Officers armed with a search warrant were sent to the home of B. Sowers. Upon their arrival they found Mr. Sowers sitting in the kitchen coughing his fool head off. He had in his hand a half gallon fruit jar with moonshine and herbs in it. Sitting on the kitchen table were two more fruit jars with moonshine and herbs in them also.

Investigator George Martin, Jenkins and Troopers Moore and Gibbs went into Mr. Sowers bedroom, and found ten more half gallon fruit jars of moonshine and herbs in a cardboard box. He had a loaded .38 caliber pistol by his liquor and his bed.

Back in the kitchen he had a small cooking stove, and sitting on the stove was a boiling pot of self-brewed coffee. (that's the kind where you place the coffee in a flour sack, and tie the top of it off, then place the coffee sack in the coffee pot). Mr. Sowers continued to cough and then all of a sudden he grabbed the hot coffee pot and placed the hot spout in his mouth and drank from it, while grabbing the half gallon of moonshine and herbs and downed some of that simultaneously. He began rocking and reeling, and then exclaimed, "You think you Revenuers and troopers are tough, let's see some of you drink from this hot spout!"

Not likely, you would have to be more than tough! You would definitely have to be in the Christmas spirit, and I'm not saying that literally.

*   *   *

It was December 23, 1945, in Carrol County, Virginia, and barely in Carrol County you might say, when Sheriff Edwards and Deputy Sheriff Webb along with Alcohol Investigator George Martin and Thomas C. Wilkins found fresh wagon tracks leading from a barn on the farm of Mr. Nester.

The wagon was in the barn, although the tracks lead straight across the field, and through a swamp and then into dense woods, and lead straight to an illegal distillery. Well, Golllll...ly, when the government agents got to the still, they found it in full operation and three men were laboring very hard putting wood on the fire, filling up the still again and jugging up that "white lightning". There was a team of beautiful "sorrel horses" just standing nearby, either waiting to deliver the white gold, or for a fast escape.

One of the laborers whispered to his other worker, "I think I hear something."

"Turn those horses loose and be real quiet," the other said.

It was too late to be listening, except hearing the bushes snap as the government agents barreled in on the distillers.

Even at that, the three men made a good escape, as well as did those fine horses. Investigator George Martin, being an old farm boy himself, a former Deputy Sheriff of Pulaski County, Virginia hollered for Wilkins, Edwards, and Webb to head for Nesters barn, and they all did.

First came the horses and then about an hour later here comes Mr. Nester, Mr. Does, and Mr. Wilson. All three were taken into custody along with that beautiful set of sorrels. Horses will go to the barn every time you scatter them,

110

especially if you have been working and they haven't been fed and you turn them loose. The horses gave them away. Next time feed your animals.

Patrick County, Virginia, December 21,1952, Mr. Williams work horses got sick with the colic, so he called Mr. Turner who he had been making whisky with. He needed his advice on what to do about his ailing stud. Mr. Turner told Mr. Williams to take a half gallon of first run sweet mash and pour it down his throat.

Mr. Williams then followed his partner's advice and went out to the barn and got some whisky and as the horse lay there in pain, Mr. Williams unscrewed the lid off that half gallon of "moonshine" and poured it down the horses throat. In about a half hour Mr. Williams returned to the barn and found the horse dead. Mr. Williams met Mr. Turner and told him of his demise, when Mr. Turner told him he had given his horse the same thing an hour ago. "Well, in land's tornation, what happened to yore horse?

"He died."

He got the right medicine all right, Christmas or not, The Dying Art of Moonshine, effects animals as well as humans, and continues to do so. From Alpha to Omega, it will always be with us.

Chapter Twelve

The Hardest Date To Remember

June 23, 1960 won't be the hardest date to remember for me the rest of my life because the good Lord let me keep it. Investigator's Martin and Prillaman and I had been looking for illegal distilleries that day and had found and left for further investigation of an illegal distillery twenty five miles north of Gold Bond, Virginia far into the National Forest's, interior. There wasn't anything up there in those days except wildness and mountain moonshiners. They cut wood, made liquor, farmed, worked at the Kimballton Lime Plant.

We checked the "mash" and found it not ready to rum. "Mash" in barrels on Big Stoney Creek in those days usually took seven days for it to ferment, rise, fall and be ready for distillation. Sometimes the distiller would "smell a rat" so to speak and they would come in and "charge the mash with sugar", put lime down all around it and then wrap spools of thread around the outside of the still site.

The lime was for detection of tracks (Revenuer's), the sugar was to prolong the fermentation of the mash and the thread was to protect the surrounding area from entry. How much better security could you want? You break the thread or penetrate the lime spread, they never would come back. They set the mash to run when they wanted it to.

We worked the roads at night for high speed transporters hauling white-lighin from these big stills to the coal fields of West Virginia and other northern cities. We had just about finished up that night. Mr. Martin and Wayne had gone on toward Rich Creek where we were staying at Cardens Motel.

It was one o'clock in the morning and I was backed up behind a service station and was in the process of coming out on to US Route 460, Pembroke, Virginia in my 1957 Ford Thunderbird Interceptor.

As I started to pull out, a black 1953 Ford pickup truck, heavy laden, a canvas over the bed and two shiny chrome pipes streaming up each side of the truck whizzed by me.

I gave pursuit to the ball of fire coming out of the top of the pipes and "he was totin the mail". I was nearly asleep and it took me a few minutes to get my wits, so a little distance elapsed between us. I "hammered down" on the gas, I checked the overdrive toggle to see if it was all the way out. I "rammed" it to low second and heard the drive shaft sing when I dropped it back.

I wasn't gaining but he wasn't leaving me at this point. My high-beams were glaring off his shiny-hiney. I continued to accelerate lapping up the steep hill this side of the old Ripplemead Bridge. The heavy laden truck seemed out front a bit...I continued to gain speed, perhaps too much. We started down the long straight stretch leading to a ninety degree turn to the left onto the bridge. He jockeyed that truck loaded with liquor onto the bridge and I lost sight of him momentarily but continued to floorboard the gas pedal.

I felt like a pilot in a nose dive with the ground coming up at me. I was going so fast the gravitational momentum had over-taken my ability to judge. I could see the east end of the bridge coming at me, staring me in the face. I saw I couldn't make the ninety degree turn onto the bridge because my front wheels were sliding in gravel, inertial force was pushing the car straight ahead into a huge rock at the end of the bridge. I tried to turn the car up big Stoney Creek or RT 635 but I kept plowing ahead breaking the huge boulder and plummeting end-over-end, five times backwards, approximately one hundred thirty one feet below, landing in the New River.

When I came to, I could feel the engine rammed up against my legs but I wasn't pinned in except the doors were smashed closed, the overdrive toggle was jammed against my right knee. Blood was "gushing" from my nose. It had lathered my cotton greens with blood foam and water. My T-Shirt was so soaked with blood it was running down in my wet boots. I felt for my legs to see if they were there and they were stuck but I was able to free them.

I lay down in the seat on my back and finally kicked the left door open and water just swirled into the bottom of the car. The blood had coagulated in my nose and knee and I felt like I would not die from loss of blood, although I had lost a lot. I wished I could have given it to a good cause rather than to the ground.

The radio was out, I couldn't communicate with anyone. I ran a mile to a phone on the side of 460 above Ripplemead. My partners came back and got me and the car was a total loss and smashed to pieces. My injuries were the least of my worries. I never went to the hospital or doctor. After viewing the car I needed to pray, and did, thanking my God for sparing me. I needed to further pray because I knew I was in trouble about the loss of that car.

The tires had left the rims and were scoffing and skidding. I laid down two hundred eighty three feet of rim marks and one hundred seventy five feet of scoff-skid marks. My supervisor was called after Trooper Fraley had made his investigation. Mr. A.L. Fulcher didn't believe what had happened and really neither could anyone else.

Other people had gone off the same end of the bridge and never lived to tell the stow. I appreciate to this day what Trooper Fraley did and apparently it's indicative of his personality and abilities. He recently has been promoted to Captain with the Virginia State Police in Richmond and had been progressively promoted since that faithful date.

Mr. Fulcher requested that Trooper Fraley reinvestigate the accident and naturally I was summons into the Richmond office and was admonished by a very fair and considerate man, the Director of Enforcement, Mr. Clyde Saunders.

In those days you didn't just wreck a car or disregard equipment or cause any conduct unbecoming a gentleman. You were fired unless you had a pretty good story. Whether they believed me or not, Mr. Saunders was a compassionate person.

They found me somewhat at fault, made me pay for the car, five days suspension, to remain on duty without pay and twelve month's probation.

I sold the motor to a moonshiner (see photo following page) and big transporter for three hundred and one dollars, the differential for seventy five dollars and the rest came out of my check. There was nothing else left except a smashed hull and tattered safety harness and that made me think of:

Buckle Up

Me in my belt and you in yours
Down the road I went without the doors.
The windshield smashed, the tires slashed.
I flipped and flopped, it rolled on its top.
The motor was driven to the back lid deck,
They pried the steering wheel from my neck.
Seat belts will save you from the wreck,
Buckle them up and have an air bag,
See how they protect, if you want to be around to brag.

Time stands still not even for bridges that get old. The Ripplemead was closed in 1975 by the Virginia Department of Transportation and traffic flows over a new concrete span much more comfortable to pass on four lanes. Several others had gone off the old bridge over the years and never lived to tell the story or the story was never told.

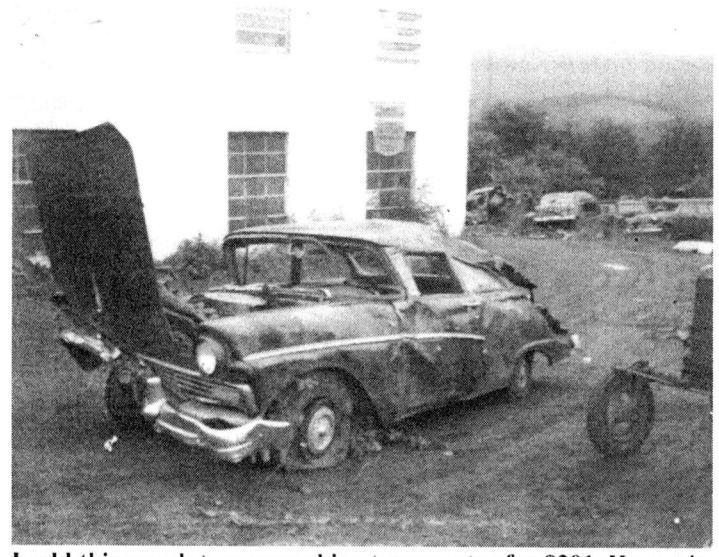

I sold this wreck to a moonshine transporter for $301. He put it in a 1957 Ford pickup and we caught it in West Virginia a month later.

I had my wife and two little daughters with me one cold night going to my office in South West Roanoke. We were crossing the Low Water Bridge in Smith Park when we met a noted transporter driving a heavy laden car. My lights flashed into his windshield and I immediately recognized the driver to be a noted violator and big transporter. I "bootlegged" the 440 Chrysler around and gave chase. He was operating an old DeSota, four door sedan. He had big air lift shocks to keep it from sagging with a heavy load on it and riding stiff, with a short bounce to it, meaning it was loaded with something heavy.

He proceeded to the intersection and turned right and went straight up to the Division of Motor Vehicles on Eighth Street S.W. where my wife worked and abruptly turned left into an alley and proceeded up the alley for a way and I guess he thought we would block the alley, and would have in due time but he "bailed out" and ran. Where were my wife and two little girls? Lying down in the floorboard of the car until we stopped. As he ran up the alley and me right behind him, I could see his gold watch and I knew who it was by his watch and demeanor.

He ran in between some houses and we lost him. By this time Roanoke City's finest had arrived and with a new police dog, a beautiful white German Shepherd puppy. It had the appropriate name "Tarzan". He was well trained, fast, alert and went right to work for the handler. The police dog master put "Tarzan" up in the car to get the scent and he leaped out of the car and started up the alley with his nose to the ground, sniffing and growling.

Just then a small black dog came down the street and above the intersection of the alley and Eighth Street she met the almighty "Tarzan". "Tarzan" was greeted with a swift smell and "Tarzan" returned the nose treat. "Tarzan" for some reason or another ran back down the alley a short way and pissed on a telephone pole and we couldn't get "Tarzan" to get the scent again. I know the transporter didn't let the little black doggie out but it served its purpose anyway.

I said I identified him by his watch and I later got a warrant for him based on the fact I had known him for years and the fact of the gold watch. He hid out for three months and I finally arrested him and he brought in motel receipts that he was in Ohio during that three months and the Commonwealth's attorney would not prosecute. Old "Tarzan" went on to make many good solid drug and sniffing out the mountain dew cases but not losing smell of a sweet little old black puppy.

The old Wildwood Goose Club, Roanoke County, was famous for gambling, liquor sales and running a roulette wheel, blackjack table and general poker games long before we had the lottery. It was a constant thing for "bootleggers" to be outwitting the law by providing a place for people to relax and lose their money in the sum of thousands of dollars, their homes, cars, property and anything else of value. We hauled them in every now and then and the court would teach them a lesson. In December 1967, just for a Christmas present, we seized large gambling paraphernalia, a huge cache of whiskey and fifty five persons, charged with various offenses of gambling and liquor violations.

The principle issue was probable cause for the issuance of the search warrant since someone "bored a peep hole" in the side of the building and there the raid officers saw gambling going on by many of the participants, to some degree.

Mr. Harvey Lutins, the famous defense attorney, attempted to discredit our testimony by saying it seemed impossible for anyone to determine something through a "hole the size of a dime." The "Late" Honorable Judge Moyer said, "I disagree with you sir, I've seen a lot though a key hole." Judge Moyer was good to the gamblers and just fined them. On March 4, we raided the same place, same bunch of gamblers, bootleggers, seizing a pot of money and this time Honorable Judge Moyer said, "Apparently you haven't behaved and you don't know when to quit." He again fined them. The next time bandits seized their forty five thousand dollars and wallets, clothes, jewelry and flattened their tires. Not a peep of who did it!!

Captions in the *Roanoke Times* and *World News* in the late 1960's read like this "Trap Snares Load of Shine." "Roanoke Policeman Knocked Down by Automobile" "Two Convicted of Booze Haul, One Called The Brain of The Sauce."

The automobile chase and case almost went to civil action thirty years ago January 6, 1966, this case in which a Roanoke City policeman was knocked down was taken under advisement by the municipal police judge. After police and ABC investigators had arrested two men for hauling untaxed whiskey, a third man later was arrested for trying to run down Vice Sergeant Jack Heath and two ABC investigators by assaulting them by automobile.

Naturally I was accused of being responsible for the problem but at the time I thought we were doing good police work. After the capture of the James Brothers and seizure of one hundred fourteen gallons of whiskey and their car, we found out that they were not Jesse and Frank but two James boys from Henry County, Virginia near the North Carolina line.

After the seizure and arrest of the James Boy's we started out of the dark driveway and into the alley when another car came flying out of a driveway with two people in it. It was a black '55 Ford that didn't have his lights on at the time. Another investigator and I attempted to stop the car by showing our badges with a flashlight shining on it but the driver of the car "floorboarded it" and we jumped aside.

We ran for our car being driven by Sergeant Jack Heath. Our car was a Black '55 Ford, Cadillac powered—seized whiskey car. Jack was a helleva driver. We pursued the other black Ford and determined it had an old woman in it.

The suspects car stopped and let the old woman out of the car. Sergeant Heath stopped behind the suspects car and thought we could jump out of our car and take the suspect out of his. At this point the suspect sped off knocking Heath to the ground, spinning his car around the corner, saying get out of the way "mother." The other investigator in the front seat pulled his revolver and shot at the fleeing car. Apparently the bullets were "duds" and fell in the front floorboard of the car and the next time he shot it jammed the gun. It reminded me of the Keystone Cops. We were right on the bumper of the suspects car going east on Shenandoah Avenue, one o'clock in the morning and he decides to turn left into then, Moores Super Stores wire front gate, crashing it into the steel pipes. We wrestled the suspect out of the car and he began to fight and we had to subdue him. We really never physically hurt him but all our clothes were somewhat creased.

Come to find out his passenger was his ninety year old mother who he claimed we scared nearly to death. He claimed and testified in court that he thought we were the Klu Klux Klan and the Nazis because we had on those green field clothes with no insignias. The judge dismissed it after a year of it being under advisement and their attorney now a great, general district judge, filed a civil action against everyone except me. The case hung-fire for two years and defense dropped the suit. Thank God, and you Judge George Harris!!

I had been staying at the Monta Vista Hotel in Big Stone Gap Virginia while working undercover assignments in that coal mining area. We had to share a community bathroom down the hall and the hotel was so old that the bathtub tilted at a forty-five degree angle. We could sit up in the air and take a bath. We stayed at the Hill Top when we worked in Wise County Virginia and they should have called it the Mountain Top. We slept late one morning waiting on another informer to show up to work with us. Investigator Wayne Prillaman and I woke up and we hadn't had a bath for a week or shaved so we decided to clean up. We sat on the side of the bed and drank a whole pint of 1889 whiskey and smoked a pack of straight camels waiting for the water to come up the hill and squirt through the spigot.

We proceeded to Pound, Virginia to break up an illegal whiskey operation and large "cock fighting" arena who was having the South West Cock Fight Rodeo. They were coming from several states and from many walks of life.

Cock-fighting in this country today, is centered not in Mexico but in ten states mostly south of the Mason Dixon. Virginia is one of the states that contribute to fifty million dollars of illegal activity along with the cruel punishment of the beautiful roosters when those steel spikes severe their brain. I had never been to a cock fight legal or illegal and probably will never go again, at best not like that time. At one time I thought I was one of the fatal roosters.

Several others joined the owner Mr. Cantrell and questioned us. I told Mr. Cantrell we just wanted to have some fun and bet on the roosters and that we were all right. "All right Hell!!" He said, "You need someone to 'vouch' for you." We had nobody and started to walk away from the door when this Ohio car drove up. Three people got out and they were pretty wild looking. Mr. Martin started to talk to one of the guys with a "hook arm". I started to talk to a man who had a .45 caliber army pistol sticking down in his belt.

After some conversation with the guy who had the gun down in his pants, they seemed to relax for the moment. He talked to Mr. Cantrell and others. Finally they let us in on these 'thugs' say so. Mr. Cantrell stamped us with a metal ring through our coat button hole by clamping or riveting into our coats. This was suppose to be safe passage, we thought.

I said I was armed with two fifths of whiskey but I lied a little because I had in the small of my back a 38 caliber squeezer revolver and a 25 caliber automatic in my watch pocket. We thought that would be all there was to it.

The vast arena was busy with professional cockfighters, students working their way through college, doctors, lawyers, novice betters, gamblers, bootleggers, thugs and us. The participants never seemed to be satisfied with our presence. They were after us all the time.

They kept following us around from one seat to another asking us questions about who we were and again what did we do. We tried to convince them that we were there to watch and bet on the "cocks". I looked down through the bleachers and two thugs were trying to look up under our coat. Naturally they didn't know we were armed but they were curious to see what was under our coats.

They never paid any attention to the two state police investigators who were there placing bets. One guy came up the bleachers to the top where they were and asked Mr. Martin to get on the loud speaker and tell everyone we weren't the law and Mr. Martin told them he wasn't a public speaker. He couldn't do it. They turned to me, a student at East Tennessee State University and said, "I hope you aren't the law because I'm working my way through college fightin cocks and selling moonshine whiskey."

I said "good luck and I'm here to make money and have a good time." He was carrying two roosters, one under each arm; a gray one and a red one. I bet on the big red rooster to kill the big gray rooster. He went down into the center of the ring and conditioned them and then turned them loose for the kill and the gray one killed the one I bet on. That pretty red rooster laid there with one of those cold steel spikes through its brain, "plum dead." I had to fork over my money to that senior at the university. I finally went down to the concession stand to get something to drink. The guy at the stand was a little reluctant to serve me. Then a man standing there with a hawksbill knife said, "If you son of a bitches are the law, I'm going to carve you up." I backed up against the wall and just as I started to reach for my "squeezer", one of the guys that helped us get in said, "If you ain't the law you will give us a drink of liquor." Rather than chance buying some from Cantrell and company I said, yeal, "We have some in the car outside. Let's go get it." The three of them searched the entire car and found a fifth of 1889 under the seat. They told me to get it out. I did and took the first drink and gave it to the guy with the "hook arm", he took a big "slug" and then gave it to the guy with the gun.

The guy with a railroad brakeman's stick took a big drink and grinned and almost polished that fifth off. He turned to me and said, "You bastards your car has West Virginia licenses plates that have expired." That unknowingly took some of the pressure off us for a while. They went back into the cockfighting arena. It wasn't over for us by a long shot. I began observing down in the "pits". That's a place where cock fighters have side fights and bets. One guy told me and gave me a matchbook that stated he was running for sheriff of Wyoming County West Virginia and that he was an ABC inspector in West Virginia. I got lucky and finally bought some untaxed whiskey from one of Cantrell's boys and some legal whiskey from another "flunky" they had selling whiskey.

They got to seeing us in too many places and started to ask questions again about, were we the law and they wanted to search us fully. We refused that little deal because if they found a gun or badge on us it would have been "good by Jack".

The matter was getting serious now. We couldn't find the state police undercover guys, Mr. Pollard and Mr. Pugh, anywhere. The cockfighting arena and the "pits" were full and more coming with no place to put them. It's getting close to midnight or one in the morning. Did Mr. Pugh and Mr. Pollard make it to a radio?

No "troops" and the guys that were watching us were getting drunker and drunker. They were calling us names and wanted to see our badges. Some people wanted to leave and couldn't. We wanted to leave but we couldn't. All of a sudden we heard tires spinning and even glass breaking outside. It was eighty state troopers and they were skidding and throwing rocks with their tires trying to get into and around the complex. There were three hundred fifty people in the arena and immediate area. The sheriff's candidate and ABC man from West Virginia wanted to be processed first so I took him and his five thousand dollars worth of cockfighting spurs and other items to then the Captain of and Commander of State Police, Wytheville, Virginia and later the Colonel of the State Police. Mr. H. Burgess.

*   *   *

We arrested seventy five for various law violations and seized thousands of "roosters", "steel spurs", whiskey and thousands of dollars used in this illegal operation. The "roosters" were in crates and were loaded on trucks, taken to the sheriff's office in Wise County. There they were held for trial without bail or heat outside the jail in fourteen below zero weather. All that danger, the "cocks" froze to death and the "fighters", a ten dollar fine!

Working with a "Holiness" preacher wasn't the most religious or the most "wholesome" thing I ever did in my life nor was it the best Christmas. The preacher was a mighty fine man who didn't know who he was working with.

It seemed appropriate at the time that if everything had been tried, and Investigator Richardson had used every trick in the book to catch bootleggers in Smyth County, it would be unusual to put an undercover man with a preacher and not let anyone know you were there except the Chief of Police Boone.

*   *   *

In those days a stranger standing around on the street by himself stood out like a sore thumb. Today with the homeless and transits no one would think twice. Even working with a preacher it seemed odd since he had nothing in common with bootleggers and some two bit dope dealers. There was some "crack" or speed, bennies and black beauties out there, even then on large scale for those days and you can see how it has escalated since those days, beyond comprehension, since 1958.

The preacher worked for the town of Marion, for the water department. I arrived and was given a job by him as his helper, reading meters in the town of Marion. I arrived in a snow storm and he found me a boarding house. It had a wrought iron fence around the front of it and it was a big two or three story house. I got a room upstairs for three dollars a week. Lots of men stayed there.

By working with the preacher in the daytime, I could concentrate on the bootleggers and dope dealers at night. It seemed that everyone in the town of Marion was selling liquor or dope except the business people and they allowed knowingly or unknowingly for some of them to stand around in their places to make contact. There were cabs and service stations that were selling illegal commodities.

They had to wear badges to keep from selling to each other. I hung around a place called the "Club Cafe" in those days. I don't know if it is still there. I haven't been back since they ran me out of town. I had to hide my car some several blocks away and would only go to it to start it, to keep the battery charged up. I could walk from the boarding house to the beer joints, "Tea House" another beer joint on the west end and the Cafe. Most of the traffic milled around these places, service stations and taxis.

All those men at the boarding house would look at me and one guy asked me, "Why is a young guy like you living in a boarding house." I told him I didn't have any money and I didn't. We all ate at a community table in a large dining room. The lady who kept the house would always ask me if everything was alright and if the food was good. That boarding house food was country and delicious, homemade biscuits, gravy, eggs over light, coffee and supper was superb too.

Those men would ask me where did you come from. Your hands don't look like someone who has been doing hard work. I passed it off that I had been in the Navy and had a good job and would just be passing through. I told them I was from all over. I finally got where I would cut some of the meals to cut down on the "chatter". Sometimes I wonder if later events stemmed from my being a stranger. The preacher was suppose to get me acquainted with the people and I would be seen and be okay. I was seen alright.

The place was full of "meth" dealers, now they called the sophisticated version made in bedrooms, bathrooms "ICE". Ice is not like the old "crack, speed". This high powered powder is addictive first time. After that you need it now and forever. It has a term of fourteen hours first smoke and then addictive to the user.

       *   *   *

Bootleggers stood around on the street and fulfilled their name that was given to them in the prohibition era. Some of them had it stuck down in their boots and one guy had two World War I trench coats on and the linings were filled with pints of bootleg liquor. I saw in the paper not long ago where he died. He must have been at least eighty five years old. He was an old man thirty years ago. It apparently was a longevity type of employment.

I finally made contact with some of the bootleg network and one individual took me to his apartment or his room in the basement of a large house. He got a gallon of liquor out of a barrel and brought it inside out of a sleeting rain. It took him a while to fish it out of the barrel. It was hard enough to be working with a preacher and making buys on my own at night. I had been drinking some before I met him and then took a big drink out of this jug and finally bought it from him.

For some unusual reason he became apprehensive. I was sitting on his small bed and he was sitting on a straight back chair by a dresser with a mirror over it. We sat there and talked, in hopes of getting him to take me to other places. They didn't sell to strangers, you needed someone with you to get you in. A friend of his arrived and he didn't like my looks at all and immediately told me, "I'm here for another reason. Who are you?" "Why would a stranger stay here a week or more?"

I told them that I had just gotten out of the Navy and was looking for a job. In fact, I was wearing my Navy Peacoat this night. I told them I was just passing through more or less and needed work. That didn't satisfy them. This bootlegger's friend was just passing through from Arkansas and that I looked like the law to him.

I told them I didn't know what the law looked like so I couldn't tell them anything. The guy from Arkansas was sitting in the chair and the bootlegger on the dresser top. All of a sudden the tall guy from Arkansas pulled out an Italian Stiletto, a sharp long two-bladed switch blade knife.

My Navy Peacoat was open with the collar up, covering up a tight khaki shirt and dungarees. He made a lunge at me cutting the khaki shirt across my stomach. I felt cold blood run down into my belt line. The bootlegger had a hawkbill knife and the two of them stuck their knives into my back and said, "We are going upstairs to a phone." they took me up the steps to a hallway in the main part of the big house. He picked up the phone in the hallway and called someone and talked to them. The guy from Arkansas now has the switch blade thrust through the Peacoat and into my back.

After telling the party on the other end of the line, "This is a brave bastard, we don't know who he is." I knew they meant business. I whirled around knocking the little guy down the steps toward his room. His hawksbill knife went with him. I ran out of the house via the hallway, jumped a metal fence and found myself in downtown Marion near the Club Cafe.

I went in the beer joint and got a cup of coffee and then came out and who was waiting on me, my Arkansas friend with his long thin knife. I told him I was going to stick that knife where the sun don't shine. He lunged at me and stabbed me through the left arm. I told him I had a gun but this time I didn't have it. I was told by my superiors that I didn't need anything on me whatsoever.

There was a policeman checking doors and heard the commotion. He spotted the Arkansas knife and heard the conversation. He immediately drew his service revolver and told the knife swinger to drop the knife, he did. He had his gun cocked, grabbed me and placed it behind my head.

I can still feel that ice cold gun barrel jumping up and down against my head. I said, "Please don't let that thing go off." It appeared that he was just a little nervous. He said, "Get your hands up and asses across and up the street," marching us up the hill to the Courthouse. He took us into the jail or docket office. The jailer, while making out his report, asked me who I was and I told him I was a farmer. He told me, "Don't give me that shit and hand over some ID." I told him I didn't have any but I had a billfold with some cards in it and pulled out one with Willard D. Parsons name on it. It was a construction union card.

He threw me against the radiator and pulled out his blackjack and grabbed my pocketbook and found a drivers license in it with my name and my address in Roanoke, Virginia. He said, "You lie to me again and I'll bust your head. Your arm and stomach won't be the only thing bleeding. You son-of-a-bitch, you."

I vaguely remember a uniformed state trooper came in about that time. I think his name was Norris. Thanks for the trooper showing up when he did because I didn't know what might have happened. By this time another deputy had come in and they took me handcuffed to a cell with no phone. They wouldn't even listen to me and finally a town policeman called Chief Boone and I tried to talk to him. When I told him who I was, he hung up because the biggest bootlegger there in town was a guy named Powell, who ran a pool room. The nice little policeman who took me to call the chief through Captain Blevins, escorted me back to the cell and said, "That's the last damn phone call you will get Mr. Smart-ass." I kept banging on the cell bars with my tin jail cup that had cold coffee, by the way I kept that cup in my Peacoat and believe it or not I have it. I kept demanding to see the Chief of Police Boone or Captain Blevins. Another police officer came around and delivered another drunk and told me if I kept banging on that cell he was going to bust me in the head with his blackjack.

Every police officer should spend at least three days to a week in jail to understand both the prisoners and the police standpoint of being in jail. You would have thought that after a while I would have become missing in action (MIA) but no one cared, you were on your own. Today superiors would be sued or fired or visa-versa. Someone finally called Chief Boone and told him again and again I was an undercover agent. He finally sent for me and then my supervisor showed up and instructed me to pick up my car and go back to Roanoke.

My supervisor advised me he would conduct an investigation and let me know what the results were. In my own mind, I knew I would be facing disciplinary action and about six weeks later my supervisor told me we were going to Richmond and all they would do is fire me. He wanted me to quit but I wouldn't. After a grilling by the director of enforcement, I was escorted into the office of the chairman of the board who was from Marion, Virginia.

The chairman of the ABC board those days was called "God". He greeted me and assured me that I wouldn't be fired. He said, "It looks like your emotions overrode your thinking." Well again, I had a wife and children and needed the job, so I was ready for any discipline. I was used to it and got more used to it. I got sixty days probation. Again I never went to the doctor or hospital or received any compensation for the injury or loss of one Navy Peacoat and khaki shirt and dungarees. After all they sent me to do the job, without backup or any security, radio, beeper or any other means of help.

Then, when you got in any trouble, yesteryear they always say you were lax-in-judgement. Today there is a direct contact with an agent by wire, cellular phones, fiber optics, female partner and four to a raid team.

Chapter Thirteen

Smokey Joe

Those days are gone and so is the oldest moonshine-bootlegger road house owner, junk dealer, bible totin builder of his house and even a guitar picking ballad singer. His name was "Smokey Joe". Smokey Joe passed away at the age of eighty three in 1981. I used to stop by and talk with him between the times we raided him at his place on old Christainsburg Mountain Road, RT 460, East of Christainsburg, Virginia.

He once told me "revenue man I made a million dollars and let it slip through my hands some of it right here in this hollow." Smokey had a sound mind and body that let him work right up to his dying day. Former bootlegger, farmhand, junk dealer, roadhouse owner, gambling den owner was a rountuer of note with plenty of tales to tell. He outwitted Jim Crow and lawmen, the law itself, made a million and lost it all on women, gambling, Cadillac's.

Smokey Joe, tall, lanky, raw boned always with a grin beneath his neatly trimmed mustache. During our many chats he always had a smile on, many times quoting the bible saying such things as this. "Its not by your good works Jack but, do you believe in him with all your heart and openly profess him—I mean Jesus Christ" and he would be jumping around almost in a pray.

Smokey's tales were evident of his name. He told me and others, "One time I had a lawyer named Calhoun who defended me on a charge of making whiskey. Then they called me baby Joe because I was the last boy born, but the lawyer made a mistake during his closing argument and called me 'Smokey Joe' in open court."

"I beat the charge and when I came out of the court house everybody was laughing and clapping and shouting 'Smokey Joe' his name spread like mayonnaise. I lost on some of those charges at times and had to serve time. I sold moonshine for forty years bringing five gallon tins of liquor from Floyd County and Montgomery County Virginia. I hid it across the road from my old house and sold it all." He later built a new house a few feet down the way. I watched him build the new one from the ground up. It was a spacious house and he built it with his bare hands. He was up in his seventies and ailing with arthritis.

In the earlier years he would pint and quart and half gallon then what folks thought was good whiskey. He told me he was the only retail man at the foot of Christainsburg Mountain. He would hop aboard the number one passenger train here for the Norfolk and Western Railway. It would come through at ten in the morning and get into West Virginia in the afternoon. He would hop off and take it to his sister's house and by dark all of it would be gone.

He said, "Jack I strapped hot water bottles full of bootleg whiskey to my body and rode the trains across the state line. I hauled it in suit cases when I could afford a ticket on the train or otherwise I hopped a freight. I never was caught at this. I handled only the best whiskey. Jack if you ain't never drank none, don't never, ain't none of it good."

Later years Smokey stuck to selling government whiskey. Buy it from the State Store and resell it for a profit. He always had something brewing at his house. His favorite was dandelion and grapefruit wine. He bottled it and sold it making a pretty good living at that.

Smokey didn't like telling the story about revenue men coming by his house one day when he had a big poker game going and two crocks of homebrew, working right in front of the front door of his house. As they passed by Smokey was in the process of selling a pint of home brew for a quarter. They saw the card game going on and the sale right through that open front door.

It was in the summer time and you could see all the way through the house. "They jumped out of their cars and ran into my house and grabbed the pint of dandelion wine and the quarter out of my hand. I had several other crocks of home brew sitting behind a door and Powell turned them all over and the wine ran down through the cracks of the house."

"I beat them in court and my lawyers threatened them with a civil suit. They turned around and got several buys off me and sent me to Bland Correction Farm. I never forgot it but I never held a grudge." Smokey continued to live on two hilly bleak acres in this hollow on US 11 or 460 at the foot of old Christainsburg Mountain, Montgomery County. He built it from cinder block and wood after a flash flood washed his first house away years ago.

The property had been in the family almost continuously since the 1800's, when his father purchased forty acres for three hundred dollars. He reared six children on that property which in the old days was three miles from the nearest black family in one direction and six miles in another.

"Smokey Joe" and his family got along well but there was one catch, Jim Crow Laws made the opportunities less than equal. He made it a point to tell this story many times and once to Joe Kennedy, a newspaper reporter of the *Roanoke Times* and *World News*, so it would be publicized and people would know about the Jim Crow Laws.

"Smokey" told me many times as he told the newspaper people, that he was born on this rather little rocky farm in the foot hills of the Allegheny. "We were four miles from any colored school, down in the village of Shawsville. An old white gentleman, named Mr. Lane, used to drive the school wagon—two horse covered wagon—to the white school on the way to our black school. I lived right on the route that the school wagon was traveling but never would they let me ride." "It wasn't that they didn't want too." "It was the law, the Jim Crow Law which was the separation of races in certain places." the Civil Rights Laws rectified these matters in the 1960's as a result of a Supreme Court decision.

"Mr. Lane was a neighbor that couldn't pick me up." "I would watch my play boys and girls, waving as they went by." "Smokey" went to school for just two years. "I learned to count so no one could cheat me and I learned to write so I could be understood." "Smokey's" family moved to Pennsylvania. He often said, "I knew it was unfair but I couldn't do anything about it. My daddy didn't stay long up north because it wasn't much better up there. He quit the railroad up in Pennsylvania and came back to our little place in Virginia. We went to work for Mr. Correll, my daddy worked for him for seventy five cents, for a ten hour day. I worked right along side him for twenty five cents a day. We lived in a one room log house on our little farm and we children had to sleep beneath the rafter roof. It would leak and when it snowed, lordy it would blow between the boards coming in on us."

"I was lean, young and quick then. We got seven dollars for clearing and sawing wood." "When they would bring water to the fields they would have two different dippers, they would drink out of one and we would drink out of the other." "They would go in and eat and we would wait on the porch or under a shade tree until the whites ate and then we would go in and eat." "If it had been today I wouldn't have eaten a bite but I had to do what my parents told me to do." "I wasn't but ten years old."

"Smokey Joe" remembered a neighbor who spent many nights drinking and eating and sleeping at his house. One day that neighbor asked him to come to his house to chop wood. I went up there and helped chop wood until twelve o'clock and then he said, "Lets go eat." He went inside his house and there wasn't anyone but he and his wife. I waited outside and he finally came out and said that I could go in and eat. I said, "You done eat," he replied "yea". I said, "No thank you and we never chopped wood together again but he would still come down here and eat like a boy with me."

Smokey always called me "lawman" except once in a while he would call me "revenuer". In a sincere chuckle he would say "Mr. Lawman, the lord watches over us all and he will take you and me to heaven someday."

I was the first one ever to open up a Wayside Inn between Roanoke and Tennessee. It was called the "Speedway Lunch". We sold barbecue food and bootleg liquor, lodging, a forty by forty foot dance floor, poker, dice and good looking women. I had to close it in 1940. The law was hot after me all the time. I naturally drew the attention of lawmen.

The one I really worried about long before you was Mr. Graham, a revenuer, who would shoot you over a pint of whiskey. He shot three of them escaping from a still and killed one fleeing with liquor from a raid on a liquor joint. Others would look the other way when given a half gallon of brandy at no charge. We were afraid of Mr. Graham. I got caught more than any of the others but I never payed it no mind. I had Powell's picture, I cut it out of the newspaper and I hung it in the kitchen and Johnny house. I had signs saying no credit, no checks just cold cash.

I couldn't get a winks sleep, people wanting government liquor, beer, home brew, wine. There was someone knocking on my door all the time. I guess that's what wore me out and jail time. Smokey went to the fullest extent at age eighty one and he said of the liquor business,—" it was against two laws, Gods and man's." Long after he quit it all, he said, "It was wrong and I paid for it but it was better than going out and breaking into someone's house or robbing banks." "When a man goes to the fullest extent, he don't want anymore livin, I'm sick from chronic illness. I'm just plain worn out and want to meet my God."

At eighty one, the last time I saw Mr. Smokey Joe, he was still six foot four inches, maintained mental clarity although he suffered from emphysema, hardening of the arteries and high blood pressure. He strummed on his old guitar to these tunes and words:

My bootlegging and gambling, pretty girls are over,
My Lords going to put me up there in the clover,
I'm preparing for a better world and that's my goal,
The important thing is to get fight with God and your
soul,
Serve him and he will take care of you without strife,
Give you water to drink out of the fountain of life,

I believe Mr. Smokey Joe did just that and is in that land of undiscovered of which there may be no return for the legendary or anyone else. You can rest a sure there are no Jim Crow Laws.

Smokey was closest to becoming the oldest bootlegger in the trade, however there was a woman nearly one hundred years old selling government liquor and had been since the state went wet in 1933. Ms. Jones alias Ms. Woods or something like that, sold liquor along with her husband who sold it for seventy five years right in the Star City of the south. I bought liquor from her for the last time in 1973.

The Honorable George B. Dillard, Municipal Police Judge, advised her if the warrants had alleged previous convictions he would have had no choice but to send her to jail. The judge's generosity and compassion kept her from any sentence. By the way when you brought in moonshine whiskey you never needed an analysis because he was from Franklin County and knew whiskey.

Chapter Fourteen

Playing With Snakes

A one hundred year old woman is rare but to be selling liquor illegally at that age is as rare as someone playing with snakes. There are people who do handle snakes, religously and otherwise. I don't even like them when they are made into belts or fixed as a specialty to eat.

I was working in Big Stone Gap, Lee and Wise Counties Virginia. I was posing as a laid-off coal miner. I was hanging around a beer joint there in the middle of Big Stone Gap Virginia and met a guy who was driving a Coke truck waiting on a load of Coke from the Coke ovens of Norton. During his break he asked me if I wanted to go back to Illinois with him and bring another truck back to Virginia. He wanted to give me a job since he though I was laid-off. I thanked him and bought him a beer.

We took a booth and was sitting there when a man came in the place in a paint hat, white paint pants and short sleeve shirt. He was carrying a paper bag and came over to our booth dancing around shaking the paper bag up and down. It had a terrible rattle about it. He leaned over our booth and told my acquaintance and I, "I have a surprise for you" and opened the paper bag and started to pull the bag over when we both jumped up and my acquaintance ripped part of the booth off and railed the guy across the head sending him reeling backwards.

He ran out the door and down the street and the truck driver right after him and me after the truck driver and the chief of police who happened to see what was going on came after all of us. The guy got away rattlesnake and all. The truck driver and I both went to the bathroom and the chief was still looking for the snake handler. It's a felony in Virginia to put a live venomous snake on anyone if they don't get killed in the process. I'm sure if my friend had caught the snake handler he might not have fared so well.

I didn't fare as well when ATU Tom Gibbs found a big black pot still just off the parkway and we went to it one hot October afternoon to see if the mash was ready to run. Agent Gibbs and Mr. Martin went one way and I was to wait at a given point until they returned. I started to step over a huge log when a large brown long configuration leaped from the other side of the log. It was a big Copperhead and I jumped backwards and nearly fainted.

I couldn't shoot because if anyone had been at the still site, they would be gone. I picked up some rock and pinned the big snake under them for a bit then it moved the rock away and started over the log as if it knew who I was and was going to have me for supper. I picked up a large stick with a knot on the end and frailed the snake but the stick was half broken into and when I struck a hard blow, it broke into pieces, throwing me off balance and into the snakes coiled position. At this time I pissed in my new field greens.

The big Copperhead lunged from its coiled position but I had fallen backwards and was moving on all fours backwards when Agent Gibbs came back to get me. He was an excellent shot, he exercised his ability and blew the snakes head off. From the time he was town marshal of Rich Creek, the last town marshal to be exact, in Virginia, state trooper in Floyd County and an ATU agent in Roanoke, he was the only law officer that I knew or know who shoots with both eyes open, he couldn't be out-shot. We all tried but we lost.

Bootleggers wanted you to lose more than a shooting match so they did some trifling things to attempt to protect their cache and "fix your little red wagon" in the process. One such character hides his liquor in post holes and hoped you would find it. He dug post holes and put the half gallon mason jars of bootleg down in them and then would put steel traps set and cover the hole up with leaves. If you came along unexpected or uninvited, you may lose a hand or so. We started carrying a walking stick to punch in the holes and set off the traps.

He had an old Coca Cola cooler buried down in the ground, across the road from his house. He worked during the day at the Radford Powder Plant and sold bootleg liquor on weekends and evenings. He was an ingenious person and knew how to keep out the devil from his full half gallons of moonshine. He put a big rattlesnake on top of the jars and then leaves and straw. If you opened the cooler top - bingo you get the prize. He did some other good tricks such as dynamite caps in stashes of liquor and when you reached into one of those traps, you had kucklettes.

Ever since that Arab girl gave me that necklace in a movie in North Africa when I was in the Navy, I have been the most blessed person on earth. That "hand of faith or fate" has been with me for the better part of my life. Gave me a pretty wife, two beautiful daughters and two fine son in laws, six grandchildren, good health, had a good job in the mountains and that's where I nearly got it but that hand of faith or fate was with me.

*   *   *

July 11, 1967, Floyd, Montgomery, Roanoke County lines come together. Trooper Johnny Holt, upon our request dropped us off near the home of a noted liquor violator and my partner and I had just got out of Trooper Holts car and started up a little bank. It was thundering and lightening that day and an electrical storm was brewing overhead. "Cigar" was behind me and just as I stepped up on the bank, I heard something rattle between thunders. This was thunder alright...it lunged out three feet struck my knee, barely touching my field greens at the knee. It recoiled.

Before it could strike a second time, my partner "Cigar" (that's what those bootleggers called him in Roanoke City) was famous for carrying two guns, which he quickly drew and opened fire on this great rattlesnake. The bullets never exited its body. It recoiled and struck again. Naturally we were out of range. I drew my service revolver in defense of me. Shaking as I was I shot the thing between the eyes. "Cigar" had been a city police officer for eight years before joining up with us enforcement investigators. He had made his mark there before he came with us and assumed that nickname.

Trooper Holt picked us up and we brought the snake to Roanoke and a picture was taken of it by the *Roanoke Times* and *World News*. I have the fifteen rattlers and one button in my dresser drawer along with another one we got in Gile's County one morning going to a still and I stepped on it and it rolled out from under my foot and struck at me in the dark of that morning. Trooper Lee and Trooper Heck both shot it and when we got to the still, there was no one there except the pure copper still and cooling barrel running over with cold water and a spout of whiskey was coming out of the coil running into a Coca Cola fountain jug. There was no Coke in the jug, just 142 proof mountain dew.

That seven rattlers and one button probably saved our lives that morning because about ten feet from the still was a single barrel shotgun with no stock. It was laying in a notch cut in a log. Did Troopers Lee and Heck save our lives by those moonshiners getting away because they shot that snake out from under my foot? I haven't seen any bigger rattlers than that one on the Tri-line near Floyd County. Sergeant Reynolds of PD (retired, deceased) Roanoke made a belt out of the rattler. I never want to encounter one like that ever again. We had one investigator that played with them. We threatened to take him to the "funny farm". Just kidding Melvin!!

We used dynamite to blow stills "high in the sky" for years and then the government got tight with the use of explosives because of the criminal elements obtaining explosives to enhance their causes. We stopped using it for a while and went back to the axe or "the devil". That's what old time bootleggers and temperance groups called the revenue officer and his trusty axe. In those days they rode horses, wore spats, campaign hats with a tassel. Stuck down in their saddle was a breech loaded carbine, a bandoleer of ammo. Tied to the saddle bags or horn was a medium hatchet, blade, painted red, with the word devil burned printed into the handle. Later they had to carry an axe because the stills were getting larger and larger.

For this operation we were still using the axe, just field greens, jeeps, cars and very limited explosives. We had found this "four-pot" operation in Floyd County's Topeka Community section. After checking the mash and found that the still would run soon, like tomorrow, we waited in the woods nearby. Daylight was breaking and we heard a "still buggy" coming. They backed the old truck into the still and two white guys and a real small black guy got out and started unloading fruit jars and sugar.

They went right to work using chestnut rails to fire the still. The little black guy started dipping up the mash and filling up the number one pot. They got the pot boiling and the vapor condensing into "white lightin". Two of the stills had to be remashed and were empty. We waited a while for the operators to settle down then we raided the still. The two empty stills were sitting on cinder block and there was a cinder block step up to the top of the stills. We caught the two white guys immediately and brought them back into the still from a short chase into the woods. Out of the corner of my eye, I thought I saw the little black guy go up the cinder block steps to one of the big pots. Apparently he had gotten down inside of one of them. We didn't go directly to the still and pretended all was secure. He thought he was safe inside that big black pot nestled inside and we would go away.

Finally I called to one of the investigators to get us seven sticks of dynamite "that ought to do it, I said. That still started rocking and rolling. It sounded like thunder in that big tin elongated device that looks like a tank without tracks, with a big hole cut in the top of it. His voice echoed, you could have heard it for a mile. "Oh!!! Hell!!!, he screamed, don't blow me up captain, I'm coming out." Out he came too, white as a sheet, his pants were wet all the way down the front.

The three of them got probation and the little black guy never made liquor again but the other two we caught several times in larger stills. They worked for big distillers who had to get their product out. Mr. Keys decided he had, had enough.

It seems there was dynamite everywhere. No wonder the government restricted the use of it by its people and law enforcement officials. Our men were always getting some kind of threats from law violators, including moonshiners we had caught.

One August morning forty three years ago just before daylight, there was a terrific explosion at one of our investigator's house. It blew the windows of his Rocky Mount, Virginia home. It blew the wheels and doors off his enforcement car along with all the windows. The suspect investigator told our enforcement director that he wasn't going to be run out of Franklin County by any bootleggers or illegal distillers. He vowed he would get the son-of-a-bitches who "wired" his car.

He was interviewed by the director and a district supervisor concerning the "bombing". He was interviewed for beating still hands when they caught them and was returning them from the woods.

As late as 1957 when I ran my first violator from a big still and caught him way out in a field, when he pleaded with me "don't whip me like Mr. Harry used to do." I didn't know what he was talking about.

Mr. Harry finally admitted he put the explosives in the hub caps, doors, and under the gas tank that blew his car to smithereans in hopes he would be transferred. He was permanently.

*   *   *

Can you imagine twenty years before this last incident when agents needed a fast car in the early 1930's, say a high speed roadster that was being operated by big time bootleggers in certain areas. The agents would spot a nice Buick Roadster with a "rag top" parked in front of a cafe without the "wheelman" and revenue agents would put several jars of untaxed whiskey on the bootleggers car and wait for the gangsters to come out and drive off. Prohibition agents would pull them over and find the liquor on the car. They would seize it. It happened time and time again, I had been told by old time revenue agents. There were several shootouts and the famous Carroll Doctrine arose from these agents conduct. By the way the Carroll Doctrine has never been repealed. We have had all kinds.

Then we had "tombstone" Johnson who made more arrests than anyone in the outfit. He was a whirlwind of an investigator with more information and seizures than the office could count. Our director began to wonder what the other investigators were doing. Mr. Johnson was outwitting the bootlegger and moonshiners and our men. The director sent his best investigator out to look into the matter. Mr. Gaulding began to check on the names of the people the investigator was sending in on the arrest record card. Mr. Gaulding apparently followed Mr. Johnson to a cemetery where he gathered certain names from tombstones. These people had been dead for years. He wrote them in his little book and then filled out an arrest card, sent it in and waited ten days to see if the person appealed to a higher court. Mr. Gaulding went on to become the director for thirty years himself and "tombstone" Johnson went on to driving a cab.

There was one investigator who put the enforcement car in an auto race in Bloutville, Tennessee. Investigators tracked the car to a hotel in Bristol, Virginia, where it was "heaped up" in the rear parking lot. It looked like it has been put through a recycle machine. They found the investigator "racked out with a pretty little thing". They racked the car up on a truck and took it back to Richmond. The investigator had made a lot of liquor buys and drank most of the evidence. They went to Tennessee and there he made the first entry with Virginia tags on it. I was told that he won the race but lost his ass, well I mean he got fired.

Fast cars were the moonshiners way to elude the revenue officers in the old days. The very first time I saw that Mr. Harless who used to be Mr. Harry's partner, you know the one who beat still hands. I was new and at a big still that he had "wired up" for demolition and I was helping. While I was still standing in the site, after he had finished wiring it he got the "hell box" and hollered, "fire in the hole."

He twisted the handle on the "hell box" and Boom!! Ka Boom!! The three cases of dynamite that we had put in this huge steam outfit blew pieces a mile away and the mash rained on us for an hour plus I had to run for my life with splinters from blown wood still hitting me in the ass.

Mr. Harless was a character. And a character was he and a helleva car driver too, I thought. We were going to make a still investigation in the Ferrum section of Franklin County. We were coming down state RT 623 when we ran up behind a black shiney '40 Ford Coupe. He had stopped, in fact, in front of us deliberately, I believe to see if we would give chase. Mr. Harless smoked a cigar and had a rather long one in his mouth with the smoke swirling around the rear view mirror as he puffed on it relentlessly.

I said, "Mr. Harless that guy is gunning that car and the car is jacked up in the rear with what appeared to be Monroe Load Levers or Adjustmatic Air Shocks." Mr. Harless chomping on the cigar said, "I don't give a damn what he has under that thing. I will catch him when I want too." the car was sitting there shaking so bad, it appeared the paint was going to fall off.

The Ford accelerated, tires burning rubber, screaming and he shifted into second, a ball of fire came out of the rear and that's all we saw of him until he was waiting again down the road for us. Mr. Harless was driving a '55 Ford, two door enforcement car with "red heads" on it. No doubt he knew we were after him and he was toying with us with a '40 Ford Offerhouser. Waiting again he was. This time Mr. Harless was slightly pee-ooed. We gave chase again and he left us waiting again. He would stop in the road and wait for us to catch up and then take off but this time we floor boarded our car and we saw him go around a sharp curve. We attempted it and went through a pine grove, riding down dozens of pines and they lapped back on us. It took us hours to cut our way out.

The reason we went through that pine grove was, the hood flew up and all that muddy water covered the windshield and came through the windows. We didn't have air in those days and the hot scalding water flew through the windows, we could have shaved with the lather of mud on our faces. It looked like the Laurel and Hardy days. We didn't have chain saws in those days to immediately saw our way out. We had to rely on our so called "devil". I told Mr. Harless I wasn't riding with him anymore but I did, one more time. A '56 Black Ford one day while we were working the roads in the Endicott section of Franklin County passed us with a lcad of shine and Mr. Harless was driving the same '55 Ford Redhead with twin carbs on it and a Columbia rear end.

Mr. Harless told me to get my revolver out and "git a tire when I get along side." Mr. Harless didn't get near him he stayed ahead of us. I swear, I believe he was the same driver as the other one except he had a Cadillac Ford with trip curbs on it and it was rigged high and loaded up full. He would go around a curve and you could see the liquor on the front passengers side up to the top of the seat.

Mr. Harless was bearing down on that cigar and saying that son-of-a-bitch is not going to get away this time he's on a road that comes out below a fork and we are heading across the cut through and we will be waiting on him. I thought we would get over there somewhere and pull up on the side of the road and wait for him to come along and take chase but Mr. Harless just went "Hee!!, Hee!! And said, "yea we'll be waiting on him alright." I was holding on for dear life, the "redhead ford" was toting the mail. Every time we rounded a curve, it would throw gravel thirty feet in the air and the tires were smoking so bad you couldn't see behind us. It rattled the windows completely out of a shack when we went through that guys yard glazing his corner porch.

Mr. Harless had beat him across the cut through and there was a little hump in that narrow secondary road. Mr. Harless said, "Jack he has to hit us in the ass end or turn over going to the left down an enbankment. He is not going to the right because he will have splinters in his ass if he hits that barn." it was like the movies, we heard him coming, those carburetors changing progressively to make a distinct honeing sound. A lump had come up in my throat as well as my pants when, Mr. Harless said, "He's hammering that ford, jump Jack, jump…jump damn't." I did, he came over that hump, instinctively turned to the right and went through the man's barn and out the other side.

He got away and I asked Mr. Harless if he was going to call the state police or the sheriff and report the incident or accident. He said, "Jack what did we see and what or who could we identify?" "Hell no, we aren't calling anyone. We wouldn't want anyone to know that some damn mountaineer moonshiner had outrun us smart revenue officers." He made plenty of sense. He was a good guy but he met his "waterloo" just like his partner, Mr. Harry.

149

Jack Allen Powell

Revenue officers have gained a reputation over the years as being rowdy, rough, tough and in the old days you had to be something a little more than a bible totin preacher.

Their escapades have been far and wide as you have read but one of these sticks in my mind as indelible. We stayed in a motel between Abington and Bristol where we were conducting raids on bootleggers and moonshiners in the late 50's and early 60's and had really torn up the motel shamefully. It's a wonder we hadn't been charged civilly.

We had played poker all night long and drank enough liquor to float the battlewagon Iowa. When it became daylight, we raided the bootleggers and moonshiners and found whiskey and stills in attics, basements, chicken houses and barns. We rounded up about one hundred violators and left the rest to history.

But as you well know history usually repeats itself. Years later I went back to the same motel and asked for a room, while on another assignment. The manager asked me who I was with and I told him I was an enforcement agent. I have no room for you or any other enforcement agents. You stayed here a long time ago and burned the carpets, tore up the rooms and walls.

The manager said, "I know you people, when you came into the motel you ask where is the women?" "drinking from a bottle of bourbon, pissed in the sink and wiped your ass with a wash rag. No motel rooms for you or any other enforcement agent."

Chapter Fifteen

Revenue Officers Creed

Not a very good reputation for law officers to create but realistic. That's keeping with revenue officers creed live fast, drink plenty and play poker when you can't or aren't catching moonshiners, bootleggers. Well, most of us was playing poker in motel in Lynchburgh in 1970. We were there for a state enforcement school to learn new techniques and more legal aspects. Three of us arrived wearing new business suits. It was in March and the swimming pool had a sheet of ice on it. The wind was blowing fiercely. Someone dared us to dive off the diving board, we killed a fifth of 1889 and we all three dived into the icy water.

Things really got going in the evening when someone attempted to blow the side out of the motel and flatten all the tires on the supervisor's cars. One of our new agents and his brother got into a fight and tore a room all to pieces and smashed the new television that had been installed in their room. I already was on probation and I guess they thought I did it but I had witnesses, my poker pals. I wasn't near any fireworks or didn't know the brothers although the new agent I met crossing the motel parking lot had just left the room they had tore up. He grabbed me by the tie and asked me where I was going and said, "I heard you was on probation 'cowboy'."

I knocked his hands down and told him to get away from me. He did and kept going somewhere. The Director, Mr. Gaulding called a "muster" immediately after the room smashing and threatened to fire the whole damn bunch. To this day, I don't think they know who did the "fireworks" deal. They fired the new agent and made him and his brother pay for the damage to the motel and room.

I went to the funeral of another investigator with Supervisor Blackburn a few months ago and we talked about the incident but he didn't know "who did it". Yes, I mentioned being on probation again from a similar incident involving a restaurant and motel in Giles County. This incident had happened five year before this, so you can see I wasn't to get into any ruckus. I was on indefinite probation since 1965.

My motel incident happened in Giles County, Virginia at the T-T Restaurant and Motel. The manager of the licensed establishment was a big guy, ex-marine, not a bad fellow, if he's on your side but he and his buddies ran the place the way they wanted to.

We had raided a still that day and had gotten a motel room at the motel adjacent to the restaurant. We were having a mixed drink after we drank a couple straight. I went over to the restaurant to get a "chaser" and when I walked into the restaurant, the owner was standing behind the counter with a mixed drink in a glass himself which was a violation. I had been drinking but I asked him about the drink and told him that it was illegal for him to have any alcoholic beverage except what he was licensed to sell, beer and wine.

I identified myself and showed him my badge. He replyed by saying, "That's the trouble with you goddamn ABC men, who do you think you are anyway." My reply to him was simply this "rats ass to you to cowboy." Investigators for years called me "rats ass cowboy". It was "jump back Jack then". About that time he reached across the counter and grabbed me and his two buddies, one a former boxer and the other a racecar driver, the three of them grabbed me and threw me through the front screen door out into the gravel. I got back up and went back in and before I could say arrest, they were waiting inside the door, grabbing me and throwing me through the door again further out into the parking lot. This time I ran to my room to get my gun when Mr. Martin, the group leader drove up, and Mr. Mac went to meet him and tell him what had happened.

He said, "I want him fired, suspended or electrocuted whichever comes first." I stood there blood running down my arms from the gravel raking. My nose was bleeding and I was still going for my gun when Mr. Martin stopped me. I told him I was going to arrest them but they had already called the Commonwealth attorney through their lawyer Mr. Dillow and pleaded their story. The Commonwealth attorney said it would have to be worked out administratively, that he wasn't going to prosecute. They worked it out all right. I was Richmond bound again. I kept the Gray Hound buses in business in those days.

I was back seeing Mr. Wright again. This time he wasn't sure if he was going to let me ride the bus back home or use the old thumb. He didn't fire me and because he was from South West Virginia, I guess he was compassionate. He was a good man. I had two children now and needed a job even more so. Sometimes I think I would have been better off if he had fired me. I got indefinite probation and was told not to ever go to the restaurant and motel again. I didn't but I did have the last word with Mr. Mac. He ran another place in the town of Narrows and failed to run it right. This time we cleaned the place out and him with it. He lost his licenses.

I am the only man with the enforcement division that ever served twelve years probation before another board member, Chairman Honorable Jack Bruce, Farmville, Virginia released me saying it was pathetic for anyone to be on probation indefinitely and not release him in a reasonable length of time. I'm the only man in the enforcement division who served a thirteen year probation, two months five days suspension to remain on duty without pay. Made to pay for two cars, jailed, abused by authorities, nearly shot several times, snake struck four times (twice by copperheads, twice by rattlers), a dozen fiasco-skirmishes, fifteen automobile fender benders and three totals (completely destroyed). I may be one of the few who have received five commendations for outstanding and meritorious duty. God has been holding the hand of faith over me and guiding me all my life. I thank him for allowing me to be a survivor.

*   *   *

Everyone survives something—not so was the case of Ms. E. a native of Vinton, Virginia a small town with a lot of good people in it. It didn't have a big police department in those days. It had come from a town sergeant to a chief and a sergeant and two patrolmen. They worked everything from murder to burglary, accidents and domestics and liquor enforcement with revenue officers. It numbers about fifteen now. Sergeant Iddings worked liquor a lot and he was forever getting information on bootleggers in Glade town.

There was a woman who would run and hide every time we would raid her. She would hide in the bed and cover up. This particular time Sergeant Iddings got the information he called me and said his informer told him that Ms. E. would jump in the bed and hide the liquor under her gown, completely covering up with the sheets and cover. Ms. E. wouldn't open the door because she was too busy running and hiding the liquor and her in the bed. We used forceful entry and went to the bedroom and there she was lying in the bed saying, "You can't pull those covers back I don't have any clothes on." we didn't have any police-women in those days to take with us so I told Ms. E. to get up out of bed and give us what she had under the cover. She said "Go to Hell!. You look under this cover and you will see more than you bargained for." I told her once again to surrender what she had under the cover. I pulled the cover back and I pulled her hand away from her gown and several pints of untaxed whiskey fell out. Oh!!, Yes and we saw more than we bargained for.

Sometimes you get more than you bargain for whether you wanted it or not. Behind the part of what is called Elm Park Estates, Hunting Hills and Tanglewood Mall was Slate Hill, Starkey Road and Southern Exposure. Trooper H.J. Meade, then called the terror of 220 called me and said he had a search warrant for a Mr. Hale who resided on Slate Hill.

Mr. Hale was a man of about sixty five or so, thin, mean, hated the law, drank all the time and liked revenue officers less. It was a hot Saturday afternoon and the informer had told Trooper Meade that Mr. Hale had gotten a load of shine in and was distributing it at his home. Investigator George Martin, who was in charge of the territory, told me to pick him up and we met Trooper Meade on the old Starkey Road.

We executed the search warrant but we jumped the gun, we got there too soon or too late. Mr. Hale wasn't there. We searched the house and did what the law instructed us to do, post a copy of the search warrant on the front door of his house. We were about to go to a shed he had out back when he came in. He was driving an old pickup truck. He was drunk and had a pint of whiskey sticking out of his bibbed overalls. I ran over to him, asked him what he had in his pocket and he said, "Corn Whiskey and its mine." I told him he was under arrest and he would have to go to Salem, Roanoke County Courthouse.

There was a chop block with a doubled bladed axe sticking in it. It was razor sharp, gleaming, just from the reflection of the sun.

He broke and ran grabbing the handle and drew back and said, "You son-of-a-bitch, I'll cut your head off." "I'm not going no Goddamn place with you. "I immediately drew my service revolver and told him to drop the axe or "eat lead". Trooper Meade and Investigator Martin jumped in front of him and saved his life. He was drunk and crazy and the judge took that into consideration when he fined him. Mr. Hale lived to be a ripe old age and finally quit selling corn liquor, when the Lord called him. I'm glad Trooper Meade and George jumped in front or grabbed him around the arms and waist because I didn't want that haunting me if I had fired a fatal shot. Sad part about the whole thing was Trooper Meade and I fell out over the incident. At the time I didn't think they should have jumped in front but what if he had let fly that razor sharp two blade axe that I'll bet you money you could have shaved with it?? I might be pushing up daisies. Maybe they thought I might shoot one of them. Time cured our difficulties and we finally started working together again. He was a helleva trooper, Mrs. Meade.

*   *   *

The little ones have the axes and the big ones don't need anything. Their size compensates for a blade or a bullet or does it? He was a monstrous man, six feet seven inches tall, weighing approximately four hundred fifty pounds. I had never seen Mr. King until one of our investigators had bought moonshine whiskey from him. My new partner had in fact bought from him on several occasions. Mr. King had just been released from Mill Point, a federal penitentiary that housed most of the nations moonshiners in the 1950's other than Atlanta. I was cautioned that hot May day that Mr. King was mean and wouldn't be taking a liken to us bothering him.

He lived in a little frame house on Little Stoney Creek in Giles County Virginia with his wife and many kids. There he sold illegal whiskey, government whiskey and traded whiskey for surplus food. He had been in the whiskey business all his life. We arrived at his house a little after lunch, Mr. George Martin and Mr. Walter W. Elmore. Mr. Martin, Chief ABC Investigator had the search warrant and arrest warrants in his hand. Mr. King was standing in the doorway. He took up all the door jam and then some. His large separated buck teeth stood out. You could put my thumb in between them. He had a faint smile that quickly vanished into a bear voice saying, "I don't give a damn how many warrants you have for me, I'm not going back to Milpint, I've had my last stay there." "Now you guys just go on back home and leave me alone." Mr. Martin reached for his blackjack and I made a dive for Mr. King's huge arm. I couldn't move it. Going through my mind was my 38 but before I could reach it, Mr. Elmore told Mr. King, you are in our custody so head for the police car.

Mr. Elmore had been a federal ATU agent for twenty years and was the first state trooper to ride a motorcycle along US RT 220 chasing moonshiners into Roanoke and North Carolina. He was one of the first to carry a .357 Magnum, six shooter in a custom made holster with shell loops all the way around the belt.

The .357 and Walter's thin trimmed mustache was his trade mark. He was a small man but had big character and wasn't afraid of the devil. Mr. Martin had been chief deputy sheriff of Pulaski County before being the chief investigator in Roanoke's enforcement division of ABC. Mr. Martin had proven he was tough. He had a heck of a reputation while working the rural areas of Pulaski and Wythe Counties dealing with moonshiners, bootleggers and sawmill hands who had off-beared all week at mountain sawmill and wanted action on the weekends, weaning themselves from a half gallon of bootleg liquor and were looking for a fight.

I guess Mr. Elmore was kind of my mentor. He and Mr. Martin "broke me in" in this revenue business. Mr. Elmore told Mr. King, "Goddamnit King you are under arrest and the next thing I saw was a "41" over and under Derringer. Mr. Elmore cocked it and Mr. King ran for his life to the car and sat down in it rocking it sideways.

I asked Mr. King what changed his mind and he, splattering spit all over me through those big buck teeth, said excitedly, "I could hear the rachet falling on that Derringer. I didn't want those forty one holes in me cause, those green bullets canker and will cause lead poisoning.

Mr. King never went back to Mill Point Pen again. He paid a lot of fines and served some time in the local jail, worked construction work and sold a little wine until he died many years later.

Mr. Burke had never been to Mill Point but he had served time in the Montgomery County, Virginia jail. Mr. Burke was an old time bootlegger who had more surprises than Houdini and had them in the shadows of every corner of his merchandising store on RT 114 between the Powder Plant and Radford or Fairlawn, Virginia. He was a little man with big survivor commitments. He kept everything. He sold everything including bootleg liquor, legal liquor and drugs and you name it. He had rows of merchandise and buckets of money sitting around.

When you bought something he threw the money, if coins, into buckets. If it was paper money he would put it in a cash register. He sold everything from overalls to light sockets. We would raid him when an informer took our investigators there to buy liquor but the investigator would never know where he went to get the liquor. On one occasion after executing search warrants, we started looking for illegal whiskey, drugs and legal whiskey. I was searching behind a counter full of women's dresses and I had a cigarette in my mouth. I pulled up a half dozen fifths of legal whiskey and placed it on the counter running over with overalls. I reached down and pulled up eight sticks of dynamite with the exudates running out of them. It scared the living stuff out of me.

I was going to look in the cash register when I noticed a string running from the cash key to the rear of the cash register and behind that conglomeration of merchandise was a shot gun attached to the string. Push "cash", you git it, Jack!!

He had a hole cut in a door leading out the back door and a string running up to the top of it on the other side with a double barrel shotgun sitting on top. Open the door and the string pulls both barrels as you go into the next room or oblivion. He had a huge pile of coal in the basement and in the center of the coal was a large bear trap made. Good thing I used a shovel to dig into that coal or I might have an arm or foot missing. Mr. Burke had been broken into several times and the boys had gotten away with a bunch of his merchandise so he decided to set "booby traps" to put a stop to it. He took the law into his own hands but it was explained to him by the judge that setting "booby traps" was a felony in Virginia. He was fined and given probation and went on setting traps and selling whiskey until he died. He never knew what he was worth.

We had another bootlegger in Wise County, who was a Vietnam veteran and got into the whiskey, drugs, explosive business and he set an entire hillside with "trip wires" and "bungle traps". ATF, ABC and EOD agents had to carefully "demine" his orchard and fields. Of course they aren't the only ones who blew up explosives. We blew up a still in Franklin County and the concussion traveled up a strata of rock shattering the windows out of a former deputy sheriff's house windows while he and his son ate lunch. The explosion shook his table and chairs to pieces. The knives and forks jumped off the table. He filed a recovery complaint. He recovered from shaking and civilly too.

There was the isolated bootlegger across the swinging bridge at Elliston, Montgomery County, Virginia, Johnny was his name and selling bootleg whiskey was his game. He had lived cross the Roanoke River for forty years and had made a good living bottling booze and keeping everyone scared to death.

He had served time in the penitentiary for many offenses back in the 1930's. After being released from prison he found it more profitable than construction work to make and sell whiskey. Life was tough in the 30's and 40's. He got caught at a still in 1948. There were three of them, he and two other guys were making whiskey in the Breaks Alleghany section of Montgomery County, Virginia. One morning about daylight, ABC, Martin and Mr. Conner, ATU Agent Stevens surprised the three of them and handcuffed Johnny to a tree and ran the other two down. Every investigator in the whole western district had bought liquor from Johnny.

He was a legend within himself. He stayed half drunk all the time. He was mean, carried two guns and watched the swinging bridge religiously for a raiding party. Johnny hated the law and more than once told me, "I'm going to lay you in the river one of these times, Jack, when you come across that swinging bridge to raid me." I took him at his word and everytime we raided him, I ran cross his bridge but you have got to know his bridge to appreciate the contraption.

The bridge was built in the 20's, repaired in the 40's and nothing else done to it except floods washed it sideways and nearly destroyed it in the 50's.

Johnny forded the river with his old Ford car that he hauled whiskey on. He was noted for hauling, selling both illegal and legal whiskey up and down the road. One of his biggest and best customers was the railroad people who worked on the tracks and stayed in those camp cars. Johnny told me many times, "They keep me awake all the time, I'm just so tired some times. I send them to Smokey Joe's. I liked Smokey even though we were in the same business. My whiskey was better than his."

You had to ford the river or walk that broken, rickety, plankless, swinging bridge that spanned the highest part of the Roanoke River area about three quarters of the year. The bridge swung high to avoid high swift water. The cable was rusted, twisted and slipping in places and the planks were missing and rotted out in places. The bridge kept a left tilt about it at all times and if people crossing it were "tipsie-topsie", they layed in the river without Johnny's help. To cross it sober is one thing but to cross it half crocked like most of us did when we bought liquor from him was near suicide.

No matter how well you tried to maneuver, the bridge would swing and sway and pitch to that left tilt. Johnny had been famous for shooting at people and had made good on some hits. The shotgun he had hung up over the fireplace mantel was handy for him drunk or sober.

One evening just about dark, he kept good his promise that he was going to try to lay me in the river. Two of us investigators and three Montgomery County deputy sheriffs went running across the dilapidated bridge. Thank God, it was nearly dark. He must have heard us coming down the high steps of the old bridge and running toward the house. My mind and my eyes were on Johnny's front door. It was twenty feet down the steps of the bridge, another fifty feet to the house. We made it to the front door and announced who we were and that we had a warrant to search and arrest for one Johnny Hall.

No one came to the door. We kicked and kicked the heavy oak door and finally it came down and who was standing, drunk with the shotgun, one Johnny Hall. His mothers picture hung above the fireplace mantel. We wrestled him to the floor and took the shotgun away from him and my partner Investigator Paul Bell said to Johnny, "That's a good way to get killed Johnny."

Johnny served a lot of time and paid a lot of money on fines. He went to his grave doing what he likes to do best— sell bootleg whiskey. I have never been back across the bridge or forded the river but I did see his wife after he passed on and talked with her. She said she loved Johnny no matter what he had done even though he kept her scared nearly to death all the time she lived with him. That's bound to be love!! Of course love is a peculiar thing it is like the dew, it falls on a rose petal just like it falls on horse manure.

Johnny Hall was one dangerous case but the "Johnny house case" is quite another. Mr. Jackson had been selling untaxed whiskey longer than anyone in Roanoke County. He had the whole Wildwood area to himself. It was wood land, narrow road and where he lived isolated with plenty of honeysuckle vines growing over top his stash of illegal whiskey. When he needed some he would come out and cross the road in front of his house, go into the honeysuckle thicket and bring sufficient amount to an outhouse or "Johnny house."

His business was better than any legal bar or tavern. Oh! We didn't have bars and taverns then, we had beer joints. These construction workers wanted "corn" from a jar. We raided the "johnny house" and put a stop to him keeping it in there. We forced him to keep most of it outside except what he needed to sell right when his customers were there. He then started hiding it about one hundred feet from his back door. He could see that clump of honeysuckles from his back window. He had been seen by an informer carrying a "gunnysack" down the road in the early morning hours.

Mr. Jackson was lean, kean and mean. He had served time for dealing in whiskey before and he put up a good fight when arrested.

One dew-laden morning we were waiting for Mr. Jackson to come to the whiskey stash and remove some from those sweet smelling honeysuckles just before daybreak. We had been there since 3:30 AM and we never saw a light on at his house. We never heard a door shut but here he came with two gunnysacks right toward us and stepped into that thicket. He bent over and placed five one gallon jugs of whiskey into the sacks. He swung them over his shoulder looking all around. He thought he was in the clear. He stepped quickly in those wet "suckes". Wayne and I grabbed him and we took him to the Roanoke County jail. Mr. Jackson hired the Honorable Robert Spessard Sr., excellent lawyer, legislator, athlete, great orator. The Honorable Edward Richardson was the Commonwealth's attorney and prosecuted the case before a jury. Mr. Ed had to be seventy then. He was stocky and conservative. He carried a derringer in his watch pocket and his hat, his white hair and mustache was his trademark. Mr. Jackson appealed the case from lower court where he was fined for possession of untaxed whiskey, while being on probation and alledged offenses on previous convictions were noted in the warrants, making the sentence stiffer. He didn't want to go back to Bland Correction Farm so he was fighting this thing like a murder case. A jury was selected and Mr. Spessard put his client on the stand and he testified that my partner and I put that liquor in his "shit house" and framed him. He was under oath. Mr. Richardson jumped up and asked for the trial to be stopped and hollered to the jury and judge "If these two investigators did put this liquor in Mr. Jacksons so called 'shit house' we need to send this jury home and seek a grand jury inditement against them and send them to the pen." It was scarey. He recanted his testimony and received a year at Bland Correctional Farm. He quit selling whiskey before he died.

Chapter Sixteen

Blue Balls Of Fire

August 10, 1958, Giles County-Montgomery County line -Gap Mills - Steel Bridge - West End. Revenuers jam bridge with two high speed Thunderbird Interceptors waiting on a moonshine laden vehicle.

Lookout agent is on high bank with binoculars and walkie talkie. Chase car is waiting beyond where the lookout is positioned. Walter W. Elmore was an experienced car driver, revenue officer of twenty years. In fact he was the first state police motorcycle driver the state police had in the Roanoke area during the thirties, before he started running "shiners" in the woods.

Walter wasn't behind the wheel of an ordinary car. He was piloting a '50, 88 Oldsmobile. He was hiding about a mile up the road from the lookout, waiting all harnessed in. The car was "shaking" and "lopping".

The idea of a "running block" is to put two vehicles on the road side by side and have a "chase" car push the "liquor laden" car into the rear of the "block" cars thus causing the driver to stop or "bail out" of the liquor car. Well, it doesn't quite work that way as you will see.

The lookout agent called, he has spotted a heavy load of whiskey on '58 new blue Ford. The liquor is packed up in the back seat and right front side. Lookout estimates about two hundred twenty gallons and that includes what he would have in the trunk.

The two black Ford Thunderbirds pull up little tighter on the steel bridge and form a wedge with the front of both cars making a V-shape with the interceptors.

Chase car has been alerted and is now pulled out behind the Ford. The Ford by the way, via informant, indicated that the '58 Ford had an Offenhouser engine with a Super-Charger on it. He's rolling about one hundred miles an hour. Walter and the chase car are attempting to gain on the Ford. The 'transporter" has now turned on a large spotlight and it is automatically directed into the windshield of the chase car to blind him. Walter advises he has shot the spotlight out.

Agent Richardson and Moore are strapped in one of the interceptors and me in the other. The chase car is calling to pull up tighter on the bridge that the liquor cars headlights should be visual and they were. They were "dancing" on the road due to the terrific speed of the "Offenhouser" Ford.

It was getting to close, he couldn't stop if he wanted to, before he hit the bridge. Richardson and Moore and I unstrapped and prepared to jump off the old steel bridge into the river below. The old steel bridge was build in the twenties and was close to the water, thank God.

Walter kept pushing Mr. Smith and that was his name. He was a big moonshiner and transporter and he was a professional race driver to. We averaged running this syndicated bunch of "bootleggers" whose headquarters was in Radford, Virginia about twice a week in those days. He liked to drive and outwit the law. Funny, Mr. Jess Carr, moonshine chronicler never mentioned Mr. Smith.

The headlights are closing now and we are preparing to jump into the river when we heard just to the rear of us tires crying and sparks flying. The Offenhouser was sliding backwards with the wheels going forward and the tires spinning forward at a terrible rate of speed, smoke covering the entire area and two huge balls of blue flames came from the rear of the Ford Offenhouser.

The '88 Olds with '53 Chrysler motor, with a blower was in a broad slide and had left the road into a field and sliding backwards just east of the bridge. We jumped into our so called fast cars and gave pursuit into the wind. Mr. Smith was gone. We raced all the way back to Dublin, Virginia and might as well have been Dublin Ireland where all this stuff started. We found no Offenhouser Ford.

Here's what happened...the chase car crowded the Ford Offenhuser and after coming down a long straight stretch he saw our headlights shining across the bridge with their beams angled into each other and the tail lights angled out to a sixty degree angle. He "ground-looped" or some old timers call it "bootlegged" the Ford Offenhouser causing him to slide backwards two hundred eighty five feet, with the wheels going forward and he continued to accelerate singeing a set of tires and finally burning them up. We can still see that great ball of fire coming out of those large dual exhaust headers.

Sometime after all the excitement we caught the Offenhuser Ford, two station wagons loaded with "shine" and two thousand gallons of illegal whiskey in a barn off RT. 8 near Riner, Virginia. The two station wagons ran into some apple trees and wrecked. They both had one hundred eighty gallons of booze each and the officer was sitting still guarding the two thousand gallons. The two station wagons were bound for Winston-Salem, North Carolina according to reliable information.

We had more bootleggers in the town of Salem in the 50's than they have good food places now. It looked like they all settled in Salem after Andrew Lewis made the place famous. There were bootlegging places where the courthouse is now. They were at West Salem, North Camp, Cat Hill, down in the bottom where the ball field is now. East Salem, Union and Colorado Station. They sold liquor by the drink illegally everywhere long before they had a liquor store or mixed drinks legally.

They sold corn liquor, homemade wine, legal whiskey, legal wine, all illegally. They were very competitive white and black. When I first came back to Roanoke I met this mechanic for Ulcid Machinery Company. He knew them all and dressed me for the part, coveralls, axle greased my face and hands and we rode his '47 Chevrolet pickup. We rounded up twenty five bootleggers and hundreds of gallons of liquor and some dangerous drugs, narcotics and gambling operations.

Chief of Police was George Eades, his right hand men were Sergeant "Pete" Peterson, Sergeant Paul Price, Mr. Stump, Mr. Ingram, Mr. Gwualney, Mr. Smith, Mr. Peters and many other dedicated police officers that I don't want to ever forget whether it was then or the 21st century department they have now and that goes for all the departments that I was honored to work with throughout western and all of Virginia.

Some of these guys above were along on the raid at Ms. W's house. We executed a search warrant and this lady was huge. She weighed three hundred pounds. She greeted us and told us to help ourselves and search. She said, "there's nothing here but a few pint bottles in the kitchen." We looked and looked and found nothing. I went upstairs and searched two bedrooms and under one of the beds in the bedroom she said she used was a case of untaxed whiskey (twelve half gallons of whiskey in mason jars).

I called her upstairs and it took a few minutes for her to climb the steps. She was out of breath. I pulled the case of booze from under the bed and asked, "Who's liquor?" Ms. W. said, "None of your damn business." I placed her under arrest and I attempted to take charge of her by taking her by the arm. She said, "I'm not going no where with you, you mother…" I tried to take her down the steps and Mr. Ingram and Mr. Stump were trying to come up the steps and assist me. She balked and I attempted to free her hands from the banister. I finally freed her hands and we again started down the long stairs.

She shoved me down the steps with me hanging onto her dress and arm. She was a big, big woman and her dress flew up and parachuted over my entire body. She was smothering the air out of me. The muffling and the smell almost got me. My assisting officers were laughing so hard they couldn't here me hollering for help. I needed resuscitation.

My fellow police officers finally pulled her off me. I could hardly breathe as well as being embarrassed. At her trial she said, "I hope you got a look at what you came for." I said, "Ms. W. we got the whiskey didn't we."

*   *   *

My visit sightseeing in Charlotte and Lundenburg Counties and the loss of the government owned Ford-Chrysler built liquor car was more than I set my sights on. I had been working around Charlotte County, near the little town of Keysville, buying untaxed whiskey from a guy that had eight children. He needed to sell liquor, or something or better than that, have something cut out. He was a pityful lot, lived way back in the woods in a weather-beaten old house. He was in his 40's and apparently had something going for him. I had left his house and had gone to a Mr. Talleys house. I bought four cases of "white lightin" from him and was coming out of his personal sandy road and onto the hard top. I was staying at the Manzel-Baugh Motel. (If that's the way its spelled and if it's still there). Those people were way ahead of themselves because there are very few, if any, motels and hotels which were only in cities and towns.

I had the RPM's turned up on that Chrysler that was progressively linked with four carburetors and the wheels were spinning. When I slipped it back into high I was high more ways than mechanically. "Dew" made the car go faster. I was headed toward RT 15 and I saw this blue and gray in the aft-mirror. I thought he was going to a wreck but he ran up behind me, like he was going to push me so I "rammed" into second and the smoke flew. The "carb's", chimed in. The radio was playing that good old country music so I couldn't hear the siren. It was the old type and if it was like the one I had it sounded like a bumble-bee in a mason jar.

I was "totin" the mail and having a good time. The trooper seemed perplexed that the old black '51 Ford with truck springs on it and air shocks was pulling away from that new '57 Ford Interceptor. Although I was playing around, I knew if he caught me I would be in a heap of trouble. I was sliding around a curve and "poured on the coal" when I heard several clicks and more funny noises along with de-acceleration. It felt like I had a parachute open behind me. The "lean" went bad on the carburetors and the shock and stress "jumped the linkage".

I was pulling to the right, I couldn't jump and run because I was the "law" too, "undercover law". The trooper slammed in behind and jumped out and drew his six shooter and ordered me, who was partly out the the car, to surrender. I had on bibbed overalls and a "doodle-bug" hat and a blonde beard. He didn't like the looks of me period. He wasn't a "rookie". It was called in those days caution and survival. I want to say his name is Meyers but I'm not sure. He no doubt by now is retired and has forgotten it. I haven't by any means after all these years and those days in jail in Charlotte County.

I don't think there is even a record of my being there (fictious name) unless there is a record of the wrecker bill. The trooper handcuffed me, had the car towed to the Keysville, Virginia Ford place and he towed me into the Charlotte jail. I tried to tell them I was an undercover agent and they needed to call Mr. V.O. Smith, in Amherst. They slammed the cell door on me and said, "rot wise-ass." I was troubled then, I prayed, I thought they had forgotten me.

No they didn't forget me. I finally persuaded the deputy sheriff to please call the state police and get Mr. V.O. Smith to come to Charlotte County and get me out of jail. He arrived a few days later. We finally got the car back and I knew ATF Agent Robinson of Charlottesville, Virginia would be looking for it. He was and later after I had made another bus ride into Richmond for inquiry as to the reason why I attempted to ellude the state trooper I wound up on the short end of the stick again driving that same car.

A team of us was going on a still investigation in Green County. My partners "Bulldog", ATF Robinson and Borman, and I were to meet Investigator "Teddy" Pangle at Luray. Our riders were Borman, Pangle, "Bulldog" in the back seat and Robinson in the front. We had just started into the town of Luray, Virginia about daylight when a police car got behind this '51 Ford powered by Chyrsler and me the driver. He blew his siren and I immediately pulled over and it was the chief of police. Remember in those days they didn't have all the police and facilities they do now. The chief was alone. He asked me for my drivers license and my license indicated I lived in Roanoke and not Harrisonburg or

Rockingham County where I was stationed. The chief asked what kind of car this was with those air lift shocks and big springs I had on it. It told him it was a Chrysler powered, a Ford 1951 and the registration was in the glove compartment and I was in hopes that Mr. Robinson would get it out and hand it to me.

"Bulldog" sitting in the back with his western hat pulled down over his eyes said, "Go to hell chief, what's it to you." The chief took offense to that and jerked the door open and threw me into the street on my shoulder which was buried in gravel. The whole damn bunch started laughing and the chief got even more perturbed. He finally let us go and we went on to that still in Green County which was high in the Shenandoah Mountains. The still and one hundred fifty five gallon barrels of apple pumice, did not run and after forty eight days we cut it up. No one came to it. There was only one way in and out of the area. You reckon they had a lookout?

Next stop was Lundenburg County Virginia. I stayed at the beautiful Hotel Victoria. Mr. Johnny Blackburn and Mr. Creedle was in charge of the territory there and knew every inch of it. I bought off every bootlegger there in three counties and had a lot of court cases. I came back a day or so early to go to court so Mr. Creedle would take me fishing and he did. Court was delayed a day or two so they decided to take me along looking for stills. I didn't have my gun that day nor any field greens. I wore my dungarees and a short sleeve shirt. It was hot that day and we split into two groups. Mr. Creedle, ABC and Mr. Kiminiski, ATU Agent stationed there. Mr. Blackburn and I were partners and I followed the boss.

We came to a swampy flat after an hour of walking. We were in the heart of moonshine country. Then to a "deer clearing" way back in the woods. As we crossed the clearing, we spotted two black males wearing overalls, one carrying a "gunnysack" over his shoulder and one carrying a double barrel shotgun. The guy with the sack cut into the woods. The guy with the shotgun was going to stop us in our tracks. He jumped up on a stump and fired both barrels. I was running full throttle toward them, no gun, in civies and howling stop, police, revenue agents. I fell half way across the clearing and I just knew I had been shot. I could feel the blood oozing out of my chest but the shotgun pellets fell short. They missed me. Mr. Johnny Blackburn, was carrying a 38 snub nose Colt pistol and opened fire on the attacker. He shot all the bullets he had in his gun except he saved one until we got into the still site. That was just in case there was someone else at the still with a firearm. We never caught anyone. We recovered the two cases of untaxed whiskey in the sack.

We went on into the still site and it was a dirty looking distillery, the type I had never been to then and have never been to one like it since then. Thirty six years of police work and raided hundreds of different kinds of stills but, none where they run the slop or spent mash into a rectangular hole in the ground and when the still is dry, they would fill it back up with water, yeast, malt, daisy middlings and oh, yea! the life blood of the moon shiner, sugar. In "Blackpots" they run it out five times, called the fifth run, like paint thinner, throw it away and start all over again, right in the "pot".

There was dead rats in the mash in that hole and twelve cans of red devil lye (lye gives mash heat and hastens fermentation). (Rats eating mash, got "woozie", fell in and drown).

Mountain Lake Hotel has always been a resort and now one of the wonders of the nation, when it comes to beauty and life style of the rich and those who just want to get away from it all for a weekend or vacation. There's tennis, horses, swimming, fishing, boatings, hot-tubbing and many many other things both with Continental Cuisine or European Entree but all those luxuries weren't available in the late 50's and early 60's.

There was the beautiful mountain lake, horses, a retreat to relax by the wealthy. They had the Continental and European styles of living. The manager was a nice man, well schooled in hotel management and a master diplomat. He did have a problem. He called the right people, Sheriff "Bill" Harmon, Giles County, Virginia, who in turn called us. The waiters and cooks were running a "skin game". I know, I had never heard of it either.

Nor had I stayed in a mountain retreat before except down the other side of the mountain in a sleeping bag on big stoney creek watching illegal distillers. We got us a fine room, second floor, in the "Alps of Virginia". We may have had the presidential suite because it was "plush" then, "lordy", only knows what they are like now. They are even making "Furrier" commercials up there now.

There were three of us who were residing there now and we were reinforced by 1889 and Bourbon Supreme. We brought plenty of money. The sheriff loaned us a couple of hundred and we each had a hundred or two. We were ready, we thought. The information was that the waiters would lure customers to a card game or better known as a "skin game" and deplete them of their funds. The "fleecing" of them didn't take long. We were to soon find out. We went to supper around nine thirty after several "high balls". We wanted to be "well oiled".

The waiter that waited our table was a small black guy with a great personality. He was prompt, cordial and never suspected us of being anyone except, fun people. We ate and talked about construction work and other matters. They listened intently. Finally one of my partners asked "where's the action".

Our waiter didn't flinch he said, "Over there in our quarters beyond the kitchen." My other partner said, what's going on? He said, "Plenty, come see for yourself." We thanked him and went upstairs and had another drink or three and plotted our strategy.

Our strategy was simply this, one of us was going to play it straight and the other two were going to cheat. The deal was if I had a bad hand I would fold and kick my partners on the leg. It either one of us had a good hand, stay and raise the others out. Well, we had never done such a thing before in our revenuer poker playing but we were told you couldn't beat these guys with a stick much less in a "skin game"; they were professionals that learned in DC.

When we got to the waiters quarters they had everything setup. They had a green felt cloth over a big oval table. It had a gallon jar in the center of the table. It was us three poker players and those four black waiters. The day was over for waiting tables and they knew we were waiting as prey.

The game of the night was the "skin game". I knew nothing about the game then and I still don't know anything about it. Right off they dealt with two decks of cards. You have to make the best out of your handful of cards. The best seven cards. Its like playing rook, the hand fills up fast with cards and everyone gets a good hand. Each one of the cards laid down must be beat until the last best seven cards remain. The head waiter cut the pot about ten dollars and put it in the big jar explaining they had to pay for the card and incidentals.

We ante'ed ten dollars a piece, four and three are seventy. I had an exhausted high hand and won the pot after all was said and done. That is after I kicked both partners on the leg. They folded and when I racked the pot, I took ten dollars and "squirreled it" (put it in my shirt pocket). The largest of the four waiters said, "You can't squirrel that money." I told him, "I won it, I can do what I want to with it." He reached over on a dresser he was sitting near and picked up a straight razor. He said, "Don't you do that again or I will 'razzoo you'." little did he know that I had a "squeezer" in the small of my back under my shirt. My partners had pieces stored away too.

I told him it would be to his best interest if he kept his razor in the dresser drawer. My partners asked for some whiskey. The little waiter said he would get it for us—fifteen dollars a fifth. We opened the fifth of Early Times and had a big buster. We went on playing and I had lost my one hundred fifty dollars to the skin game artist even after we cheated. My partners loaned me some money but they were losing fast. Time was creeping up on us, it was one in the morning and still no sheriff and investigators or state police. We had gotten pretty high off that fifth and ordered another fifteen-dollar bottle.

The chief waiter cautioned me again about attempting to squirrel money. This time he got the razor and unsnapped it with his wrist action. I could hear it sing, if he swung it at the angle he positioned it, he would cut my shirt off or more.

At 1:30 AM, the door of the waiters quarters flew open and in came the long awaited arm of the law. The chief waiter jumped up but not quick enough, he was looking down the barrel of my .38 revolver (squeezer). I was putting pressure on the trigger in hopes he pressured that razor. He then said, "God please don't shoot", "it was all in fun." I said, "Fun hell, you are under arrest."

A Dying Art II: Part II

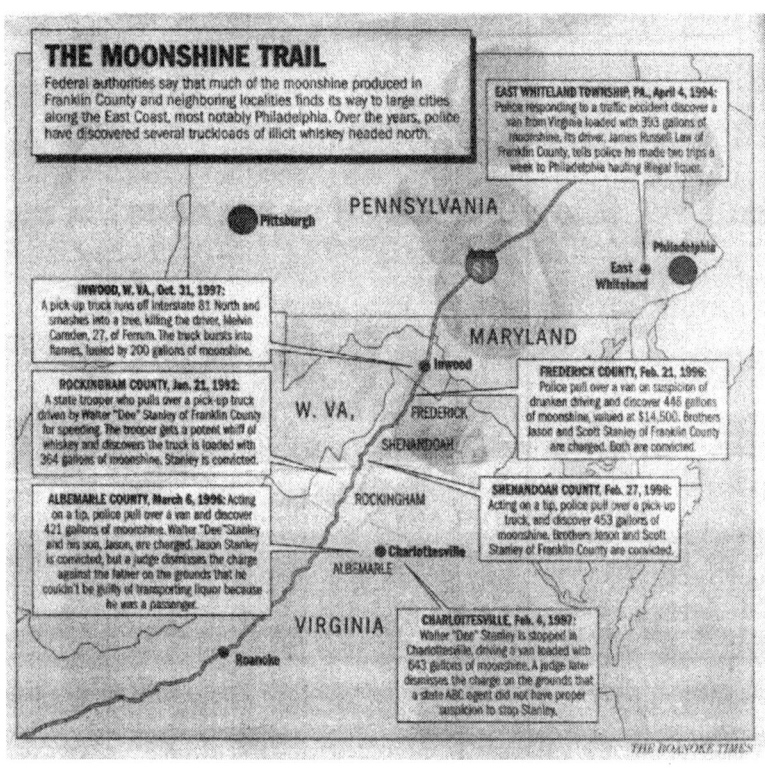

THE MOONSHINE TRAIL

Federal authorities say that much of the moonshine produced in Franklin County and neighboring localities finds its way to large cities along the East Coast, most notably Philadelphia. Over the years, police have discovered several truckloads of illicit whiskey headed north.

EAST WHITELAND TOWNSHIP, PA., April 4, 1994: Police responding to a traffic accident discover a van from Virginia loaded with 393 gallons of moonshine. Its driver, James Russell Law of Franklin County, tells police he made two trips a week to Philadelphia hauling illegal liquor.

PENNSYLVANIA

Pittsburgh

Philadelphia

East Whiteland

INWOOD, W. VA., Oct. 31, 1997: A pick-up truck runs off Interstate 81 North and smashes into a tree, killing the driver, Melvin Camden, 27, of Ferrum. The truck bursts into flames, fueled by 200 gallons of moonshine.

MARYLAND

Inwood

ROCKINGHAM COUNTY, Jan. 21, 1982: A state trooper who pulls over a pick-up truck driven by Walter "Dee" Stanley of Franklin County for speeding. The trooper gets a potent whiff of whiskey and discovers the truck is loaded with 364 gallons of moonshine. Stanley is convicted.

W. VA.

FREDERICK

SHENANDOAH

FREDERICK COUNTY, Feb. 21, 1996: Police pull over a van on suspicion of drunken driving and discover 448 gallons of moonshine, valued at $14,500. Brothers Jason and Scott Stanley of Franklin County are charged. Both are convicted.

ALBEMARLE COUNTY, March 6, 1996: Acting on a tip, police pull over a van and discover 421 gallons of moonshine. Walter "Dee" Stanley and his son, Jason, are charged. Jason Stanley is convicted, but a judge dismisses the charge against the father on the grounds that he couldn't be guilty of transporting liquor because he was a passenger.

ROCKINGHAM

Charlottesville

ALBEMARLE

SHENANDOAH COUNTY, Feb. 27, 1998: Acting on a tip, police pull over a pick-up truck, and discover 453 gallons of moonshine. Brothers Jason and Scott Stanley of Franklin County are convicted.

VIRGINIA

Roanoke

CHARLOTTESVILLE, Feb. 4, 1997: Walter "Dee" Stanley is stopped in Charlottesville, driving a van loaded with 643 gallons of moonshine. A judge later dismisses the charge on the grounds that a state ABC agent did not have proper suspicion to stop Stanley.

THE ROANOKE TIMES

Revenuer's Memories of Moonshiners

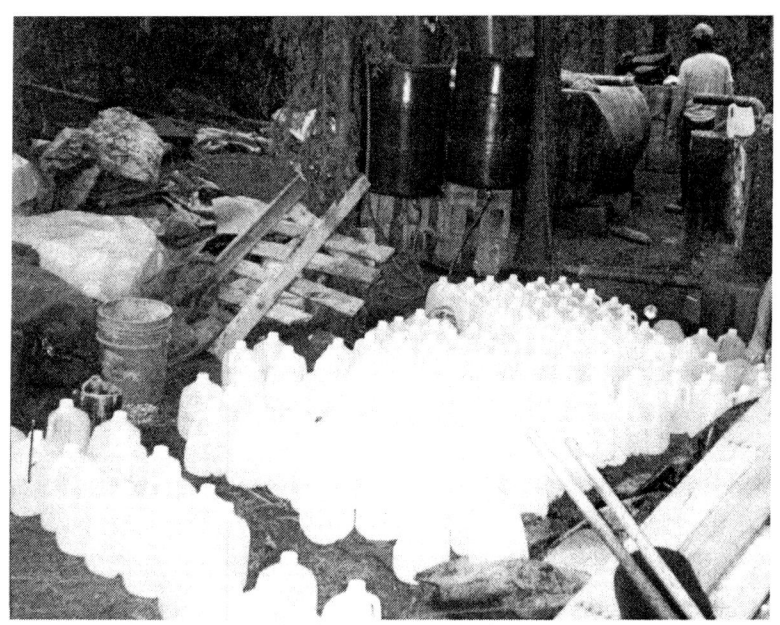

12 Pots, Franklin County, near Phillpott Lake, VA

A Pictorial Epoch

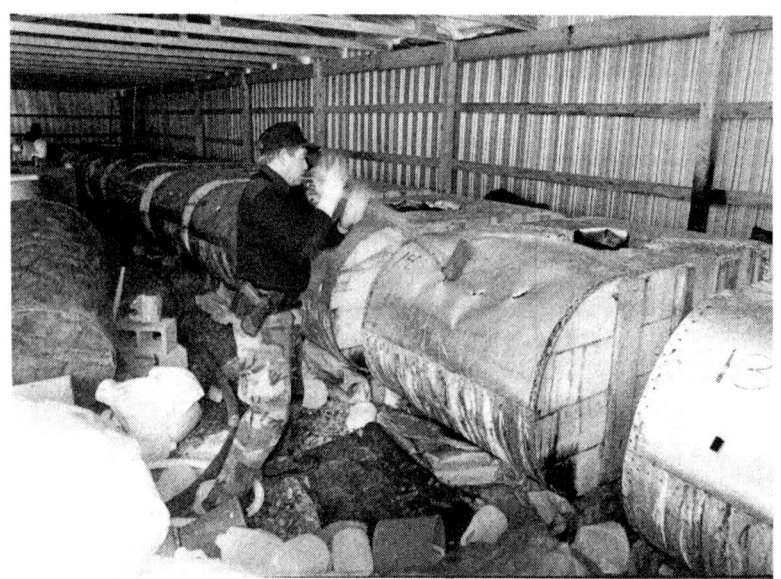

Cool Springs, Pittslyvania Co, Va, world's largest illegal blackpot operation. 36-800 gallon blackpots; 28,000 gallons fermented mash. Photo by Roanoke Times, 1993

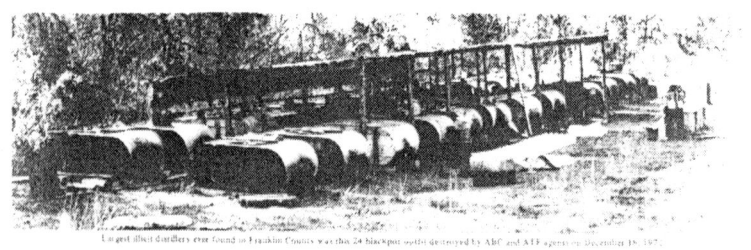

ABC, ATF Agents Destroy Holiday Spirits Factory

Second largest illegal "black pot" stills ever captured. 24 pots in Franklin County, Ferrum, VA (Photo by Franklin News Post by Keomit W. Salyer

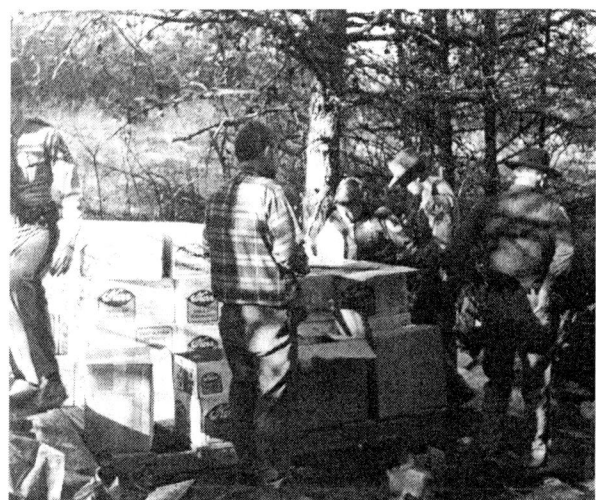

April 1973. Off Franklin Pike, Floyd, Va. Third largest black pot still in the nation at the time (not steam outfits). 22-800 gallon wood and galvanized "black pots." Pictured here: Sheriff Akers, Floyd Co.; Deputy Sheriff Yopp, Agent Jack Powell, Virginia Troopers Higgins, Abshire, and East.

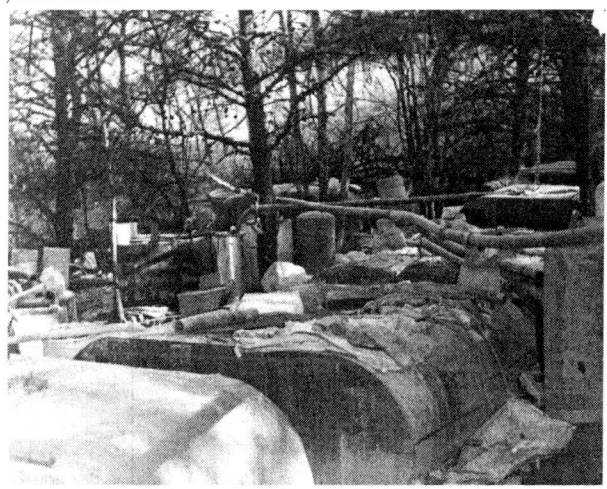

There were four jackets hanging on pine trees, four got away, but the owners were arrested. In their possession was 1,300 gallons of untaxed whisky ready for consumption. (Photos by Floyd Press.)

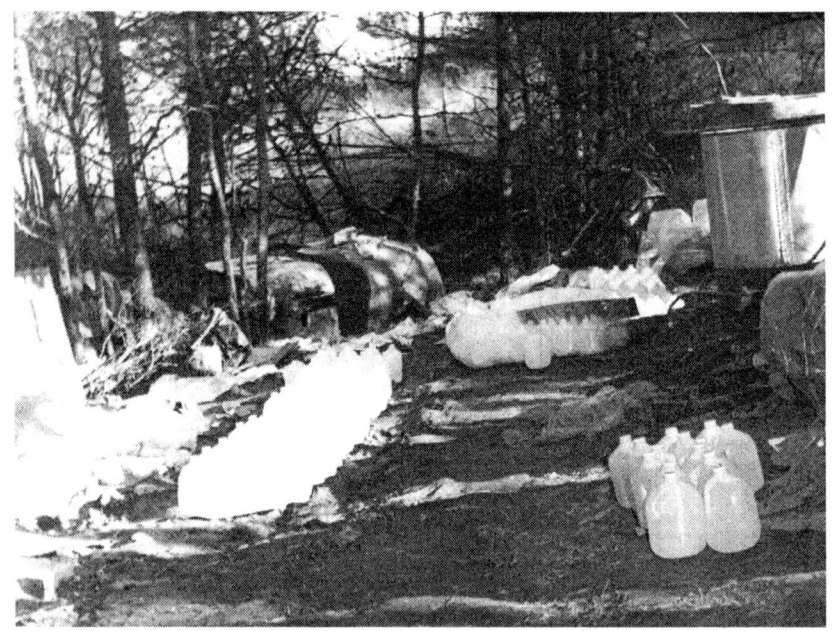

**April, 1973: Floyd County, Va. Twenty-two pots as show earlier.
(Photo by Floyd Press.)**

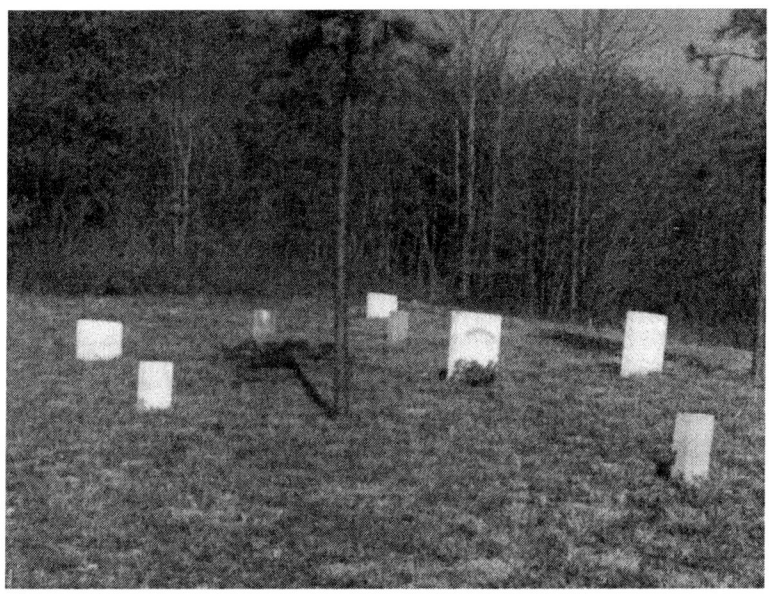

Fake cemetery above illegal underground distillery. 1982. Near Phillpot Lake, Franklin County, Va. (photo provided by State and Federal Agents.)

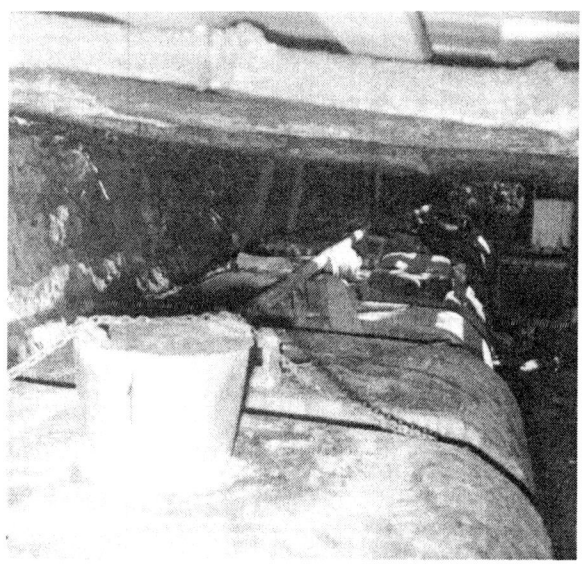

Underground illegal distillery with 18 black pots stills – 300 gallons of illegal whisky. (photo by Franklin News Post, Rocky Mountain, VA)

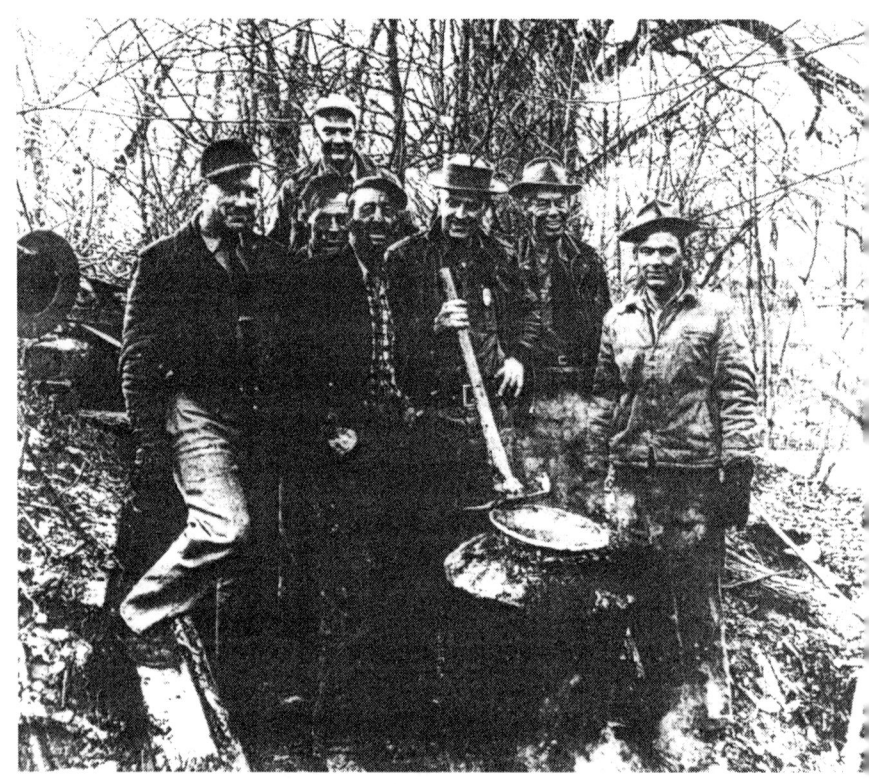

Fall 1953, Scott County, Va., Near Bull Run. A 40 gallon still of pure copper from an underground still site. Pictured here (left to right): Officer Bob Stringer, two unknown illegal distillers, ABC Investigator Joe Lee Baker (mattack in hand), ABC Investigator Henry Lane, Trooper Woodrow Ward and Trooper R.E. Giles (back row). Photo by Trooper Don Riner. (Photo by Virginia State Police Don Riner, 1953.)

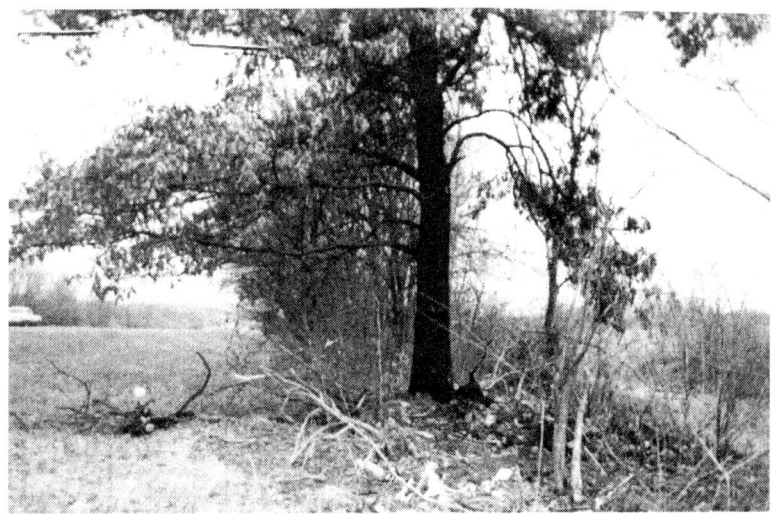

This scorched tree at Inwood, West, VA (1997), off I-81 was hit by a pickup truck, headed north with 350 gallons of moonshine. The driver was killed. (Photo by Jack Powell.)

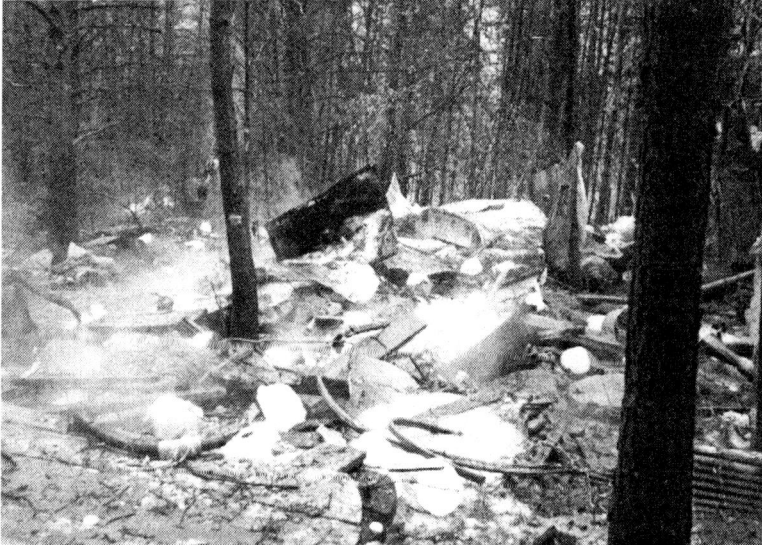

April17, 1990, where stills were "blown as high as the sky" in Franklin County, VA. (Photo by Franklin News Post.)

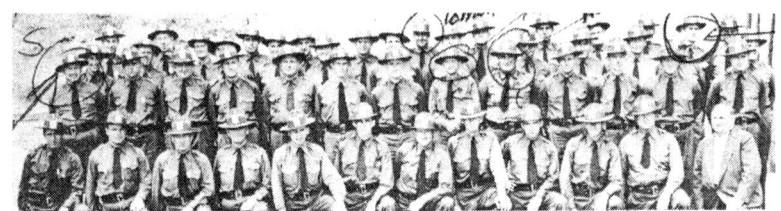

ABC Board Enforcement Officers policed the state for illegal manufacture and sale of alcoholic beverages during the 1930's and 1940's. The Enforcement and Inspection divisions were merged in 1982.

Photo by Virginia ABC Board, 1940 Enforcement Division, Rocky Mt., VA

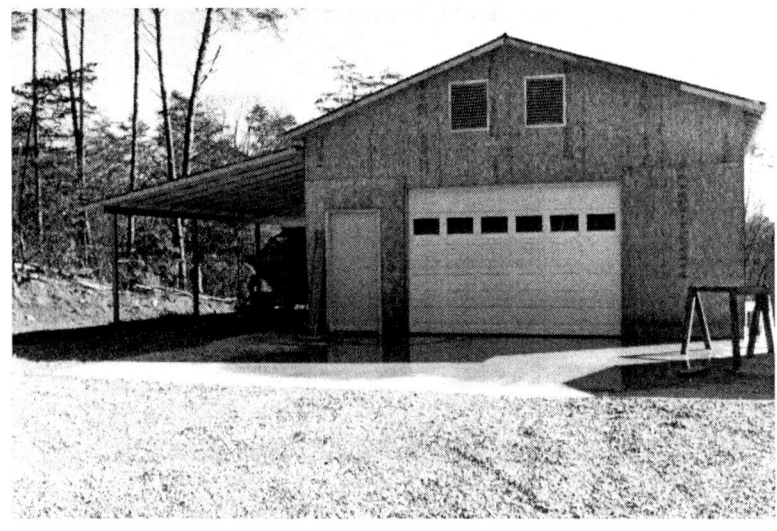

Rocky Mt., VA, large steam still under newly built garage. (Photo by Jimmy Beheler and Franklin News Post 1999.)

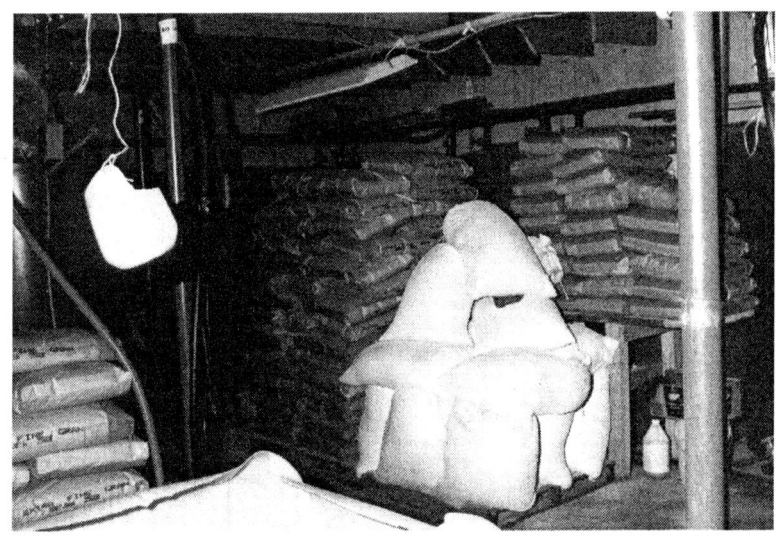

Interior of steam outfit in Rocky Mount, VA (top and bottom).

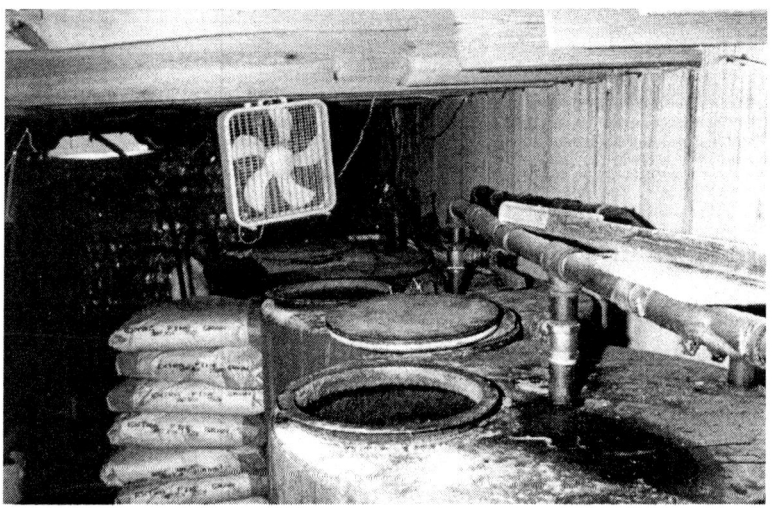

As shown on page 185, still in new garage. (Photo by Agent Jim Beheler and Franklin News Post.)

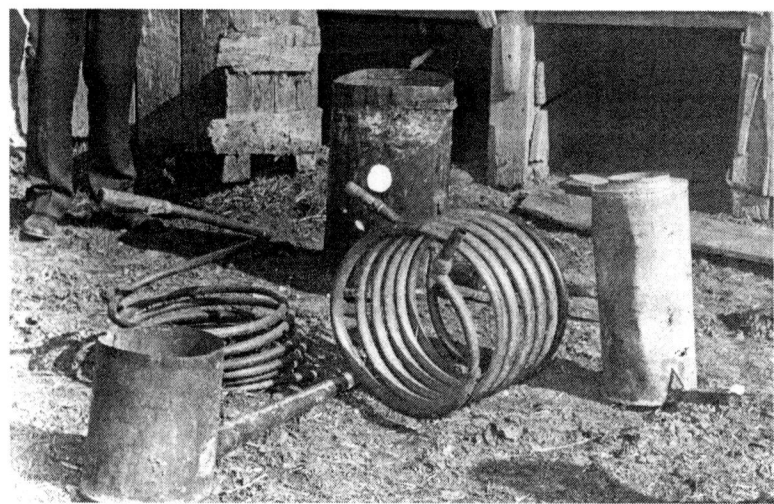

Three caps and two coils under a manure filled barn in Floyd County, VA – very unsanitary conditions. Photo by Floyd Press.

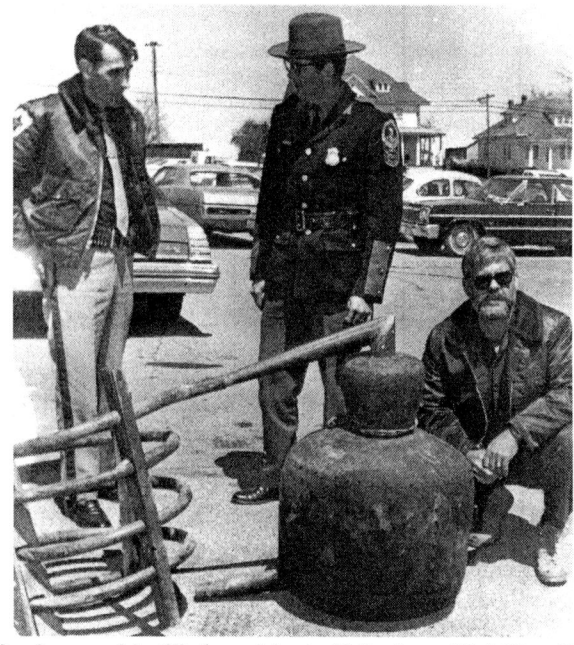

One hundred year old still, found just off the beautiful Blue Ridge Parkway, 1972. Pictured l – r: Sheriff Branscome, Floyd Co., VA; then Trooper David East; Special Agent Jack Allen Powell (Photo by Floyd Press.)

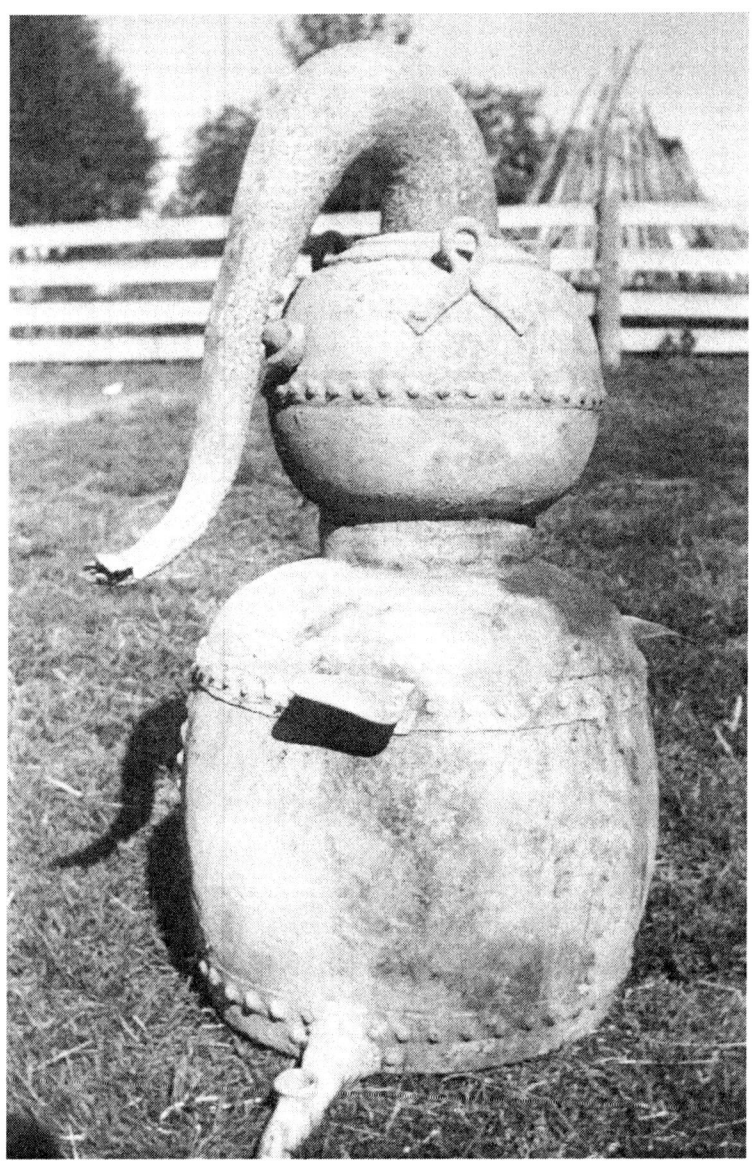

Turnip-type stills, c. 1890. Found in Loudoun County, Va.

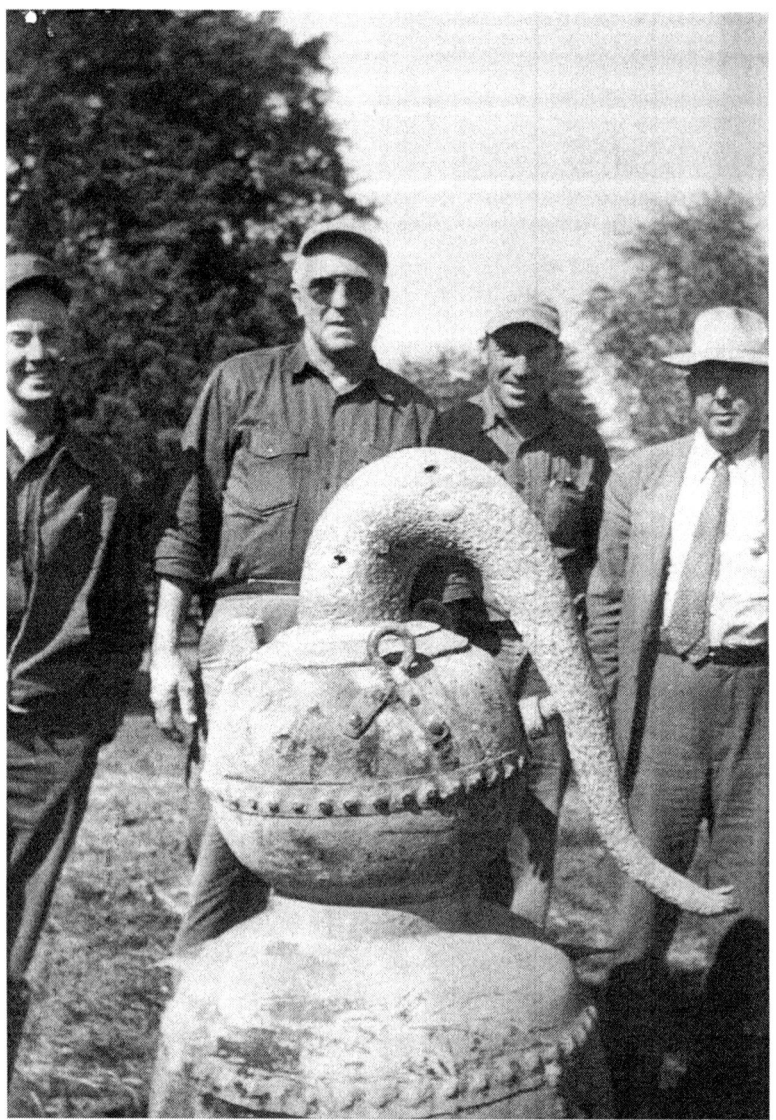

(l-r): U.S. ATU Agent, ABC Agents Hubbard and Burkhead and Sheriff of Albemarle County, Virginia.

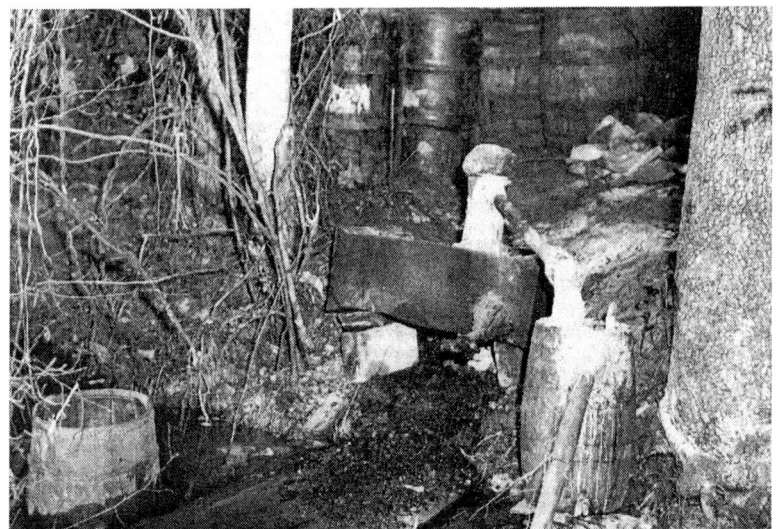

Illegal distillery in Albemarle County, Virginia, 1955.

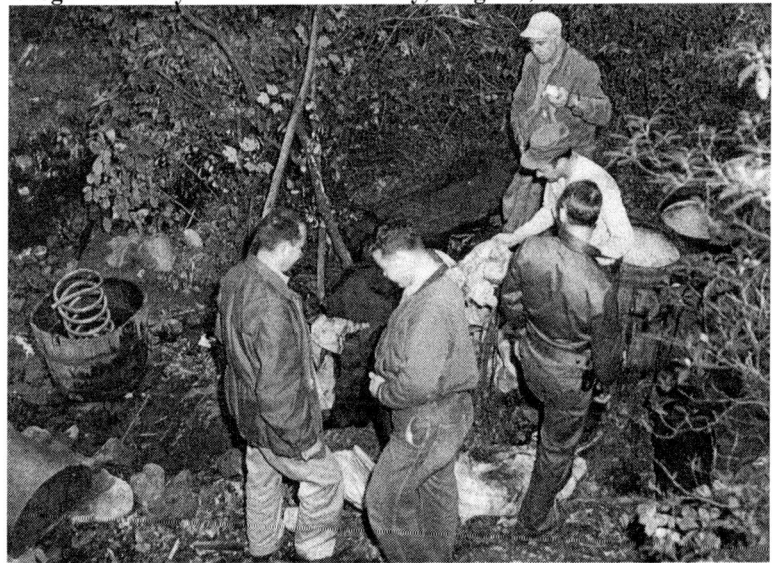

(clockwise): ABC Investigators, Hubbard, Burkhead, Royston (Powell's partner in 1957 at Harrisburg, Virginia), and ATU Agent Robertson

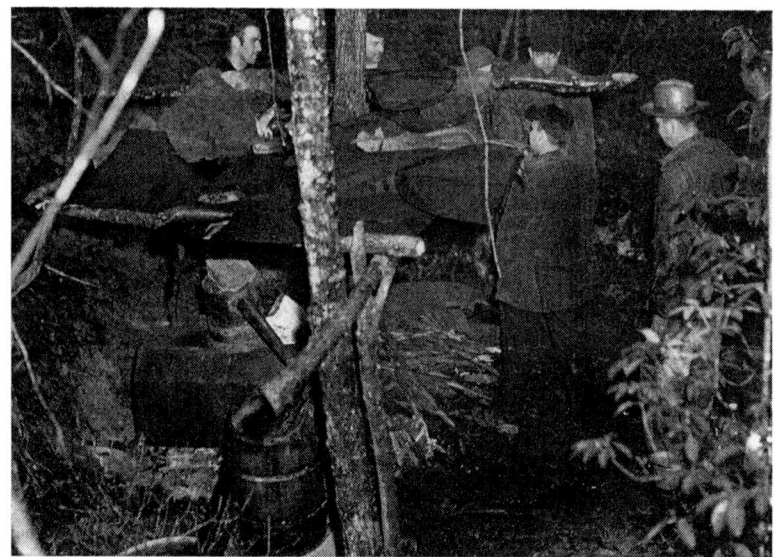

State and federal agents at Albemarle County illegal distillery, 1956.

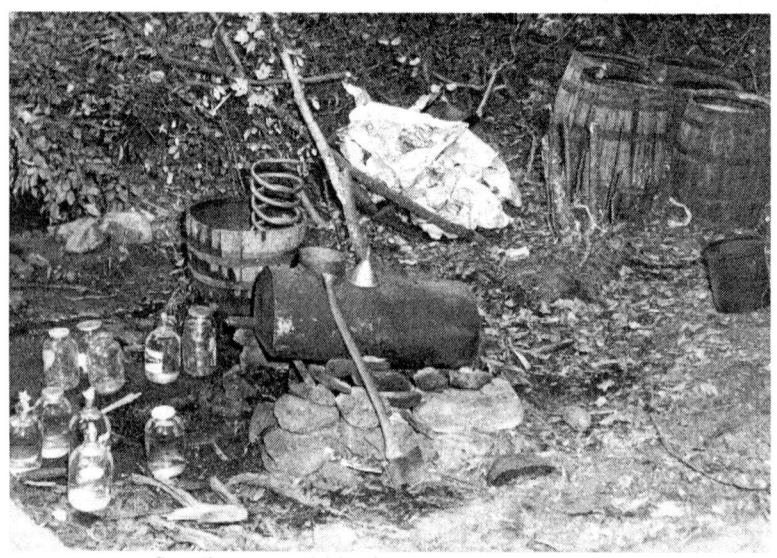

Small steam still in Charlottsville, VA, 1956

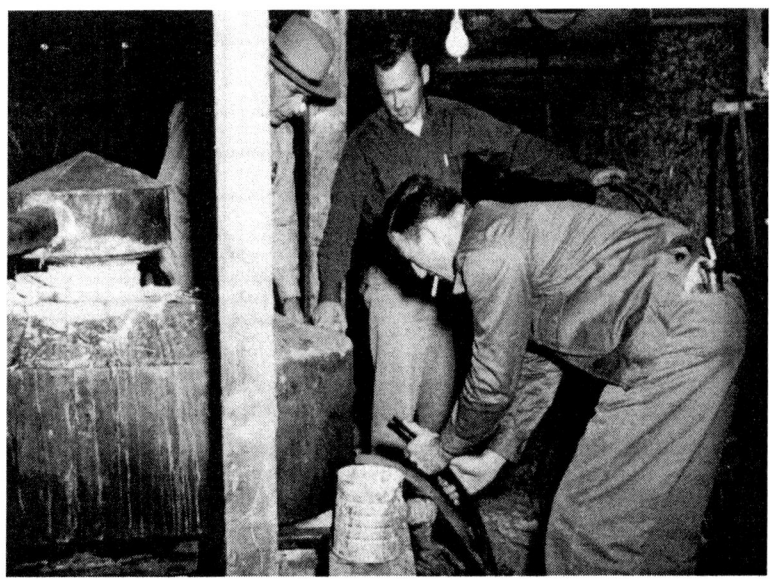

(l-r): Sheriff, Shenandoah County, Garland E. Weaver; Investigator Ted Pangle, Investigator John Wert. November, 1955.

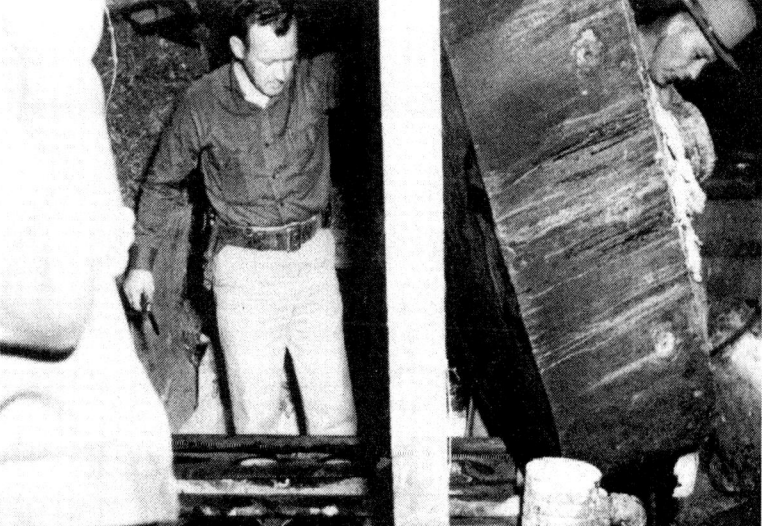

(l-r): Agent Teddy Pangle, Sheriff Garland E. Weaver.

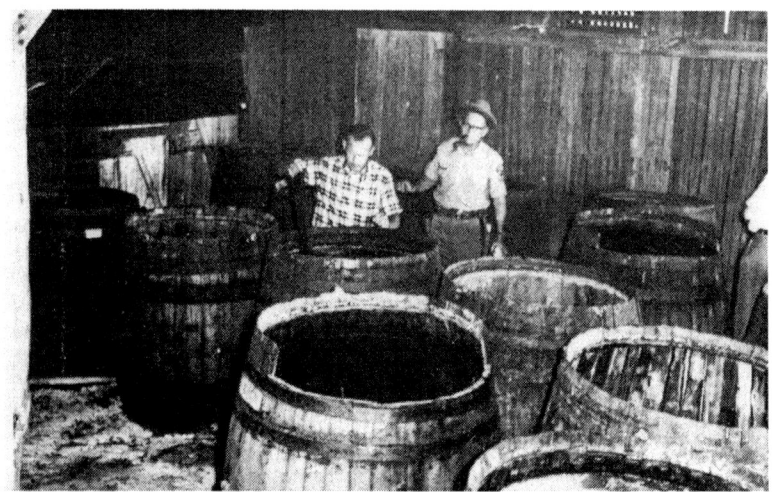

Louetteville, Loudoun County, Virginia. Teddy Pangle in checkered shirt with Sheriff Bobby Legard, looking over 22-200 gal barrels at one of the biggest stills in Northern Virginia. (Photo by Agent T. Pangle.)

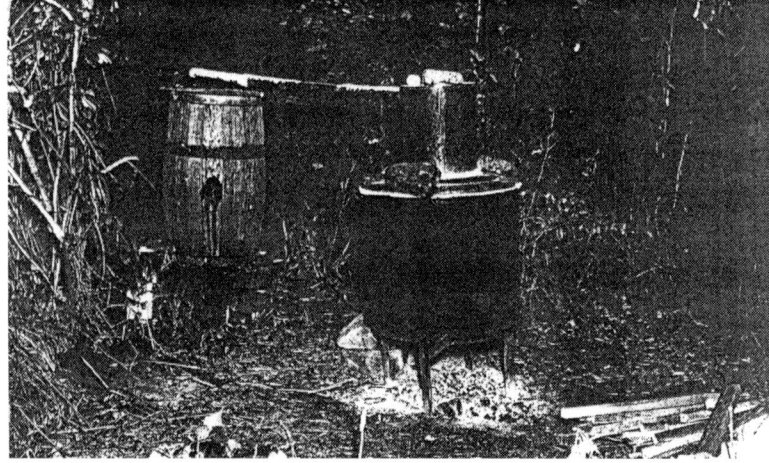

Hopkins Gap, Rockingham County, Virginia, Gilbert Morris Still. Copper-charcoal filtered moonshine. I crawled 20 yards through a creek, then through barbed wire, where I was greeted by Mr. Morris's two beagle hounds, who began yelping when I arrived. Mr. Morris ran away and fell over a pile of brush. I had fired a shot in the air. He claims his fall was due to my shooting him. (Photo by Jack Powell.)

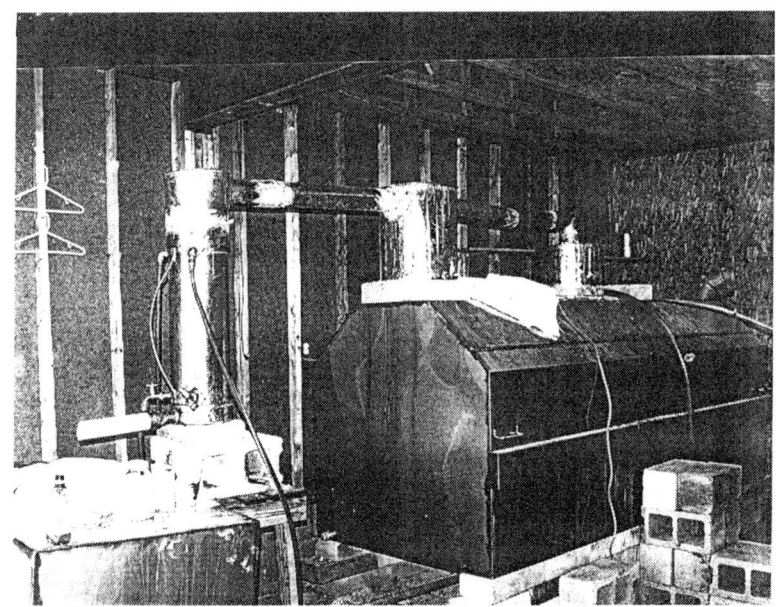

"Coffin" type still and "Shot gun" condenser (unusual type still). Found in 1995 in Sampson County, North Carolina. (Photo by Vance Jackson, ALE N.C., ABC Agent.)

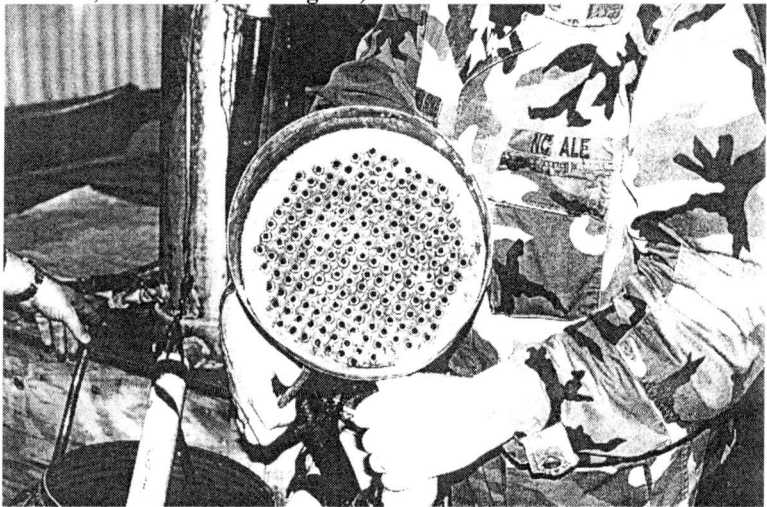

Shot gun condenser. (Photo by Vance Jackson, ALE N.C., ABC Agent.).

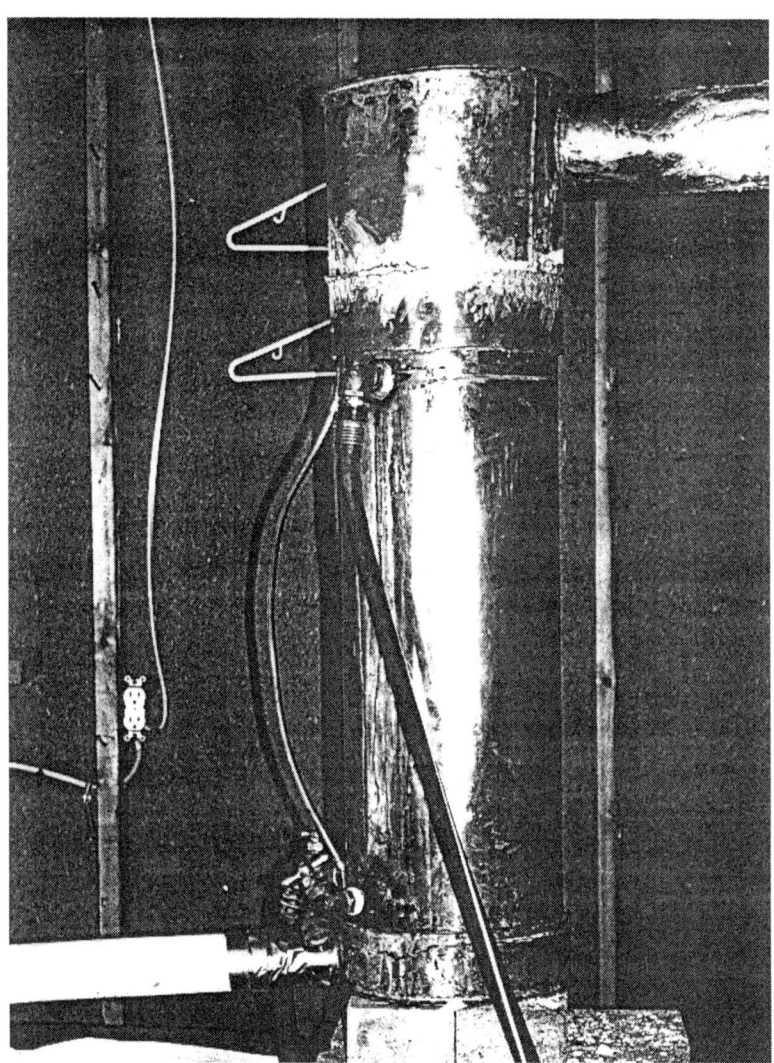

Another view of shot gun condenser. Inside this copper device is a set of baffles, whiskey vapor passes through these baffles and the cold water fed by a hose "cools" off the baffles and turn the vapor back to a liquid moonshine whiskey. (Photo by Vance Jackson, ALE N.C., ABC Agent.)

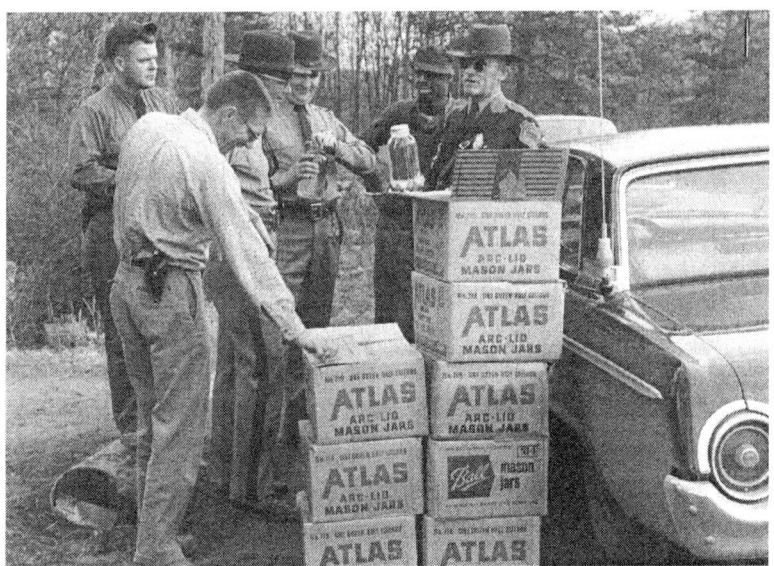

Forty-eight gallons of moonshine seized. (l-r): Wayne Prillaman, Jack Allen Powell, Deputy-Sheriff Roanoke County, Bob Wakins, Deputy Ray Henderson, Mr. Starkey, and Captain Roanoke County Sulley (?) Lynch. Photo by Roanoke Times and World News.

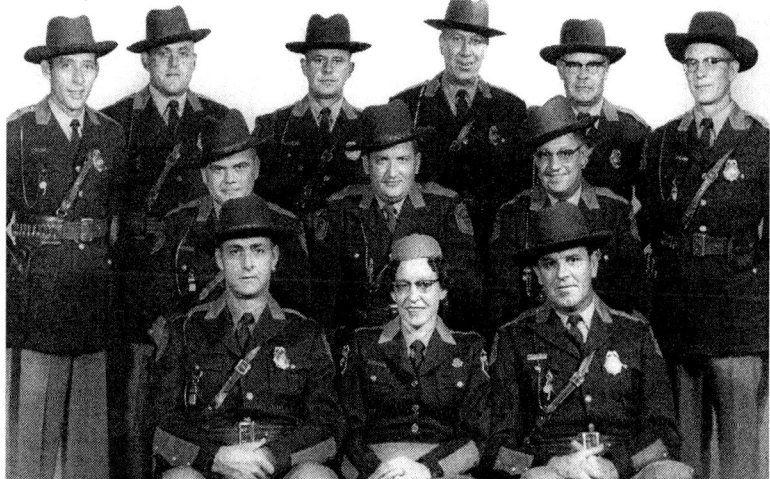

Roanoke County Sheriff Department, Liquor, Drug and Gambling Enforcement, 1966.

Museum may get antique liquor still seized in Patrick

STUART — An antique copper still seized in a Patrick County moonshine raid may live on as a museum exhibit.

The "turnip-style" still, believed to be at least 100 years old, was found by state liquor agents while they were staking out a Woolwine farm last Friday.

Jack Powell, an agent with the state Alcoholic Beverage Control Department, said the still may be donated to the Roanoke Valley History Museum.

Though rare today, turnip stills were in common use earlier in this century when moonshining was a cottage industry. Later, moonshiners turned to mass production with stills made from steel and other materials many experts regard as inferior.

The 100-gallon still was seized on the farm of Roy Eldid Lackey, 78, of Route 1, Woolwine, authorities said.

Lackey was charged with felony manufacture of whiskey, authorities said.

During the raid, liquor agents found an airstrip and two crosses that had been burned on Lackey's farm. Federal authorities say the property was the site of a 1986 meeting of white extremist groups from Virginia and North Carolina.

Lackey could not be reached for comment Monday.

Roanoke Times & World-News, Tuesday, Nov. 22, 1988

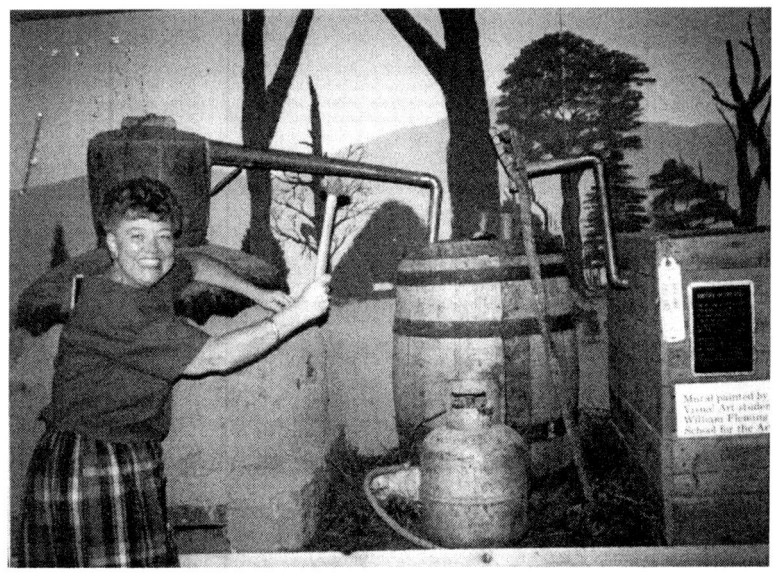

Mary Wright Powell "still busting" at copper still in the history and science museum, Roanoke, Va. (Photo by Jack Powell.)

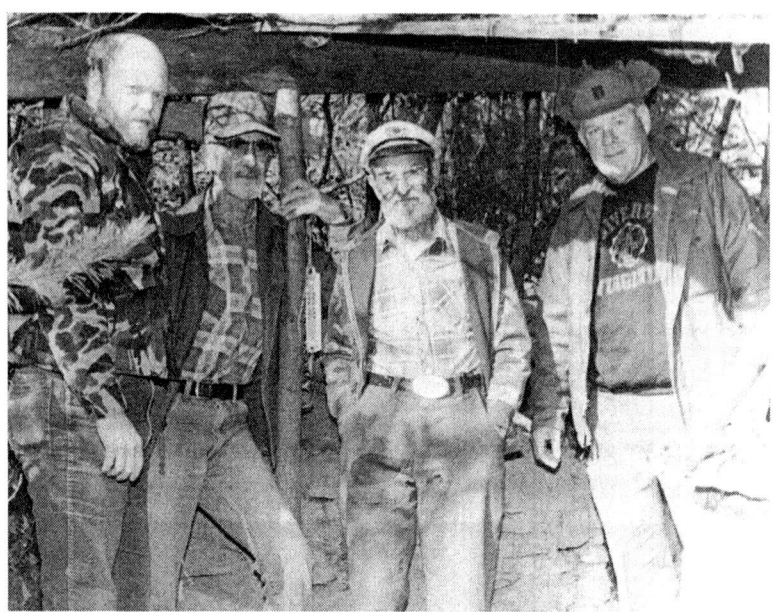

Nov. 22, 1988: (l-r) Agent B. Weddle, J. Rorrer, Mr. Lackey, and J. Powell

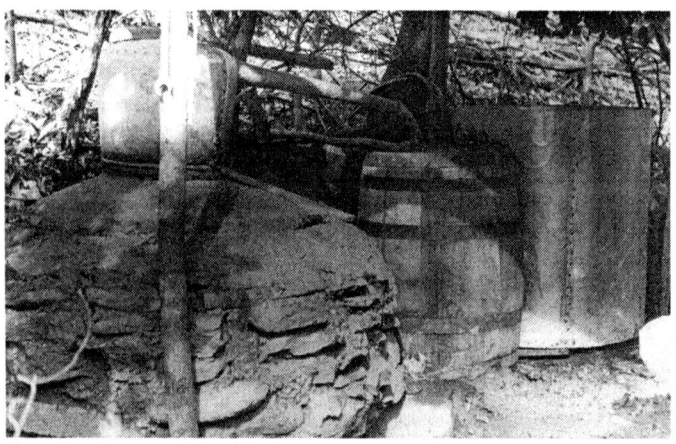

One hundred year old still that went to science museum. November 22, 1998 recovered in Patrick County, Virginia. (Photo by Ed Martin, Bugle News, Patrick Co., VA.)

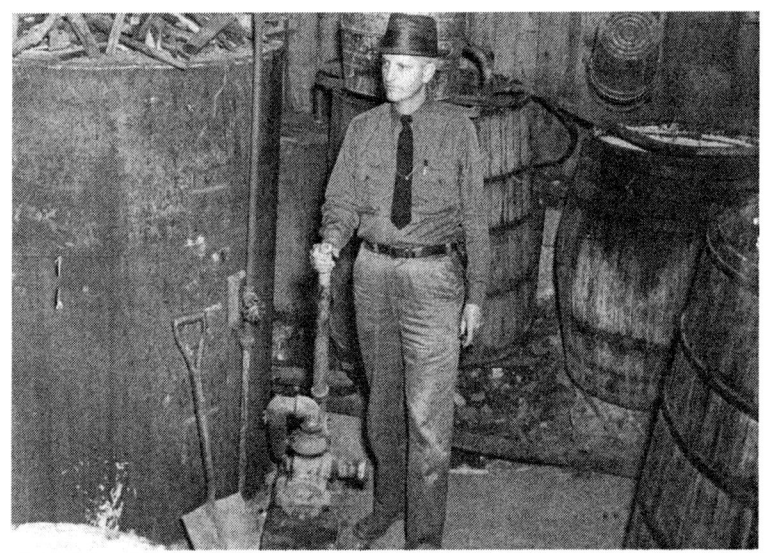

G.A. Martin apprehending 28 hogsheads, 500 gallon steam still, 7 tons sugar, 2 tons coke and 500 gallons moonshine. Sugar Loaf Mountain, 1955

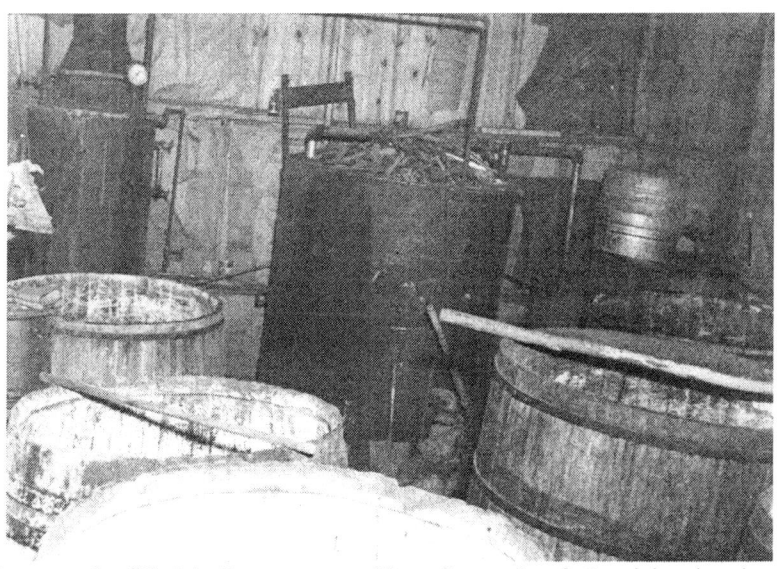

Large coke-filled boilers steam still at Sugar Loaf. Participating in recovery were ABC Agents George Martin and Wayne Prillman, and ATU Agents Waller Elmore, Cecil Kline, and others. 1955.

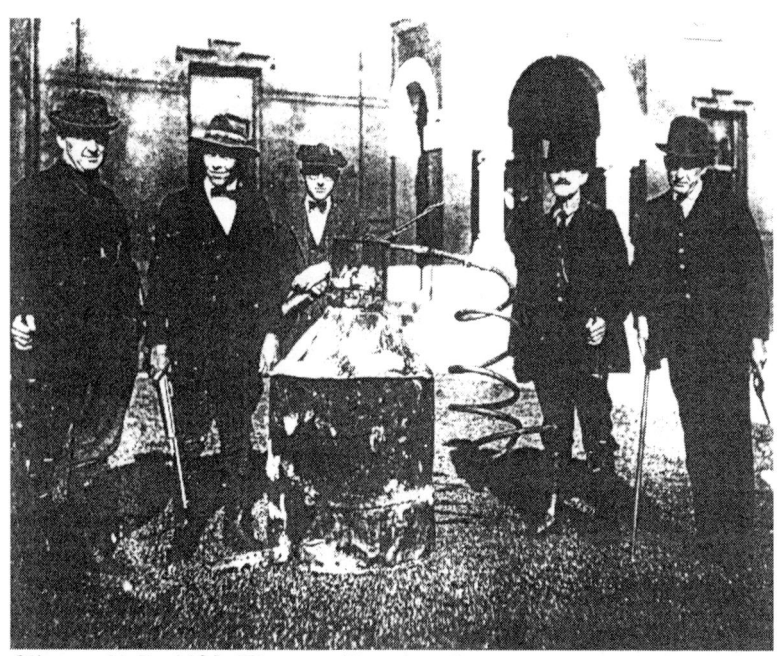

Clinton, N.C., 1928. These "still seekers" weren't taking any chances – look at their guns. (Photo by Prohibition agents, 1928.)

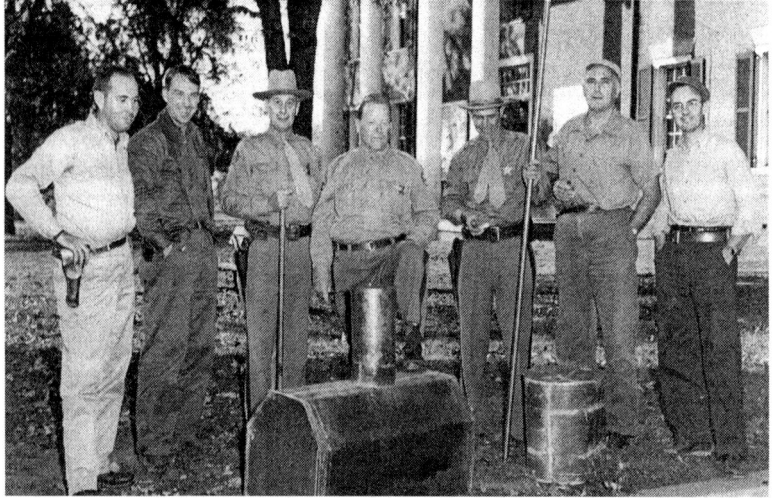

Albemarle County, 1955. Standing with copper triangular still. (l–r) ATU Agent, ABC Agent Birkhead; Deputy Sheriff; Sheriff of Albemarle County, 1953; Deputy ABC Agent Mr. Hubbard; ATU Agent Robinson.

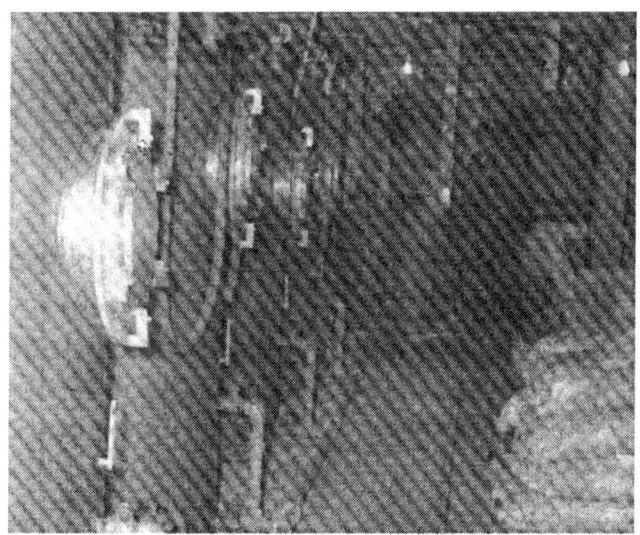

Three runs thorough these illegal still will produce an estimated $15,000 to $20,000, enough to pay for the equipment. This thirty-three stainless steel still set up, was rather elaborate and operated a mechanical engineer. His kitchen wall "pivoted" around and led to a set of steps into a large room in the basement. He had a pneumatic hose across the drive way. The stills were seized in Richmond, Va., 1965. (Photo by Richmond Times Dispatch.)

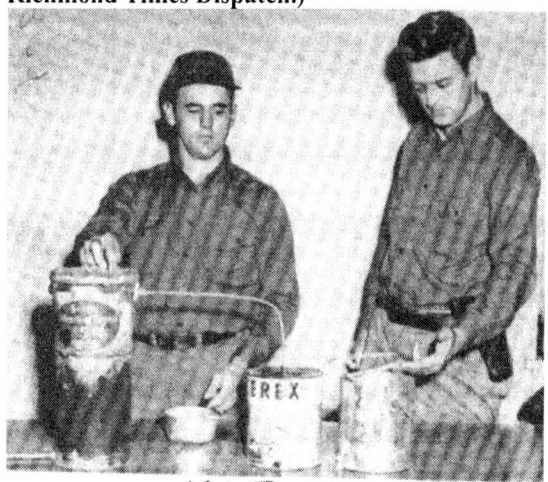

A small one gallon still located in Dickenson County in western Virginia. Pictured here: Trooper Giles (left) and ABC Agent Joe Lee Baker (right).

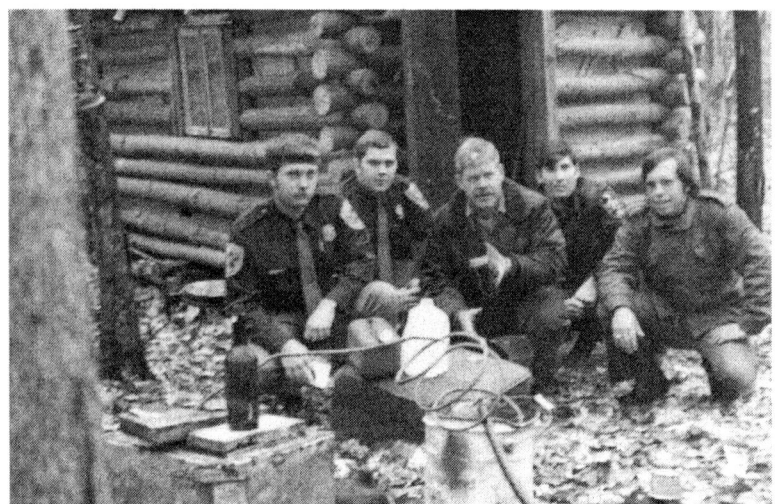

Small cabin moonshiners lived in, 25 miles west of Gold Bond, Virginia in the interior of a national forest along the West Virginia/ Virginia state line. Pictured (l-r) are: Sheriff J. Hopkins, Jr.; Deputy Mann, Giles County; ABC Agent J. Powell; Deputy Langford; and ABC Agent Mike Cassada. (Photo by J. Powell.)

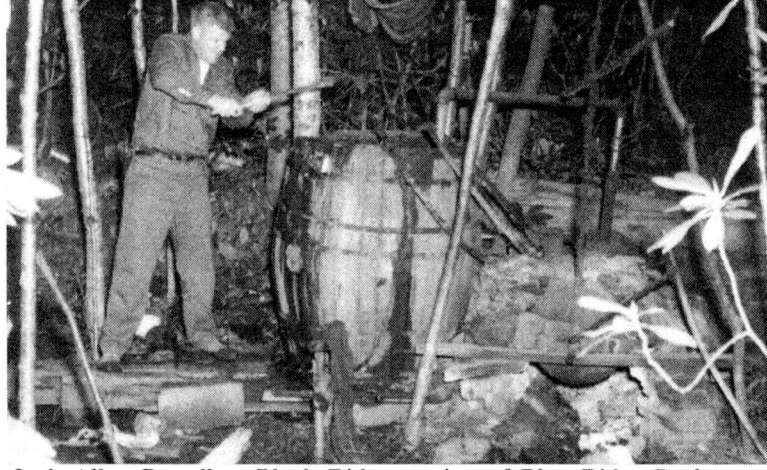

Jack Allen Powell at Black Ridge section of Blue Ridge Parkway, Floyd, Va., 1966. Two were arrested here for making apple brandy 47 gallons and two cars seized by ABC Agents, Floyd Co. Sheriff Office and Trooper Gene Phipps. (Photo by J. Powell.)

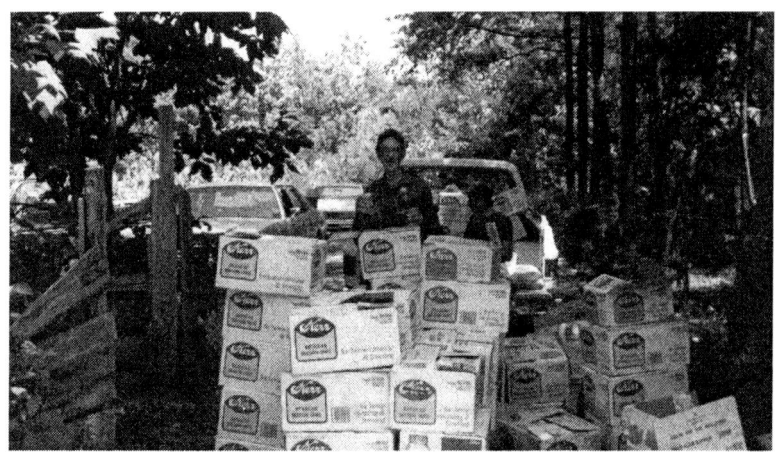

Illegal brandy distillery, Carroll County, Va. along the North Carolina line. Jimmy Rorrer shown with large number of barrels and brandy still set up (below), look closely and see many large marijuana plants in and around distillery. ABC Agents from Virginia and ALE Agents from N.C. participated in the raid. We had to use chain saws to cut down the marijuana. Defendant had his 14 year-old daughter in and around the still in cost him a fine and five years in the penitentiary. (Photos by State ABC Agents (ALE) N.C. and V.A.)

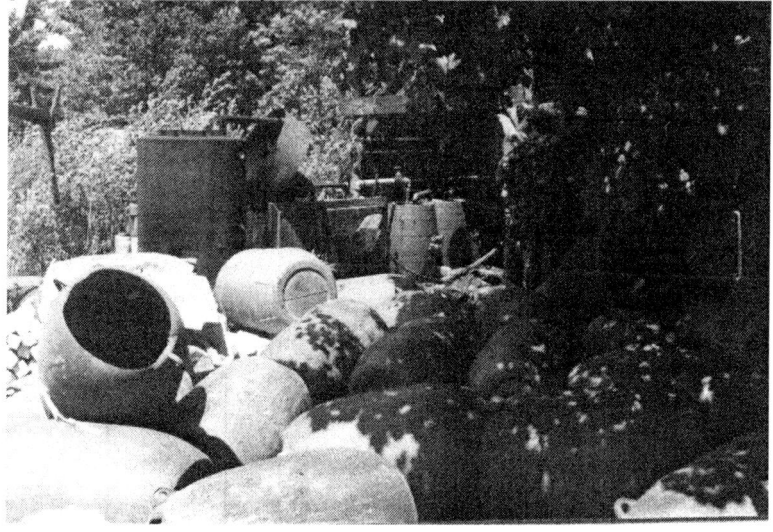

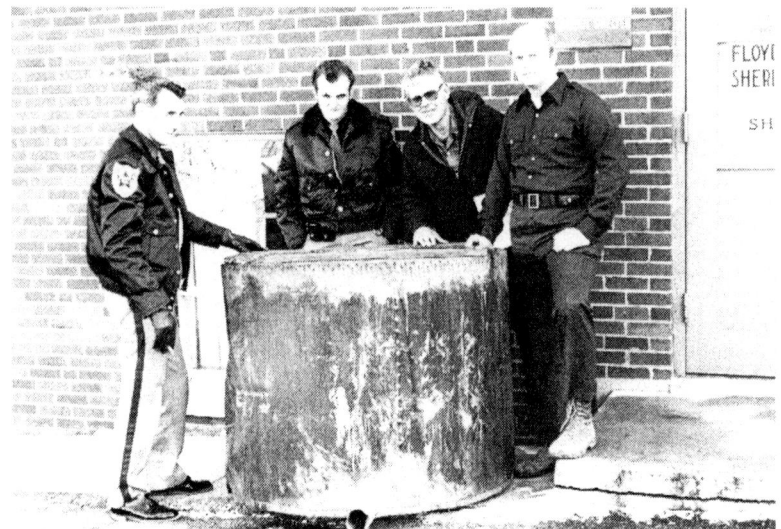

Brandy still in Franklin Pike, Floyd County, 1981. Pictured (l–r) are Sheriff G. Branscome, Floyd County; Deputy Sheriff B. Turman; and Floyd County.Investigators Weddle and Powell. (Photo by Floyd Press.)

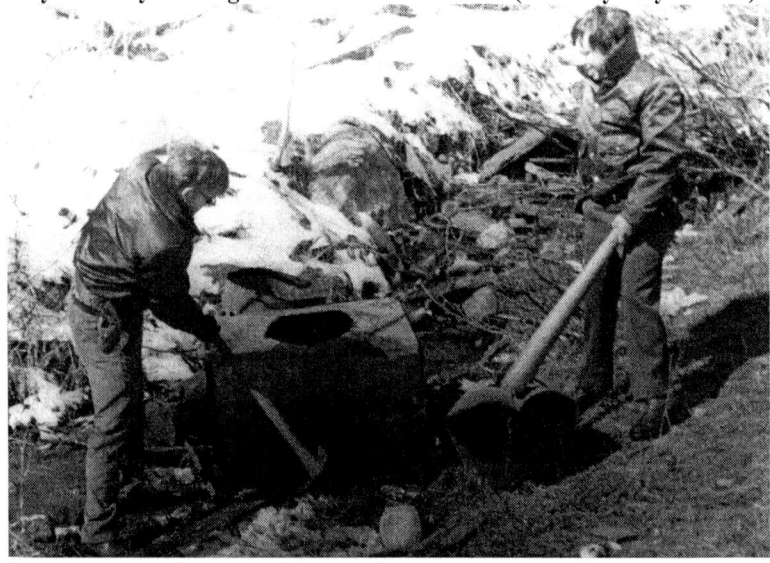

ABC Agents Mike Cassada and Jack A. Powell. (Photo by Floyd Press.)

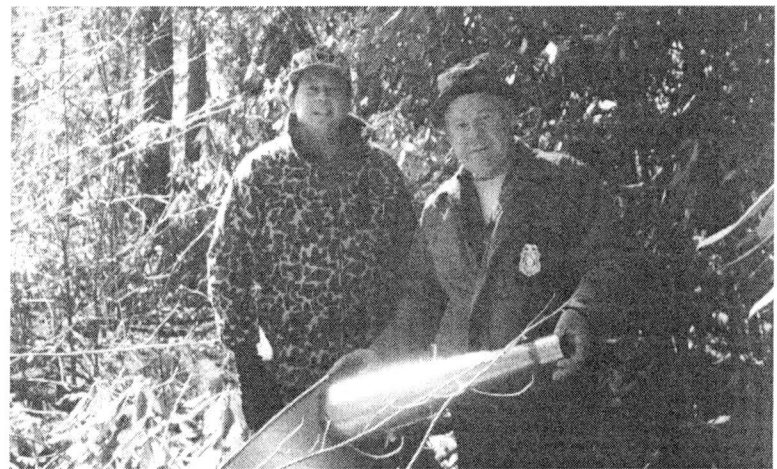

Bill Thomas ABC Special Agent and Jack Allen Powell in Franklin Pike, Floyd Co., V.A., in hand is large galvanized cap (most are made of copper). (Photo by Will Goodman, ABC Agent, 1990.)

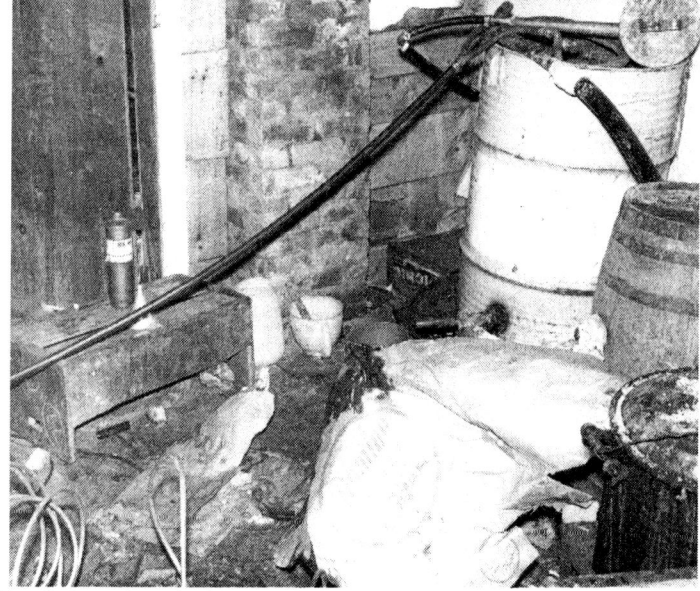

Rat infestations in illegal distillery in Floyd County, VA, off Blue Ridge Parkway. (Photo by Floyd Press.)

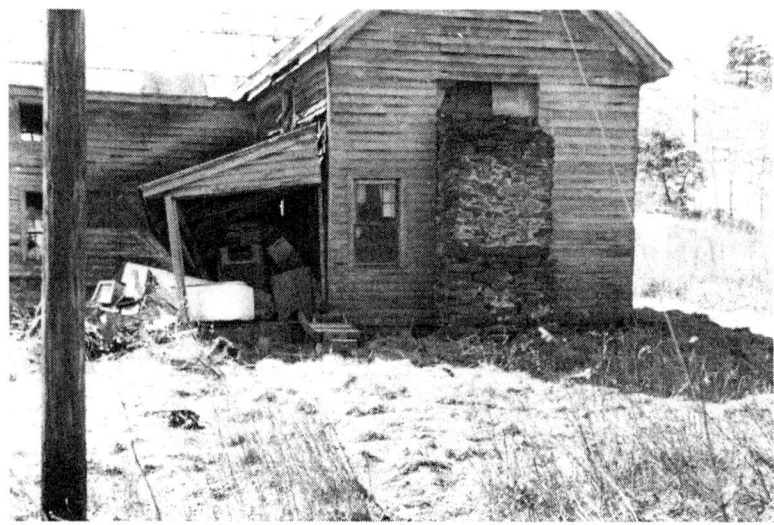

Floyd County mile post 147 on Blue Ridge Parkway. Two or three story abandoned house: three stills, two caps, two coils, several gallons of illegal whisky seized, one arrest made. A hose was run from the creek behind the house up the back side of the building and through the window. Very unsanitary conditions and poor quality whisky – takes the enamel off you teeth and makes you feel like a "swarm of bees" is coming at you. You don't see many of these today.

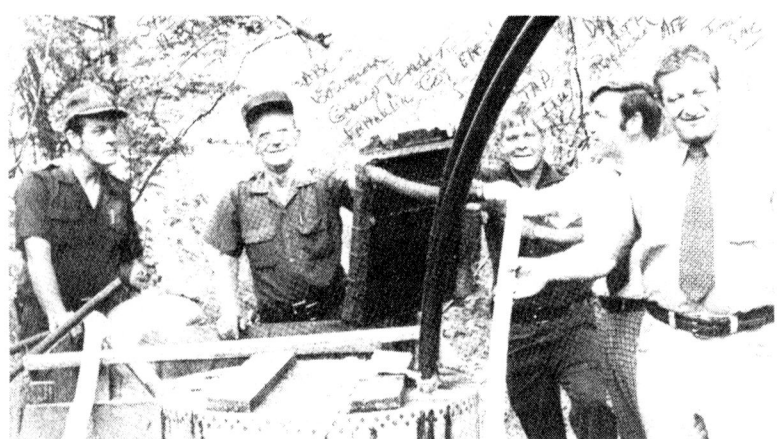

ABC-ATF "Blitz" of 1980. (l–r) ABC Supervisor Stoneman; ABC Agent Bowman; Jack Allen Powell; Special Agent in charge Douglas Testerman; Richmond; Jim Hunt SAC, Roanoke, VA. (Photo by Franklin News Post.)

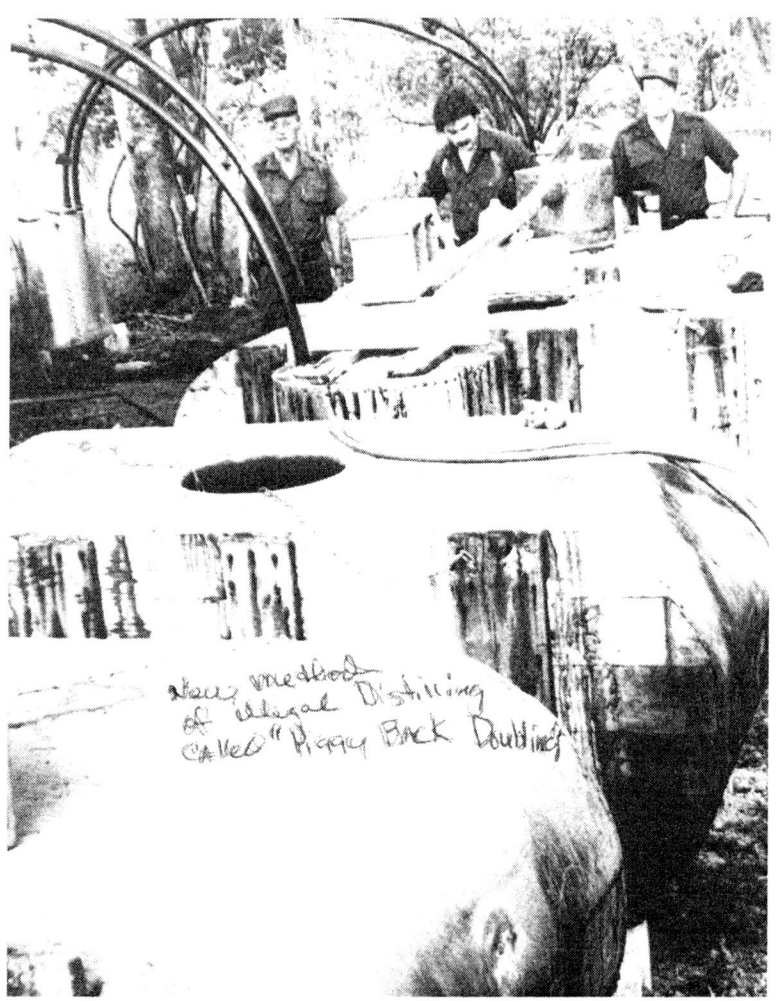

New method of distilling called "piggy back doubling." (l–r) ABC Agent Jim Bowman; ATF Agent; ABC Agent, Supervisor Ken Stoneman. (Photo by Franklin News Post.)

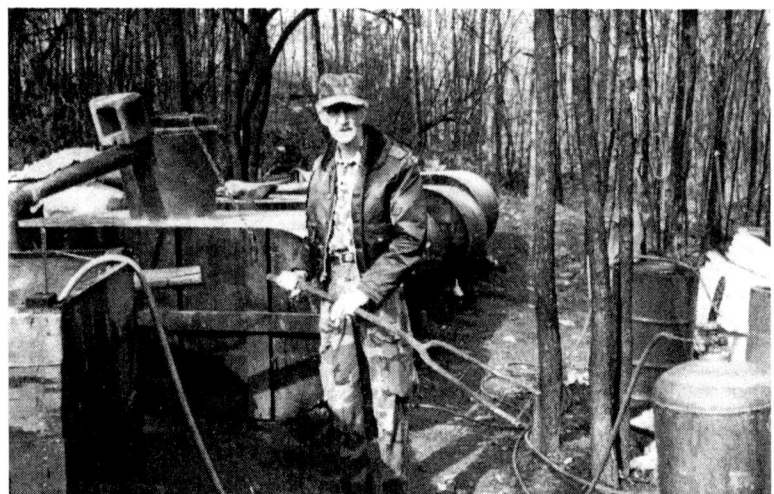

Jimmy Rorrer, ABC Agent shown in Patrick County with four black pots seized. 1990. (Photo by J. Powell.)

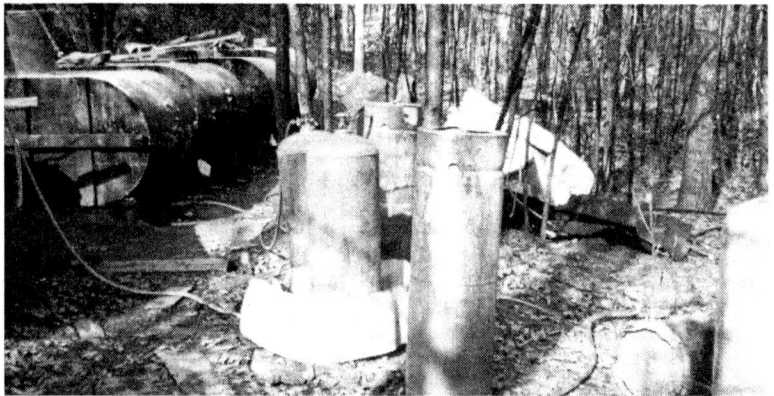

Four black pots located behind a saw mill. While we were observing the distillery, a man came out of the woods to answer to the call of nature. He had had a small dog with him who looked all around and ran toward us. The moonshiner knew his dog smelled something, but pulled his cap down over his head and slowly went back into the illegal distillery. Once he got down in those thick laurels he hollered, "It's the damn law." Two of them vacated the still very quickly. (Photo by J. Powell.)

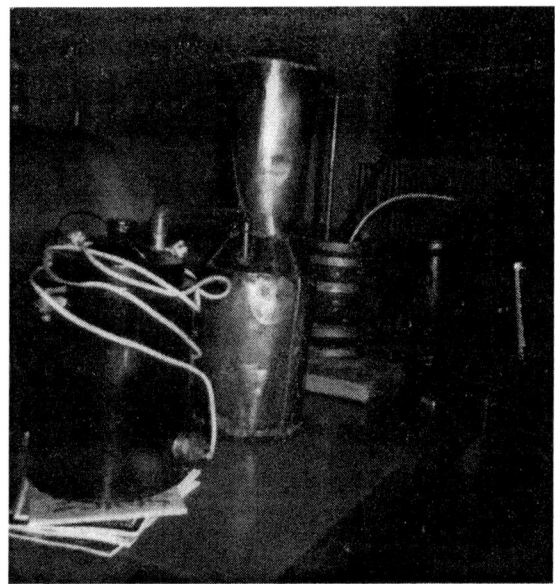

Community (Poteen) Still Buchanan County, Virginia, 1949.

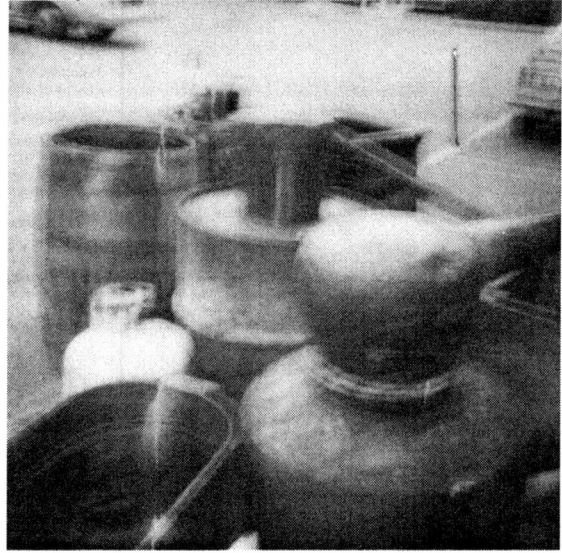

Community mountain still: turnip old fashion copper type still and 55 gallon drum modern type still.

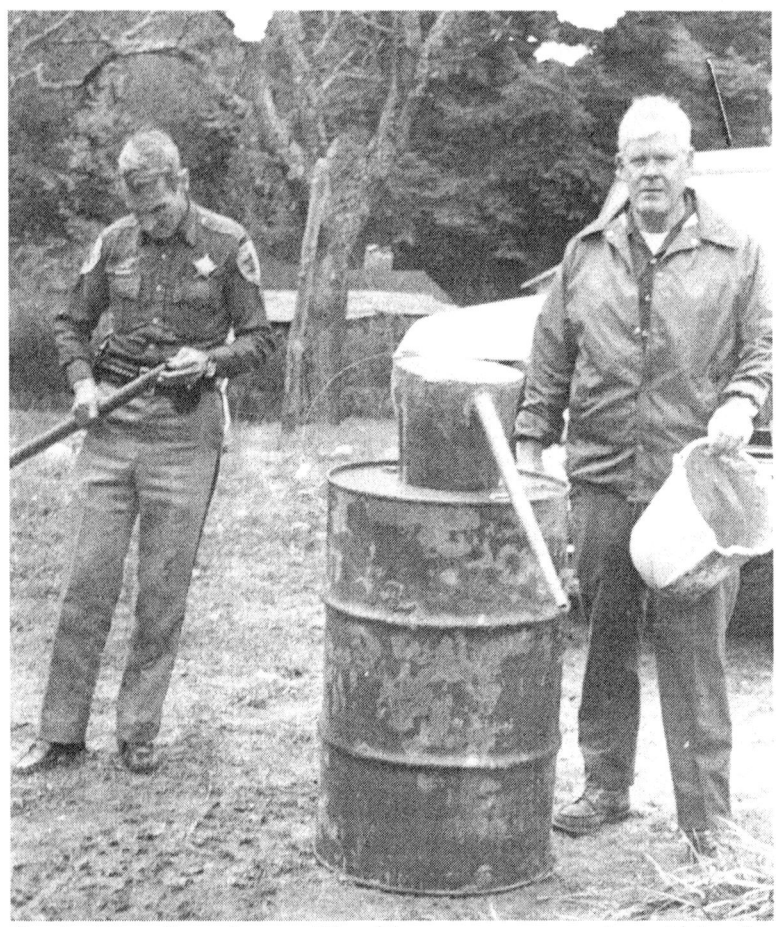

Crude 55 gallon drum still with copper cap make whisky for Thanksgiving and Christmas. Floyd County, Va., Nov. 3, 1983. Sheriff of Floyd County, George Branscome and ABC Agent Jack Powell. (Photo by Floyd Press.)

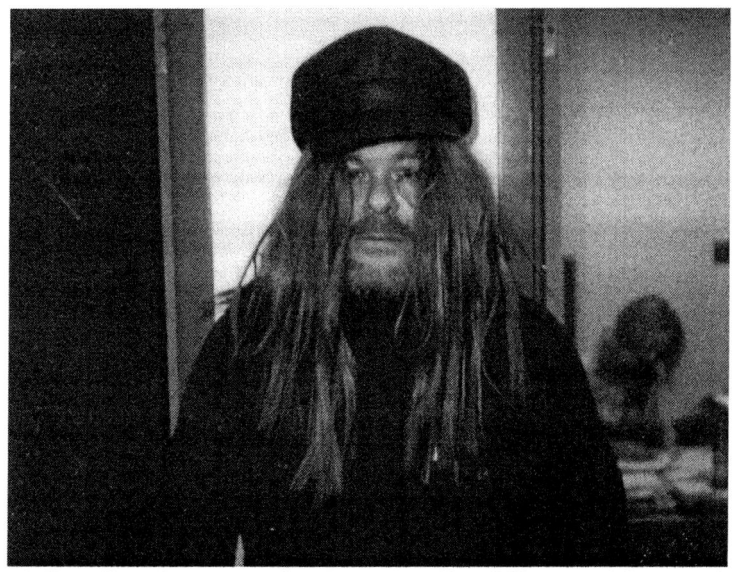

Jack Powell undercover with Roanoke Vice Officers, while working liquor and prostitution area motels and hotels. A Vice Officer (RPD) was in a Motel Room with a prostitute and I was outside in a "pimp's" Cadillac when the Vice Officer triggered his radio for the uniform cars to come in for the arrest. The "pimp" in the Cadillac reached under the seat for a weapon and I stuck a .38 snub nose in his ear and told him to turn off the motor. He was attempting to back the car out of the motel parking lot at a high rate of speed. I slowed him down and we arrested a bunch of prostitutes and pimps, liquor violators as well. (Photo by Vice RPD Officer.)

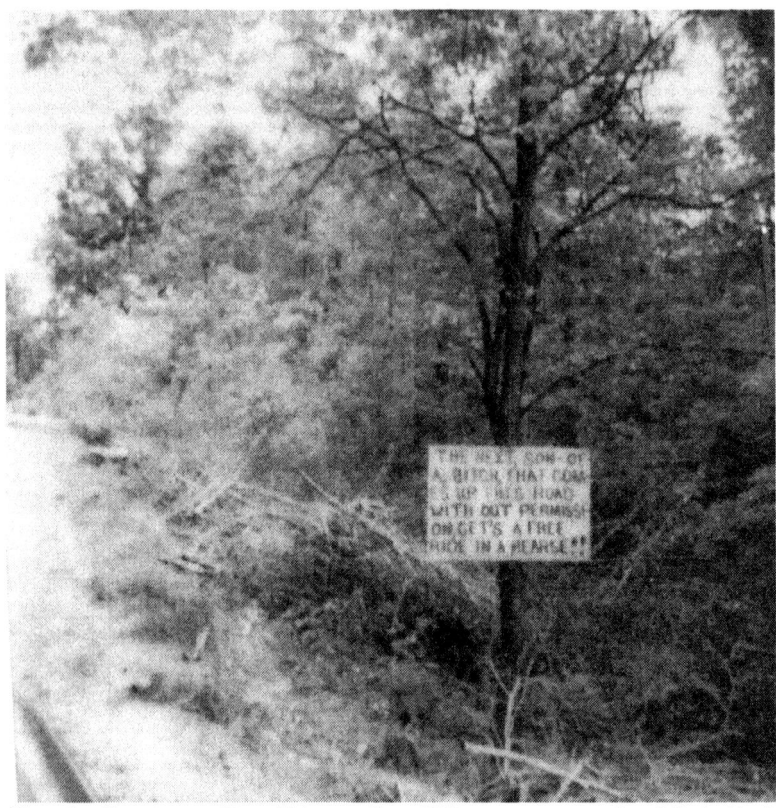

Sign in Botetourt Co., VA reading "The next son of a bitch that comes up this road without permission gets a free ride in a hearse!!" Encountered while agents J. Powell and B. Weddle were looking for a "still" and marijuana in 1989. (Photo by J. Powell.)

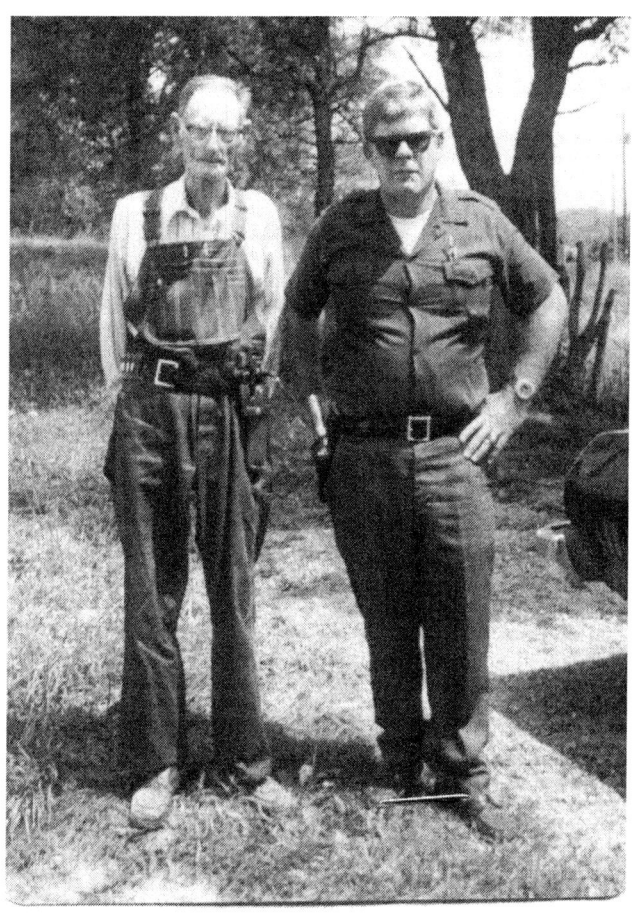

Walter Bryant, self-proclaimed woodcutter and revenuer with J. Powell from 1978–1984. He liked to walk in the woods and check "creeks" for distillers' signs. He was proud to work with me. (Photo by Detective Denver Stuart, Montgomery County, VA Sheriff's Department. Photo released by Mr. Bryant, with permission to print in 1978.)

Jack Allen Powell

Though the making of whiskey is illegal in Virginia, beer and wine is not. The author is not in the business of making wine and beer, however, the recipe can be obtained at the Franklin County Historical Society at Rocky Mt., VA

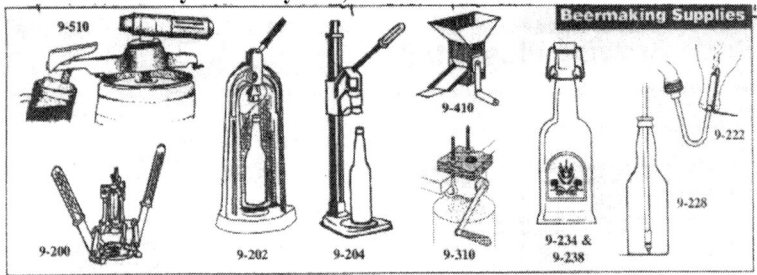

Beer Bottling Equipment

Double Handle 'Wing' Cappers - Lever action makes these cappers easy to use. Magnet holds cap for capping (deluxe model).
No. 9-200 Deluxe Capper Shp. Wt. 2 lbs. $16.95
No. 9-400 Brev Capper Shp. Wt. 2 lbs. 14.95
Colonna Capper - New design Italian capper. Heavy duty, caps all sizes of bottles, easy to use. Best capper available.
No. 9-202 Shp. Wt. 6 lbs. $35.95
'Slide' Capper - The capping mechanism on this capper slides up and down to adjust to bottle size. Fast to use.
No. 9-204 Shp. Wt. 9 lbs. $28.95
'Hammer' Capper - A padded hammer or mallet is used on this capper to drive the cap onto the bottle.
No. 9-208 Shp. Wt. 1 lb. 8 oz. $5.50
Bottle Caps - Commercial quality caps, plastic lined for the best seal. Two styles. Shp. Wt. 1 lb. 8 oz.
No. 9-210 Plain Caps (144) $2.50
No. 9-213 "Real Beer" Caps (144) $2.99
No. 9-212 Oxygen-Barrier Caps (144) $3.95
'Grolsch' Bottle Seals - Replacement rubber washers for ceramic cap bottles. Package of 25 seals.
No. 9-214 Shp. Wt. 3 oz. $2.50
Plastic Bottle Filler for Beer Bottles - Automatic shut-off valve.
No. 9-228 Shp. Wt. 12 oz. $2.50
No. 9-228A Adapter to fit 6-145 spigot. Shp. Wt. 2 oz. $.75
Phil's Philler - All brass construction.
No. 9-230 Short Filler Shp. Wt. 1 lb. $13.95
No. 9-236 Long Filler Shp. Wt. 1 lb. $14.95

Immersion Type Wort Chiller
Reduce the temperature of boiling wort in 10 to 20 minutes using cold tap water. Fits in your brew kettle.
No. 9-301 Shp. Wt. 9 lbs. $49.95

Counter Flow Type "Brew Chiller"
Includes all hoses and copper syphon tube.
No. 9-303 Shp. Wt. 11 lbs. $79.95

Mini-Keg Draft System
Use 4 of these 5 liter kegs for 5 gallon batch, prime and dispense with injector assembly using CO₂ cartridges (8-105).
No. 9-510A Injector Assy. & 1 Mini-Keg Shp. Wt. 4 lbs. $44.95
No. 9-510B Additional 5-liter Mini-Keg Shp. Wt. 2 lbs. $7.95
No. 9-511A Spare CO₂ Adapter Shp. Wt. 2 oz. $1.00

Beer Bottles - New beer bottles for home brewing. Cappable, not twist-offs. Should be sterilized before use. Case of 12 bottles (22 oz.) or 24 (12 oz.) or 12 "Grolsch" type (16 oz.). Single one liter (33 oz.) Grolsch-type also available.
No. 9-220 Case of 12-22 oz. Bottles Shp. Wt. 16 lbs. $8.95
No. 9-232 Case of 24-12 oz. Bottles Shp. Wt. 16 lbs. $9.95
No. 9-234 Case of 12-16 oz. Bottles Shp. Wt. 16 lbs. $19.20
No. 9-238 Single 33 oz. Flip-Top Bottle Shp. Wt. 2 lb. $2.80
Beer Labels - Gummed-back, decorative labels for your brewing efforts. Available in 'Lager,' 'Ale' or 'Stout.' 25 per package.
No. 9-216 Lager Labels (25) - Shp. Wt 2 oz. $1.99
No. 9-217 Stout Labels (25) - Shp. Wt. 2 oz. $1.99
No. 9-218 Ale Labels (25) - Shp. Wt. 2 oz. $1.99
No. 9-219 Blank Labels (25) - Shp. Wt.2 oz. $1.99
Bottle Washer - Heavy-duty, brass spray-type washer to rinse bottles and carboys. Attaches to garden hose-type connector (order adapter for kitchen sink use). Lifetime warranty.
No.9-222 Bottle Washer Shp. Wt. 6 oz. $10.95
No.9-226 Sink Adapter All Metal Shp. Wt. 4 oz. $2.99

Hand-Crank Grain Grinders
No. 9-110 Corona Mill Shp. Wt. 14 lbs. $49.95
The old standby.
No. 9-310 The Phil Mill Shp. Wt. 10 lbs. $89.95
Features single, adjustable roller.
No. 9-410 The Glatt Mill Shp. Wt. 10 lbs. $139.95
Heavy duty stainless steel construction. Two adjustable rollers. Best mill on the market.

Propane Cooker
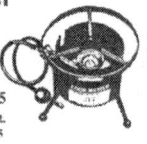
135,000 BTU Propane Cooker with regulator boils your wort in 1/4 the time, AWAY from the kitchen. Propane tank not included.
No. 9-930 Shp. Wt. 15 lbs. $56.95
Extension legs set - adds 2 ft. to height.
No. 9-938 Shp. Wt. 6 lbs. $14.95
Prices subject to change without notice 5/98

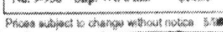

218

Beermaking Instructions

Basic Brewing Illustrated

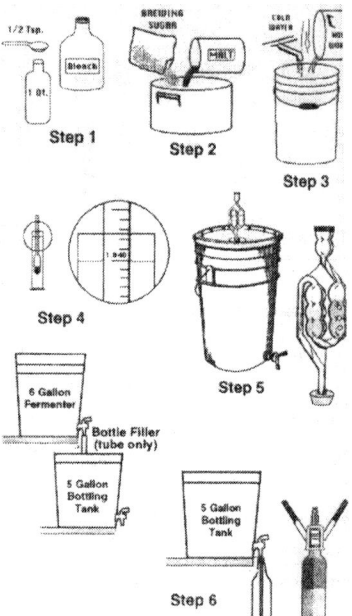

Step 1. Make sterilizer solution by adding 1/2 tsp. household bleach to 1 quart water. Sterilize fermenter with solution. Rinse completely.

Step 2. Dissolve the can of hopped malt extract and 2 lbs. corn sugar (brewing sugar) in 2 1/2 gallons of warm water and bring to a boil (15 minutes to 1 hour).

Step 3. Add about 1 gallon of cool water to the fermentation bucket and pour in the hot liquid from Step 2. Add more cool water to make 5 gallons (4 inches below rim). Cover and let cool to 68° to 72° F. This mixture is now called the "wort" (pronounced wert).

Step 4. While the wort is cooling, boil 1/2 cup of water, let cool to 80° and sprinkle the yeast on top. Sterilize the hydrometer and its plastic shipping tube. Remove enough cooled wort from tap to nearly fill the plastic tube, float the hydrometer in the tube and note the reading. It should be about 1.030 to 1.040 Specific Gravity. Discard this sample. Rinse and sterilize hydrometer and tube.

Wait until the yeast foams (15 to 30 mins.) and add to the cooled wort in bucket. Snap the lid onto the bucket and insert the airlock with rubber stopper into hole. Fill airlock 1/2 full with water and replace small lid on airlock. Fermentation should start in 8 to 24 hours. Water in airlock will begin to bubble.

Step 5. Fermentation continues for 7 to 10 days (10 to 12 days for heavier, all-malt beers). Check fermentation progress by observing water in airlock. When bubbles quit coming through the airlock, take another hydrometer reading as you did in Step 4. The Specific Gravity should be 1.000 to 1.005. If it is higher, wait 2-3 additional days and take another reading. However, do not wait over 16 days from start to finish before you bottle.

Step 6. Clean and sterilize bottling bucket, filler, cappable bottles (twist-offs will not work) and beer caps. Draw one quart of beer from tap on fermenter into sauce pan. Stir in the package of priming sugar and heat to dissolve (bring to a boil). Cool mixture and pour into sterilized bottling bucket. Place bottling bucket under fermenter spigot and allow all clear beer to fill bucket and mix with primed portion (leave all sediment behind). Attach filler to spigot (in off position) and set bottling bucket on edge of table. Turn on spigot. Fill bottles by pushing up onto filler spout as shown. Fill to top of bottle then remove bottle from spigot. Head space is now correct, about one inch from mouth of bottle. Cap each bottle immediately after filling. Clean all equipment after use.

Step 7. Store bottles at 68° to 72° F. for 1 week, then store in a cooler place. Beer can be drunk in 10 days after bottling, but will taste much better 1 month later, and better yet in 3 months.

Note: This is a single stage brewing fermentation method. Two stage fermentation requires the use of a 5 gallon carboy as a secondary fermentation vessel. Read more about this method in one of the excellent brewing books listed on page 22.

Extract Recipes for Delicious Beers

Wheat Beer

Recipe for 5 gallons

    1   can Alexander's Wheat Malt Extract
    1   can Alexander's Wheat "Kicker" Malt Extract
    1/4 lb. German Lt. Crystal Malt (crushed)
    1/4 lb. Dextrine malt (crushed)
    1 oz. Hallertau Hops (bittering)
    1 oz. Hallertauer Hops (finishing)
    1 Pkg. Dry Ale Yeast
    3/4 cup Corn Sugar for priming (bottling)
    50 Bottle Caps

Ingredient Kit for Wheat Beer
No. 10-101 Ship. Wt. 9 lbs
$19.95

Original Gravity - 1.035 to 1.040
Terminal Gravity - 1.006 to 1.012

Special Instructions - Add Crystal and Dextrine grains to 1/2 gallon water and bring to a boil. Remove from heat and let steep for 20 minutes. Strain out grains and add more water to make 2 to 2 1/2 gallons. Bring to boil and add malt extracts plus bittering hops. Continue boiling for one hour. Add finishing hops 5 minutes before the end of the boil. Proceed from step 3 above.

Octoberfest

This style of amber German beer is the best known of the "Fest" beers. Smooth and malty, a great treat anytime

Recipe for 5 gallons

    1 can Coopers Lager (yeast included)
    1 can Alexander's Amber Kicker
    3 lbs. Amber Dry Malt
    1/2 lb. Light German Crystal Malt - cracked
    1/4 lb. Chocolate Malt - cracked
    2 oz. Tettnang Pellet Hops (bittering)
    1 oz. Tettnang Leaf Hops (finishing)
    50 Bottle Caps

Ingredient Kit for Octoberfest
No. 10-102
Ship. Wt. 12 lbs.
$33.95

Original Gravity - 1.038 to 1.044
Terminal Gravity - 1.014 to 1.018

Special Instructions - Add Crystal and Chocolate grains to 1/2 gallon water and bring to a boil. Remove from heat and let steep for 20 minutes. Strain out grains and add more water to make 2 to 2 1/2 gallons. Bring to boil and add liquid and dry malts plus bittering hops. Continue boiling for one hour. Add finishing

Jack Allen Powell

BEER & WINE SERVICE

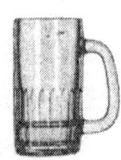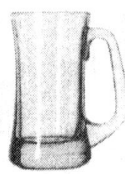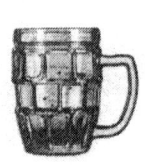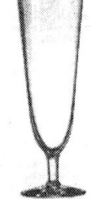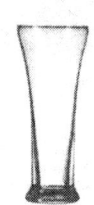

20-101 Traditional Mug
A. 12 oz. Mug-$2.59ea.
Shp.Wt. 2 lbs. each
B. 4 Mugs for $9.85
Shp. Wt. 7 lbs./4

20-102 Scandanavia Mug
A. 15 oz. Mug-$5.75ea.
Shp.Wt. 3 lbs. each
B. 4 Mugs for $20.70
Shp. Wt. 10 lbs./4

20-103 Barrel Mug
A. 19 oz. Mug-$2.95ea.
Shp.Wt. 2 lbs. each
B. 4 Mugs for $10.60
Shp. Wt. 7 lbs./4

20-104 Footed Pilsner
A. 12 oz. Glass-$2.79ea
Shp.Wt. 1 1/2 lbs.each
B. 4 Glasses for $10.90
Shp. Wt. 4 lbs./4

20-105 Flare Pilsner
A. 12 oz. Glass-$1.89ea
Shp Wt. 1 lb each
B. 4 Glasses for $6.90
Shp. Wt. 4 lbs./4

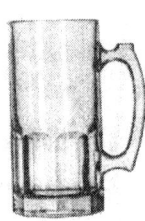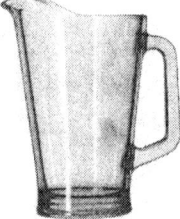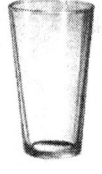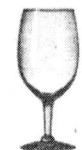

20-106 Super Mug
A. 1 Liter Mug - $6.95ea.
Shp. Wt. 4 lbs. each
B. 4 Mugs for $25.00
Shp. Wt. 11 lbs./4

20-107 60 oz. Pitcher
A. 60 oz. Pitcher · $6.75ea.
Shp. Wt. 5 lbs. each

20-111 Pub Pint
A. 16 oz. Glass-$1.95ea
Shp.Wt. 2 lbs. ea.
B. 4 Glasses for $7.00
Shp.Wt. 7 lbs./4

20-109 8 oz. Wine
A. 8 oz. Glass - $2.75ea
Shp. Wt. 1 lb. each
B. 4 Glasses for $9.95
Shp. Wt. 3 lbs./4

CORKSCREWS, etc.

Waiter's Corkscrew
Inexpensive, pocket-sized corkscrew for restaurant or home use.
Chrome-plated with plastic handle.
No.20-305 Hinged Pro Model   Shp. Wt. 5 oz. $7.25

Two-Prong Puller
This Ah-So® style cork puller is popular for its ease of use and long lasting performance.
No. 20-306 Sanbri Two-Prong Shp.Wt. 5 oz $5.95

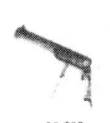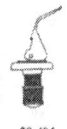

20-305   20-306   20-404

Budget Bottle Stoppers
These handy stoppers are great for champagne, beer or soda! They lock firmly in place with the flip of the lever!
No.20-404 Budget Stoppers Shp. Wt. 2 oz. $1.29ea.

220

Winemaking Illustrated

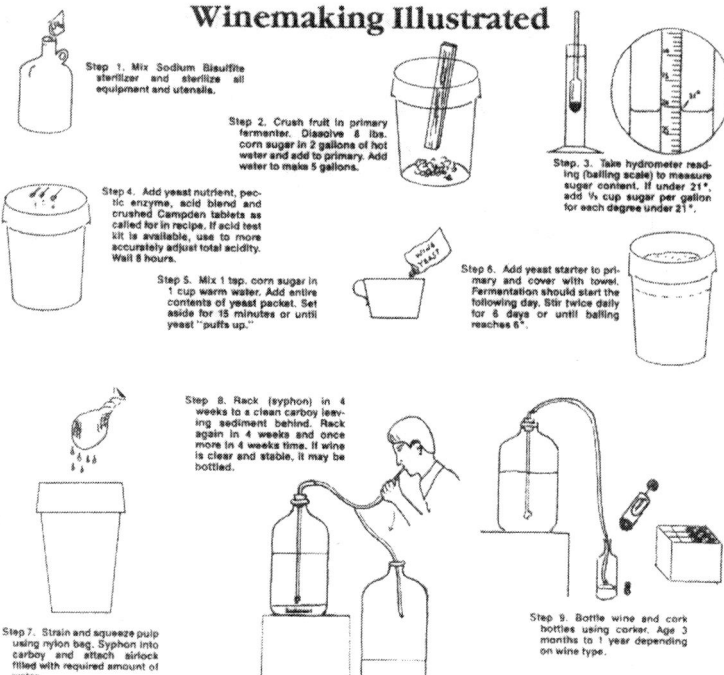

Step 1. Mix Sodium Bisulfite sterilizer and sterilize all equipment and utensils.

Step 2. Crush fruit in primary fermenter. Dissolve 6 lbs. corn sugar in 2 gallons of hot water and add to primary. Add water to make 5 gallons.

Step 3. Take hydrometer reading (balling scale) to measure sugar content. If under 21°, add ⅛ cup sugar per gallon for each degree under 21°.

Step 4. Add yeast nutrient, pectic enzyme, acid blend and crushed Campden tablets as called for in recipe. If acid test kit is available, use to more accurately adjust total acidity. Wait 8 hours.

Step 5. Mix 1 tsp. corn sugar in 1 cup warm water. Add entire contents of yeast packet. Set aside for 15 minutes or until yeast "puffs up."

Step 6. Add yeast starter to primary and cover with towel. Fermentation should start the following day. Stir twice daily for 6 days or until balling reaches 6°.

Step 7. Strain and squeeze pulp using nylon bag. Syphon into carboy and attach airlock filled with required amount of water.

Step 8. Rack (syphon) in 4 weeks to a clean carboy leaving sediment behind. Rack again in 4 weeks and once more in 4 weeks time. If wine is clear and stable, it may be bottled.

Step 9. Bottle wine and cork bottles using corker. Age 3 months to 1 year depending on wine type.

Ingredients and Supplies for Fresh Fruit Winemaking
Yield: 5 gallons

Ingredients		Supplies	
Cat. No.		Cat. No.	
–	15-25 lbs. Fresh Fruit – blackberry, raspberry, strawberry, etc.	14-107	10 Gallon Poly Tub (primary fermenter)
–	3 gallons water (use to dissolve sugar)	12-101	Hydrometer and Test Jar
11-116	9 - 12 lbs. corn sugar	13-101	Airlock and Adapter
11-100	5 Campden tablets	14-326	2 - 5 Gallon Containers (secondary fermenter)
11-102	1 1/2 tsp. Yeast Nutrient	13-115	Syphon Hose and Clamp
11-101	2 1/2 tsp. Pectic Enzyme	13-117	Racking Tube
12-201	1 package Wine Yeast	11-120	Sodium Bisulphite (sterilizer)
11-106	1/2 to 1 oz. Acid Blend		

Flip order in illustrations.
Method is hot in wine or beer making because

Franklin County Sweet Mash Corn Liquor 1940s

The Recipe

To make sweet mash corn liquor: Boil water and transfer to the mash boxes. Add about 3 bushels of ground corn to each mash box and stir with a 'mash fork.' This swells and thickens the mixture to keep the water from running out the cracks. Sprinkle dry barley or corn malt – ground shelled corn to hold the heat. Cook just under 1 hour to allow mixture to thicken. Stir to break up 'cap' on top. Continue stirring to keep mixture evenly heated, adding 40 lbs. barley malt. Bootleggers say the temperature should stay to a point where they can swipe a finger through the top of the mixture 3 times without being burned. Add 40 lbs. rye. Allow mixture to set an hour and a half "to sweeten" and cool to about 90 degrees. In warm water, dissolve a half-pound "east" (yeast) to pour into each mash box. Any hotter than 90 degrees, the mash will sour before the yeast works. It takes 3 days for the mash to "work off" and produce beer. Then remove beer and put in the still. Heat, boil and stir constantly with a "broom" (soft stir stick) to prevent sticking and a "scorched" taste. Stirring can stop once mixture reaches a rolling boil. Place copper cap on still and chain tightly in place. Connect copper cap spout to the pipe in the thumper barrel. To retain steam, paste a strip of cloth around the cap and pipes. The pressure from the beer being heated in the still blows the steam into the thumper barrel. Heat evenly lest the beer flavor spoil and the beer be thrown into the cap and thumper barrel, ruining the liquor. As the still is fired, peck on the cap to hear the clear sound that means only steam is coming through. If the "dead sound" of beer escaping into the cap is heard, immediately throw water on the fire to cool it down. Pull peg on thumper barrel to drain out the hot beer. This means the "backings" in the thumper barrel must be replaced. The backings are the last few gallons of a previous batch of whiskey, saved to put in the thump barrel to increase the proof of the next run. This is liquor but is not strong enough to hold a bead. Check for alcohol content by throwing a cupful into a fire. As long as it burns, it can be used for "backings." Once hot steam is built up in the thumper barrel, the backings in the bottom begin to bubble and make a thumping sound – one federal tax agents used to listen for with trained ears. When the thumping noise stops, the liquor has started out the copper worm. Steam travels from the thump barrel through the pipe to the slackstand where the copper worm condenses it into the finished whiskey product. A bucket in a tub under the hole at the bottom of the slackstand catches the first and strongest proof whiskey. Catch a bit in a zinc can top, strike a match to it and look for the blue flame. As the liquor runs, the strength weakens. Once the run in completed, pour all the whiskey into the proofing barrel to mix and even the proof. It usually averages 90 proof. Old-timers checked the proof by pouring liquor into a jar and "reading the bead." The product was best when the bead separated in the middle. This first run is the choice liquor for family and friends.

Save the mash for the second run. Sugar is added to make the cheaper to produce sugar liquor. Grain made the first batch ferment. The sugar makes the grain work again. Each 100 lbs. of sugar makes about 12 gallons of whiskey. Each mash box takes about 200 lbs. of sugar for the second run. Refill mash boxes with water, wait 3 days and run the sugar liquor. This can be done 3 times before the mash becomes hog slop – something hogs of yesteryear loved.

The copper still gave way to blackpot stills – so named because the galvanized tin used in construction turned black from firing. Liquor quality suffered then

About the Author

Jack Allen Powell was born in Roanoke, Virginia, October 6, 1933, just a few months before prohibition ended. Jack graduated from Jefferson High School, 1952. He served in the United States Navy during the Korean Conflict. He joined the Roanoke Police Department in 1956 and he and Sergeant Jack Heath worked out of the Chief's office (undercover-working gambling, liquor, prostitution.

He joined the State Alcoholic Beverage Control Boards Enforcement Division in 1957. He was a criminal investigator working illicit whisky, unlicensed distilleries, resale of taxed paid liquor, narcotic's and dangerous drugs.

He spent five years on undercover work in the coalfields of Southwest Virginia then, Norfolk and Virginia Beach, (called the "The Rat Patrol", a burglary detail where Tidewater ABC stores were being burglarized and the safes and best whisky taken).

In 1978, he was promoted to Assistant Special Agent In Charge, Roanoke, Va., Enforcement-Office. He has been shot, stabbed, jailed, snake-bit, 10 auto crashes and three totals, suspended three times, five meritorious awards.

In 1960, while chasing a pickup truck loaded with untaxed whisky, he failed to negotiate a sharp turn and went off the east end of the Ripplemead bridge, Giles Co. Va. And plummeted, 131 feet end over end, five times into the New River and lived to tell about it but he paid. Thirty days later a moonshiner, in a pickup truck hit him head on, while he was operating a 58 Ford undercover car, near the Va.-Kentucky-Tenn. border.

1973, another tremendous auto crash in Floyd County, a 1972, Plymouth, Enforcement car demolished.

Graduated from Institute of Applied Science (Scientific Crime Detection). Graduated, Virginia Western College, 1972, (law enforcement degree). Graduated from LaSalle Law School, Chicago, Ill, 1973. Graduated, 1972 BNND School, Old Dominion University. Graduated from numerous other Police Schools in the United States.

1981, graduated from the FBI Academy, (Executive Law Enforcement, Session 126th, 3rd Sec.). He has a Private Investigators licenses and Private Security Instructorship license, CJSD/COM/VA.

Has taught in various Police Academies throughout Virginia and has spoken to social, civic groups, colleges and universities.

Jack retired in 1991 on an early retirement. After 35 yrs. He produced a documentary "Moonshining In Virginia" 1958 to 1991. Assisted in the production of "Sniffing Out The Mountain Dew" with Charles Karalt, CBS Sunday Morning, 1987. Jack worked for the U.S. Marshals (CSO) Service 1995-2004.

He appeared with a mountain moonshiner on the "Night Watch News", CBS. Robert Pierpoint, 1989. 12-95. WSET-TV, Lynchburg, Va. with Gili Ossola, Danville Bureau, Ref: tape, "where is this moonshine going". Married to Mary Wright Powell and has two married daughters, Trenda, Andra, son-in-laws, Jake and Marty, and six grand children four boys an two girls.

Jack is featured in the History Channel's "Moonshining Bootlegging, Rum Running." He was Assistant Technical Director of filming in 2003 (last 30 minutes of film *The Law*). And also featured in CMT's most shocking moments "Moonshining Stories," which aired on October 16, 2004.

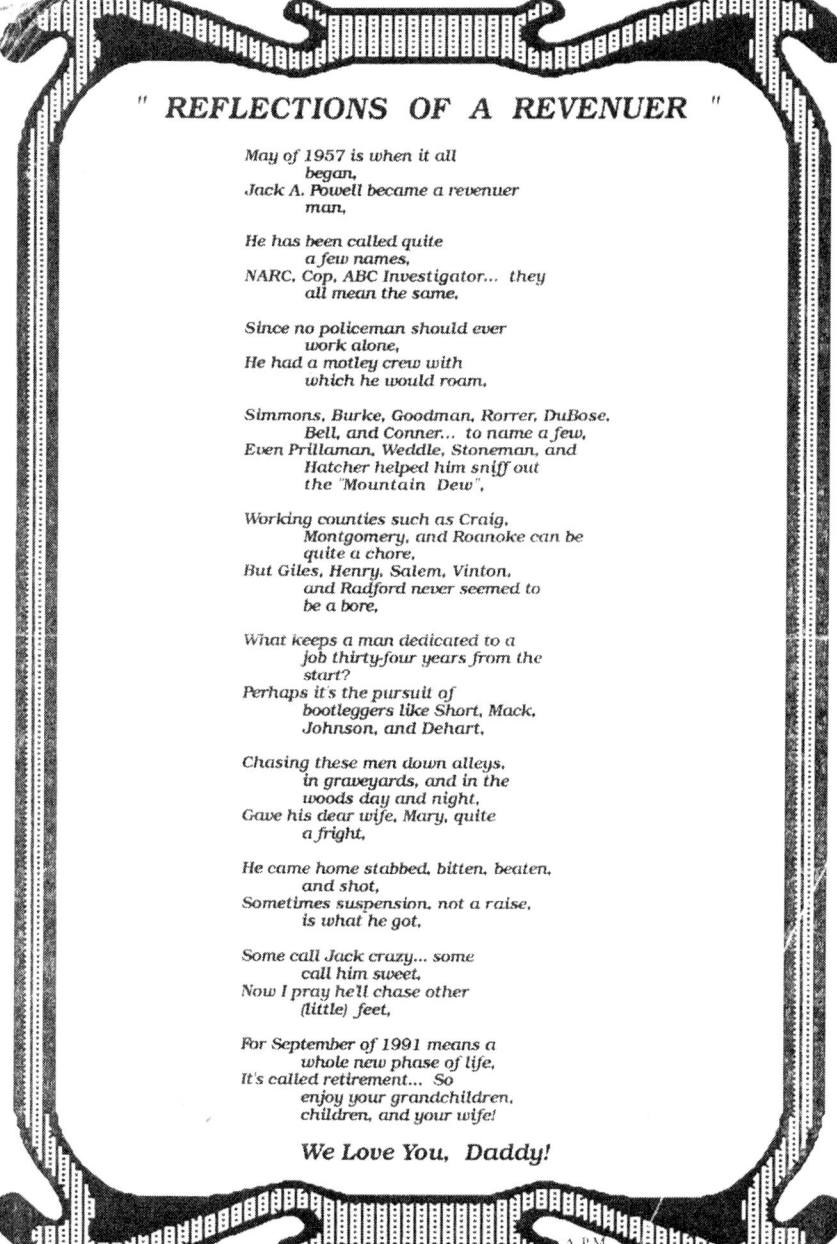

" *REFLECTIONS OF A REVENUER* "

May of 1957 is when it all
      began,
Jack A. Powell became a revenuer
      man,

He has been called quite
      a few names,
NARC, Cop, ABC Investigator... they
      all mean the same,

Since no policeman should ever
      work alone,
He had a motley crew with
      which he would roam,

Simmons, Burke, Goodman, Rorrer, DuBose,
      Bell, and Conner... to name a few,
Even Prillaman, Weddle, Stoneman, and
      Hatcher helped him sniff out
      the "Mountain Dew",

Working counties such as Craig,
      Montgomery, and Roanoke can be
      quite a chore,
But Giles, Henry, Salem, Vinton,
      and Radford never seemed to
      be a bore,

What keeps a man dedicated to a
      job thirty-four years from the
      start?
Perhaps it's the pursuit of
      bootleggers like Short, Mack,
      Johnson, and Dehart,

Chasing these men down alleys,
      in graveyards, and in the
      woods day and night,
Gave his dear wife, Mary, quite
      a fright,

He came home stabbed, bitten, beaten,
      and shot,
Sometimes suspension, not a raise,
      is what he got,

Some call Jack crazy... some
      call him sweet,
Now I pray he'll chase other
      (little) feet,

For September of 1991 means a
      whole new phase of life,
It's called retirement... So
      enjoy your grandchildren,
      children, and your wife!

We Love You, Daddy!

A.P.M.

Jack Allen Powell